The Future of Children

PRINCETON-BROOKINGS

VOLUME 24 NUMBER 1 SPRING 2014

Helping Parents, Helping Children: Two-Generation Mechanisms

Introduction: Two-Generation Mechanisms of Child Development

Ron Haskins, Irwin Garfinkel, and Sara McLanahan

Programs that aim to improve the lives of children from disadvantaged backgrounds are facing a challenge. On the one hand, scholars and policy makers agree that we must invest in children to secure our country's future and to promote educational and economic opportunity, suggesting that we should expand programs for children, especially during early childhood.[1] On the other hand, there is a growing sense in some quarters that existing programs for children are not working as well as they could.

A few widely cited models, such as Perry Preschool and the Abecedarian Project, have demonstrated that high-quality programs can make a big difference in children's lives.[2] The children who participated in these programs have shown long-term gains in educational attainment, employment, and earnings relative to their peers, and those who participated in Perry Preschool had lower rates of arrest.

The evidence from larger-scale efforts, such as Head Start and some state prekindergarten programs, is less clear-cut. On the one hand, numerous assessments of Head Start, the nation's largest preschool program, which enrolls about 900,000 mostly disadvantaged children, have found improvements in children's test scores, as well as their rates of high school graduation, college attendance, and delinquency, especially among children from disadvantaged backgrounds. Similarly, assessments of state prekindergarten programs, which have a much shorter history than Head Start, have found that in elementary school, the participants—especially those from disadvantaged backgrounds—had better language skills and were less likely to repeat a grade or be suspended.[3]

On the other hand, a recent randomized trial of Head Start found that the test score gains children experienced at the end of the program typically faded by the end of kindergarten.[4]

www.futureofchildren.org

Ron Haskins is a senior editor of *Future of Children*, a senior fellow in economic studies, and co-director of the Center on Children and Families at the Brookings Institution, and a senior consultant at the Annie E. Casey Foundation. Irwin Garfinkel is the Mitchell I. Ginsberg Professor of Contemporary Urban Problems at the Columbia University School of Social Work and co-director of the Columbia Population Research Center. Sara McLanahan is the editor-in-chief of *Future of Children*, as well as the director of the Center for Research on Child Wellbeing and the William S. Tod Professor of Sociology and Public Affairs at Princeton University.

And a well-executed evaluation of a preschool intervention in Tennessee found a similar fade-out by the end of first grade.[5] It's not unusual for gains in cognitive test scores to fade—the same phenomenon occurred in the Perry Preschool and Abecedarian projects. Still, the recent Head Start and Tennessee evaluations have caused some people to doubt the efficacy of early childhood education and of universal prekindergarten more broadly.[6]

Although it's too early to assess the long-term benefits of the new prekindergarten programs, it's hard to be optimistic that current programs can boost poor children's development enough to overcome the huge divide in educational achievement and economic opportunity between children from poor families and children from economically secure families. The United States has experienced a dramatic increase in income inequality over the past four decades, which, not surprisingly, has been accompanied by a growing income gap in children's test scores.[7] So even if the $30 billion or so that the federal and state governments spend on preschool programs and the $640 billion the nation spends on public education are having large effects, they are not large enough to compensate for the growing gap in achievement between children from high- and low-income families.[8]

The school problems of poor children stem in large part from the home environment. Numerous studies show that parents and the home environment they provide exert a continuing influence on children as they grow up.[9] Betty Hart and Todd Risley, in their well-known study from nearly two decades ago, found major differences in the home language environments provided by poor and more affluent parents. They estimate that the average child on welfare is exposed to 62,000 words per week at home, compared with 125,000 words per week for more privileged children.[10] Similarly, based on the large sample of the Panel Study of Income Dynamics, Meredith Phillips shows very large differences, all of them favoring children from more affluent families, in time spent in conversation with adults, in primary caregivers' verbal responsiveness, and in time spent in literary activities.[11] The upshot is that children from poor families show up for kindergarten already far behind in school readiness, and they fall further behind during the school years.[12]

These important differences in poor children's home environments, the parenting they receive, and the effectiveness of public schools in helping them overcome their disadvantages are certain to affect their economic opportunities as adults. Intergenerational data from the Panel Study of Income Dynamics show that 42 percent of children from families in the bottom 20 percent of the income distribution themselves wind up in the bottom 20 percent as adults, and only 6 percent of them make it to the top 20 percent. By contrast, only 9 percent of children from families in the top 20 percent of income wind up in the bottom 20 percent, and 39 percent of them remain in the top 20 percent. Equal opportunity this is not.

Purpose of This Issue

Given these sobering facts about socioeconomic differences in home environments, as well as the modest track record of intervention programs that seek to reduce socioeconomic differences in educational attainment and economic opportunity, the time seems ripe to step back and review what we know about the mechanisms that shape these differences by influencing children's development. Understanding these mechanisms of development could help us design intervention programs that boost children's intellectual and socioemotional development and that could, in turn, help close the gaps between students from poor and more affluent families. One of *Future of Children's* fundamental goals is to write about effective intervention programs for children that are based on an understanding of the processes underlying child development. Thus we decided to focus not only on intervention programs themselves, but on the mechanisms of child development that intervention programs are trying to influence. If we understand how these mechanisms work, we can use this knowledge to design or redesign interventions to boost child development.

The two-generation model is based on the assumption that serving parents and children simultaneously with high-quality intervention programs would be more effective ... than serving them individually.

A second focus of the issue is prompted by the aphorism that parents are their children's first teachers. Several foundations—including the Foundation for Child Development, the Bill and Melinda Gates Foundation, the George Kaiser Family Foundation, the Annie E. Casey Foundation, the W. K. Kellogg Foundation, and the Aspen Institute—have supported the idea that "two-generation"

programs could improve the effectiveness of preschool interventions for children. The two-generation model is based on the assumption that serving parents and children simultaneously with high-quality intervention programs would be more effective (and perhaps more efficient) than serving them individually. The rationale for two-generation programs, and the results of such programs to date (most of which simultaneously enroll parents in job training and their children in quality child care), are examined in this issue by Lindsay Chase-Lansdale and Jeanne Brooks-Gunn.

In addition to existing two-generation programs, the editors identified six widely acknowledged mechanisms or pathways through which parents and the home environment they create are thought to influence children's development. These pathways are stress, education, health, income, employment, and assets. We then asked a carefully selected group of scholars to summarize the theories of development relevant to each mechanism; explain how each mechanism is expected to influence parents and, through parents, their children's development; and review the research on whether intervention programs have been shown to strengthen each parenting mechanism and whether each mechanism does, in fact, influence children's intellectual or socioemotional development.

Overview
The following is a brief review of what our authors found.

Two-Generation Programs in the Twenty-First Century
Chase-Lansdale and Brooks-Gunn explain the theories behind two-generation programs that aim to build the human capital

of both adults and children, and they review the evidence for these programs' efficacy. A first wave of two-generation programs in the 1980s and '90s produced mostly disappointing results, but the evaluations they left behind pointed to promising new directions. More recently, a second wave of two-generation programs—the authors dub them "Two-Generation 2.0"—has sought to rectify the flaws of earlier efforts, largely by building strong connections between components for children and adults, by ensuring that children and adults receive services of equal duration and intensity, and by incorporating advances in education and workforce development. These Two-Generation 2.0 programs are still in their infancy, and we have yet to see clear evidence that they can achieve their goals or be implemented cost-effectively at scale. Nonetheless, Chase-Lansdale and Brooks-Gunn write, the theoretical justification for these programs is strong, their early results are promising, and the time is ripe for innovation, experimentation, and further study.

Stress and Child Development

Ross Thompson examines the child's early environment and how stress affects early development. Sources of stress—including marital conflict, domestic violence, child abuse or neglect, and parental depression—are abundant in the environment of poor and at-risk parents and children. Poverty itself can lead to conditions that increase stress on all family members. Thompson examines early development to understand how parenting quality and other aspects of children's environments shape the development of their biological systems, with particular attention to stress as the mediating mechanism. Research shows that children are "biologically designed" to incorporate early social experiences in their developing biological systems in ways that can "assist or undermine their coping and adjustment." Reviewing the research on stress, Thompson examines the types of experience that can undermine children's development. He then introduces the concept of developmental plasticity, and he examines research on early interventions that offset the effects of excessive environmental stress by improving children's stress neurobiology. An important finding, as Thompson shows in a review of several empirical studies, is that the parent-child relationship can be a source both of excess stress that causes developmental problems and of sensitive caregiving that prevents the negative effects of stress and even ameliorates damage done by excessive stress earlier in a child's life. He concludes by pointing out that infants quickly understand and adapt to the characteristic behaviors of their caretakers. These early social experiences "guide them biologically and behaviorally to prepare for a life of security or adversity." It follows that one of the foundations of two-generation programs is found precisely in these social experiences with caretakers and that improving both preventive and ameliorative intervention programs can be accomplished through a deeper understanding of these experiences and their consequences.

Intergenerational Payoffs of Education

Better-educated parents generally have children who are themselves better educated, healthier, wealthier, and better off in almost every way than the children of the less educated. But this simple correlation does not prove that the relationship is causal. Neeraj Kaushal sifts through the evidence from economics and public policy and reviews large national and international studies to conclude that, indeed, education has large intergenerational payoffs in many areas of children's lives, and that these payoffs persist over time. Thus the rationale for two-generation programs that boost parents' education is compelling. However, Kaushal writes, the U.S. education system reinforces socioeconomic inequality across generations by spending more money on educating richer children than on educating poorer children. By themselves, then, two-generation programs will not necessarily ameliorate the structural factors that perpetuate inequality in this country.

Two-Generation Programs and Health

Parents' health and children's health are closely intertwined, write Sherry Glied and Don Oellerich, and healthier parents have healthier children. Genetics accounts for some of this relationship, but much of it can be traced to environment and behavior. Thus programs that improve parents' health should improve their children's health as well. Yet we have few two-generation programs that explicitly aim to work this way, save for a narrow category of programs that target pregnant women, newborns, and very young children. Glied and Oellerich assess these programs, discuss why there are so few of them, and suggest ways to expand them. Their chief conclusion is that structural barriers in the U.S. health care system stand in the way of such programs. Some of these barriers have to do with health insurance, access to care, and benefits, but the biggest one is the fact that physicians typically specialize in treating either children or adults, rather than families as a whole. The Affordable Care Act has begun to break down some of these barriers, the authors write, but much remains to be done.

Boosting Family Income to Promote Child Development

Decades of developmental research have shown that there is no question that poverty disrupts child development. But as with education and health, establishing a causal relationship is more difficult, which means that it's difficult to make the case that boosting family income will have major effects on child development. Greg Duncan, Katherine Magnuson, and Elizabeth Votruba-Drzal examine whether policies that increase family income but do nothing else can promote child development. The authors also want to know whether the timing of increased income—that is, when it appears during a child's development—can make a difference. They first review three "theoretical frameworks"—family and environmental stress, family resources and investment in children, and cultural practices—that social scientists have developed to explore and explain how poverty could influence children's development. These theories all support the argument that poverty harms children's development and behavior. Reviewing the empirical evidence on whether poverty has a causal effect on school achievement, educational attainment, behavior, or health, the authors find that the causal effect is moderate, but that poverty early in life has the strongest impacts. The authors conclude that giving families cash and in-kind income supplements is likely to have positive effects on their children, especially if the income supplements come during early childhood.

Parents' Employment and Children's Wellbeing

According to Carolyn Heinrich, the bottom line is that parents' work can have both positive and negative effects on their children. For example, employment lifts family income, which has many beneficial consequences for children, and working parents can be positive role models. On the other hand, work can reduce the amount of time parents spend with their children, expose parents to severe stress that spills over into family life, and induce mothers to stop breastfeeding sooner. The families most likely to experience employment's negative consequences are precisely those where the parents work in low-paying, low-quality jobs that lack autonomy and benefits such as sick leave and maternity leave; these conditions are especially detrimental for single mothers and their children. Public policy, Heinrich writes, could bolster the positive effects of parents' work and ameliorate the negative ones. In particular, if we want low-income parents' work to enhance their children's wellbeing, we need to expand workplace flexibility, help parents place their children in high-quality child care, and help parents train for, find, and keep a well-paying job with benefits. All of these policies could be components of two-generation programs.

Family Assets and Child Outcomes

For more than three decades, there has been a growing movement in research, practice, and policy based on the view that even low-income parents can save and that if they did, they and their children would be better off in the long run. Michal Grinstein-Weiss, Trina Williams Shanks, and Sondra Beverly argue that savings could aid children's development by giving their families a cushion against hard times, reducing parental stress, helping parents invest in children, and improving parents' personal efficacy as well as their attitudes and expectations about the future. Rigorous studies show that low- and moderate-income parents will save money over the short term if their savings are matched by a third party. One study even shows that

providing matched saving accounts increases homeownership in the short term, although families that do not receive incentives for savings are just as likely to own a home after 10 years. Other experimental studies find that interventions to increase savings have long-term positive impacts on parents' education. The authors also find that automatically opening a $1,000 savings account for newborns, and then matching parent contributions to the account, can dramatically increase the percentage of families that save money. However, the average amount of money that low- and moderate-income families save in these automatic accounts is quite modest, around $100 after 30 months. The authors conclude that parents can be induced to save, especially if an account is opened for them and if their savings are matched, but it is not yet clear whether these savings improve either their wealth or the wellbeing of their children in the long term.

Even small effects can accumulate and lead to large effects.

The Promise of Two-Generation Mechanisms

The United States has always advertised itself as a nation of boundless opportunity, in which every child has a shot at taking advantage of equal opportunity to achieve financial security as an adult. In recent decades, however, U.S. income inequality has increased dramatically, and the chances of getting ahead, especially by rising from the bottom, are worse than in many other nations with advanced economies.[13]

The traditional route to opportunity is through education. To help poor children use education to achieve financial security as adults, the nation is spending much more on preschool programs than it did 10 years ago, based on the assumption that children who attend preschool will be better prepared to take advantage of the public schools. Further, the public schools themselves are in a nearly continuous state of reform, epitomized in recent years both by President Bush's No Child Left Behind law and by President Obama's Race to the Top and Investing in Innovation initiatives.[14] But despite major investments in preschool programs and the reform of public schools, poor children continue to fall further and further behind in educational achievement and in college enrollment and completion. Preschool education and school reform may be part of the road to increasing opportunity for the poor, but the experience of the past several decades shows that something more is needed.

Based on the extensive evidence that parents are a vital force in children's development, and capitalizing on the recent interest in two-generation programs, this issue explores six mechanisms that might be part of that something more. Three generalizations are justified.

First, in addition to the Two-Generation 2.0 programs, the articles here present solid evidence that stress regulation, parental education, parental health, family income, employment, and assets are linked to children's development. In each case, there is correlational evidence suggesting that these mechanisms are at the very least associated with children's development. In most cases, there is even stronger evidence from experimental or quasi-experimental studies (as opposed to correlational studies) that programs that raise the level of parents' education, health, income, etc. can have a causal impact on children's development.

Second, research shows that among social intervention programs generally, positive effects are infrequent and, when they occur, usually modest.[15] Thus we are not discouraged by the finding that most of the positive effects on development reported by our authors are moderate. The field of intervention science should learn to savor moderate success, and work to modify current programs and to develop new programs with more substantial effects. Further, even small effects can accumulate and lead to large effects.[16] For example, Isabel Sawhill and her colleagues at the Brookings Institution found that providing disadvantaged children with a sequence of five well-evaluated programs from early childhood through adolescence increased their projected lifetime incomes by roughly five times the cost of the five programs.[17]

Third, some of the fields of intervention research that our authors review are in their early stages. For example, the research on stress and developing biological systems has only just left its infancy. Nonetheless, as Thompson shows, the field has already produced effective intervention programs that help children entering new foster care homes and that improve poor preschool children's classroom self-regulation skills. Chase-Lansdale and Brooks-Gunn argue that we are now developing more effective two-generation intervention programs of the type that involve simultaneous quality preschool for children and job training for parents. Perhaps the most enticing example of promise is found in increasing poor parents' income during the early years of children's lives. Duncan and his colleagues present several research findings suggesting that income supplements early in life can have positive effects on developing children. Fortunately, a large-scale experiment subjecting this finding to a rigorous test will soon be under way.

Taken together, the research reviewed in this issue of *Future of Children* at least suggests that each of the six two-generation mechanisms we present can enhance children's development—and in some cases the evidence is more than suggestive. Moreover, there is good reason to expect that interventions based on these mechanisms will improve as research proceeds.

ENDNOTES

1. Jack P. Shonkoff and Deborah A. Phillips, eds., *From Neurons to Neighborhoods: The Science of Early Childhood Development* (Washington, DC: National Academy Press, 2000); James J. Heckman and Flavio Cunha, "Investing in Our Young People," in *Childhood Programs and Practices in the First Decade of Life: A Human Capital Integration*, Arthur Reynolds et al., ed. (New York: Cambridge University Press, 2010), 381–414.

2. Craig T. Ramey, Joseph J. Sparling, and Sharon Landesman Ramey, *Abecedarian: The Ideas, the Approach, the Findings* (Los Altos, CA: Sociometrics Corporation, 2012); Lawrence J. Schweinhart et al., *Lifetime Effects: The High/Scope Perry Preschool Study through age 40* (Ypsilanti, MI: High/Scope Press, 2005); David Olds et al., "Long-Term Effects of Nurse Home Visitation on Children's Criminal and Antisocial Behavior: Fifteen-Year Follow-Up of a Randomized Controlled Trial," *Journal of the American Medical Association* 280 (1998), 1238–44; James J. Kemple, *Career Academies: Long-Term Impacts on Labor Market Outcomes, Educational Attainment, and Transitions to Adulthood* (New York: MDRC, 2008); Raj Chetty et al., "How Does Your Kindergarten Classroom Affect Your Earnings? Evidence from Project STAR," *Quarterly Journal of Economics* 126 (2011), 1593–1660.

3. Gregory Camilli et al., "Meta-Analysis of the Effects of Early Education Interventions on Cognitive and Social Development," *Teachers College Record* 112 (2010), 579–620; Janet Currie and Duncan Thomas, "Does Head Start Make a Difference?" *American Economic Review* 85 (1995), 341–64; David J. Deming, "Early Childhood Intervention and Life-Cycle Skill Development: Evidence from Head Start," *American Economic Journal: Applied Economics* 1 (2009), 111–34; James Heckman, Rodrigo Pinto, and Peter Savelyev, "Understanding the Mechanisms through Which an Influential Early Childhood Program Boosted Adult Outcomes," *American Economic Review* 103 (2013), 2052–86; Christopher Ruhm and Jane Waldfogel, "Long-Term Effects of Early Childhood Care and Education," *Nordic Economic Policy Review*, no. 1 (2012), 23–52; Douglas Almond and Janet Currie, "Human Capital Development before Age Five," in Handbook of Labor Economics, vol. 4, Orley Ashenfelter and David Card, ed. (2010): 1315–1486.

4. Michael Puma et al., *Head Start Impact Study: Final Report* (Washington, DC: U.S. Department of Health and Human Services, 2010).

5. Mark W. Lipsey et al., *Evaluation of the Tennessee Voluntary Prekindergarten Program: Kindergarten and First Grade Follow-Up Results from the Randomized Control Design: Research Report* (Nashville, TN: Peabody Research Institute, 2013).

6. Grover J. "Russ" Whitehurst, "New Evidence Raises Doubts on Obama's Preschool for All," Brown Center Chalkboard (blog), November 20, 2013, http://www.brookings.edu/blogs/brown-center-chalkboard/posts/2013/11/20-evidence-raises-doubts-about-obamas-preschool-for-all-whitehurst.

7. Ron Haskins and W. Steven Barnett, eds., *Investing in Young Children: New Directions in Federal Preschool and Early Childhood Education*, September 2010, Brookings Institution and National Institute for Early Education Research, http://www.brookings.edu/~/media/research/files/reports/2010/10/13%20investing%20in%20young%20children%20haskins/1013_investing_in_young_children_haskins.pdf; Susan Aud et al., *The Condition of Education 2013* (Washington, DC: National Center for Education Statistics, 2013).

8. Sean F. Reardon, "The Widening Academic Achievement Gap between the Rich and the Poor: New Evidence and Possible Explanations," in *Whither Opportunity? Rising Inequality, Schools, and Children's Life Chances*, ed. Greg J. Duncan and Richard J. Murnane (New York: Russell Sage and Spencer Foundation, 2011), 91–115.

9. Ariel Kalil, "Inequality Begins at Home: The Role of Parenting in the Diverging Destinies of Rich and Poor Children," in *Diverging Destinies: Families in an Era of Increasing Inequality*, ed. Paul Amato, Susan M. McHale, and Alan Booth (New York: Springer, forthcoming).

10. Betty Hart and Todd R. Risley, *Meaningful Differences in the Everyday Experience of Young American Children* (Baltimore: Paul H. Brookes Publishing, 1995).

11. Meredith Phillips, "Parenting, Time Use, and Disparities in Academic Outcomes," in Duncan and Murnane, *Whither Opportunity?*, 207–28.

12. Valerie E. Lee and David T. Burkam, *Inequality at the Starting Gate: Social Background Differences in Achievement as Children Begin School* (Washington, DC: Economic Policy Institute, 2002).

13. Miles Corak, "Do Poor Children Become Poor Adults? Lessons from a Cross Country Comparison of Generational Earnings Mobility," working paper, Institute for the Study of Labor, Bonn, Germany, 2006; Congressional Budget Office, *Trends in the Distribution of Household Income between 1979 and 2007* (Washington, DC: Congressional Budget Office, 2011), http://www.cbo.gov/sites/default/files/cbofiles/attachments/10-25-HouseholdIncome.pdf; Ron Haskins and Isabel Sawhill, *Creating an Opportunity Society* (Washington, DC: Brookings Institution Press, 2009).

14. Steven Brill, *Class Warfare* (New York: Simon & Schuster, 2011).

15. Jim Manzi, *Uncontrolled: The Surprising Payoff of Trial-and-Error for Business, Politics, and Society* (New York: Basic Books, 2012).

16. Jonathan R. Cole and Burton Singer, "A Theory of Limited Differences: Explaining the Productivity Puzzle in Science," in *The Outer Circle: Women in the Scientific Community*, Harriet Zuckerman, Jonathan R. Cole, and John T. Bruer, ed. (New York: W. W. Norton & Company, 1991), 277–310.

17. Kerry Searle Grannis and Isabel V. Sawhill, "Improving Children's Life Chances: Estimates from the Social Genome Model," Brookings Institution, October 11, 2013, http://www.brookings.edu/research/papers/2013/10/11-improving-childrens-life-chances-sawhill-grannis.

Two-Generation Programs in the Twenty-First Century

P. Lindsay Chase-Lansdale and Jeanne Brooks-Gunn

Summary

Most of the authors in this issue of *Future of Children* focus on a single strategy for helping both adults and children that could become a component of two-generation programs. Lindsay Chase-Lansdale and Jeanne Brooks-Gunn, on the other hand, look at actual programs with an explicit two-generation focus that have been tried in the past or are currently under way.

These explicitly two-generation programs have sought to build human capital across generations by combining education or job training for adults with early childhood education for their children. Chase-Lansdale and Brooks-Gunn explain the theories behind these programs and review the evidence for their efficacy. A first wave of such programs in the 1980s and 1990s produced mostly disappointing results, but the evaluations they left behind pointed to promising new directions. More recently, a second wave of two-generation programs—the authors dub them "Two-Generation 2.0"—has sought to rectify the flaws of earlier efforts, largely by building strong connections between components for children and adults, by ensuring that children and adults receive services of equal duration and intensity, and by incorporating advances in both education and workforce development. These Two-Generation 2.0 programs are still in their infancy, and we have yet to see clear evidence that they can achieve their goals or be implemented cost-effectively at scale. Nonetheless, Chase-Lansdale and Brooks-Gunn write, the theoretical justification for these programs is strong, their early results are promising, and the time is ripe for innovation, experimentation, and further study.

www.futureofchildren.org

P. Lindsay Chase-Lansdale is Frances Willard Professor of human development and social policy at the School of Education and Social Policy, faculty fellow at the Institute for Policy Research, and associate provost for faculty at Northwestern University. Jeanne Brooks-Gunn is the Virginia and Leonard Marx Professor of child development and education at Teachers College and College of Physicians and Surgeons at Columbia University and co-director of the National Center for Children and Families.

In principle, two-generation programs have a unifying form: they explicitly target low-income parents and children from the same family. However, their structure and content vary widely. For children, two-generation programs can include health and education services, such as home visiting, early childhood education, and programs for children who have been exposed to trauma. Services for parents can involve parenting, literacy, learning the English language, earning a GED, getting a postsecondary education, treating mental health problems, and preventing child abuse and domestic violence, as well as case management and workforce development.

In this article, we focus on a specific type of two-generation program: those that intentionally link education, job training, and career-building services for low-income parents simultaneously with early childhood education for their young children. These programs emphasize an investment strategy to build human capital for both children and parents, implying an intensive, extended approach. In the past five years, the appeal of a human capital two-generation perspective has led to a number of initiatives. Evaluation evidence for these recent innovations lags behind policy and practice, but theoretical support for two-generation programs is compelling.

This article integrates theories from developmental science, economics, and education to evaluate the assumptions that underlie two-generation programs, to outline possible mechanisms through which these programs affect children, to synthesize and critique what has been tried to date, and to describe emerging programs across the nation. Our bottom line: The jury is out and will be for some time regarding whether new human capital two-generation programs can be successfully implemented, as pilot programs or at scale. Very little data are available on whether the impacts on children and families are stronger than those of single-generation programs. Yet new approaches to two-generation human capital programs are worth pursuing and testing.

Brief History

The idea that the needs of vulnerable parents and children can be tackled together is not new. The concept was explicitly introduced with the launch of Head Start in 1965.[1] In the early 1990s, the Foundation for Child Development coined the term "two-generation program" and sponsored a book on the subject.[2] At that time, innovation involved two strategies: embedding some self-sufficiency programs for parents in early childhood education programs, and adding child care to education and employment services for parents. We call these programs "Two-Generation 1.0." In the first set of Two-Generation 1.0 programs, the self-sufficiency services that were linked to early childhood programs included adult basic education, GED attainment, and strategies to obtain entry-level jobs and leave welfare. In general, the adult programs in these child-oriented settings were not intensive, widely implemented, or extensively studied. Instead, most services for parents in early childhood education programs in the 1980s and '90s emphasized family support, parenting, literacy, mental health, and access to public benefits, all of which were seen as more closely aligned with early childhood programs' primary mission: achieving positive development for children.[3]

The second set of Two-Generation 1.0 programs in the 1980s and 1990s started with parents, primarily adolescent mothers on welfare. Their chief goal was to promote life skills, high school graduation or GED attainment, employment, and reductions in long-term welfare dependency.[4] The elements of these programs that directly targeted children were undeveloped and underused, and they often involved child care of unknown quality. However, these large-scale, parent-oriented demonstration programs aimed to help in many areas of teenage mothers' lives, including parenting.[5]

Two-Generation 1.0 programs seemed to be a promising new direction in services to combat social inequality. Yet, by the late 1990s, the impetus to expand two-generation programs faded away, in part because findings from the large demonstration programs for adolescent mothers were disappointing (see below) and also because "work-first" policies had come to dominate the conversation.[6] Welfare reform under the 1996 Personal Responsibility and Work Opportunity Reconciliation Act (PRWORA) mandated that recipients work, gave them fewer education and training options, and set time limits and sanctions for not following the rules. This extraordinary legislation, combined with the booming economy in the late 1990s, resulted in the steepest decline in the welfare rolls in the history of the program—approximately 60 percent, exceeding even the highest hopes of most of the law's supporters.[7] At the same time, federally funded job-training programs for low-income adults shrank significantly. For instance, the 1998 Workforce Investment Act (WIA) primarily supported job search and placement programs rather than training and education.[8] The public policy focus on welfare dependency in the 1980s, 1990s, and early 2000s has largely given way to concern about the United States' competitive position in the world economy and the fact that we lag behind so many other countries in educational attainment at a time when education

beyond high school is essential for success.[9] With advancing technology and globalization, many jobs in the U.S. require increasingly higher levels of education and training than in the past, and low-skilled jobs that pay enough to support a family have largely disappeared.[10] Yet many members of our current and future workforce—especially low-income children and their parents—are unprepared for the demands of the twenty-first century.[11] In addition, childhood poverty remains persistently high at over 20 percent, and social inequality has increased substantially. In this context, policy makers, advocates, and scholars are seeking promising new approaches to combat economic hardship and low education, and their deleterious consequences for families and society.[12]

Philanthropists have been key catalysts for a resurgence of interest in two-generation programs. For example, in 2008, the Bill and Melinda Gates Foundation launched an ambitious postsecondary education agenda with the goal of doubling, by 2025, the percentage of low-income students who earn a postsecondary degree or other credential with genuine value in the workplace. Similarly, the George Kaiser Family Foundation collaborated with the Community Action Project of Tulsa, Oklahoma (CAP Tulsa), to fund a pilot human capital two-generation program called Career*Advance*; the Foundation for Child Development added a two-generation component to its Pre-K–3rd initiative; the Annie E. Casey Foundation launched an initiative to expand and study implementation strategies for two-generation human capital interventions; and the W. K. Kellogg Foundation is fostering innovative family engagement programs. Finally, the Aspen Institute has established an initiative through its new Ascend center—called Two

Generations, One Future—that represents significant investment in building a broad two-generation perspective in policy, practice, research, philanthropy, and the media.

Two-Generation 2.0: Central Concepts

Today, this second wave of programs—we call them "Two-Generation 2.0"—has a renewed and explicit focus on promoting the human capital of low-income parents and children in the same program. What is different about this new wave? First, it combines human capital programs for adults and children that have previously been kept in separate silos (see figure 1). For parents, education and training goes beyond adult basic education and getting a GED to include postsecondary education and certification. Similarly, second-wave two-generation programs capitalize on new directions in job training that go beyond search and placement to include workforce intermediaries, also called sectoral training (we discuss this and other innovations below).[13] Two-Generation 2.0 programs recognize the compelling evidence that high-quality early childhood education centers can have significant short- and long-term benefits for children. Thus, such centers are an essential building block for new two-generation programs. The Two-Generation 2.0 approach also considers the full range of low-income families, not just those who are on welfare. As programs unfold, their designers are giving considerable thought to which subgroups are most likely to succeed and how they should be targeted and approached. Most Two-Generation 2.0 programs are in the pilot stage, requiring innovation and experimentation. Advocates and leaders of these efforts across the nation are united in their belief that Two-Generation 2.0 programs will be more effective than single-generation

programs in enhancing healthy development over the life course for young children in low-income families.

Why Would Two-Generation 2.0 Programs Be More Effective?

By what scientific rationale might two-generation programs be more effective than single-generation programs? A number of theoretical frameworks from developmental science shed light on the assumptions underlying these programs.

First, continuity and change theory suggests how much change is realistic or possible for low-income children whose development has gotten off to a difficult start. Widely substantiated empirically, this theory states that for most children, over time, significant continuity in the environment *and* within the child is the rule rather than the exception.[14] Once young children have started along a particular path of development (for example, heightened sensitivity to stress, delays in vocabulary and numeracy), they are likely to proceed in a similar fashion, unless they encounter new opportunities, resources, or interventions. Eric Knudsen and his colleagues, explaining why early childhood education is vital for low-income children, capture the notion of developmental continuity well: "Early learning begets later learning, and skills beget skills."[15] Likewise, most home environments are difficult to change. They are shaped by parents' characteristics and experiences, such as their own education, employment, income, mental and physical health, ability to handle stress, and ways of relating to each other, their children, and their extended families. To more effectively redirect low-income children's lives, programs should simultaneously target the child *and* the child's home environment. Human capital two-generation programs go

Figure 1. Two-Generation Human Capital Programs

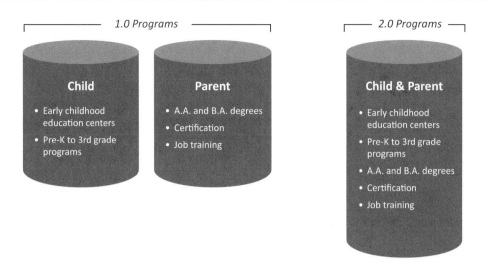

about changing the child by fostering learning and social competence through an early childhood education program, and changing the child's home environment by promoting parents' education, employment, and income.

Second, the power of "proximal" environments is a central tenet of ecological theory.[16] Numerous studies have shown that the quality of a child's "close-in" environments is most influential for later development, especially during the early years when the child's developing systems are exquisitely sensitive to environmental forces.[17] Factors that affect the environment's quality include cognitive stimulation, richness in literacy and numeracy, regular routines, warmth and responsiveness, setting appropriate limits, role modeling, and opportunities to develop emotional regulation, executive function, attention, and the like.[18] Two-generation programs, then, are likely to be more effective than single-generation programs if they mean that low-income children experience the combination of two positive proximal environments, rather than just one. A child who returns home from a stimulating

educational setting to a stressed family environment with few learning resources and parents who are worried about making ends meet is likely to do less well than a child who experiences enriching environments both in and outside the home.

The third relevant framework is risk and resilience theory, which examines how children adapt to environmental and biological challenges.[19] Supported by numerous studies, this theory posits that children can bounce back and even thrive in the face of short-term adversity, but their development is likely to be seriously hampered by chronic and cumulative stress, such as the combination of family economic hardship, low parental education, parents' poor mental health, problematic parenting, and limited access to enriched learning opportunities outside the home.[20] Empirical research has also documented protective factors in the child or the environment—such as a sunny personality, responsive and stimulating parenting, or high-quality early childhood education—that promote resilience or positive development

Figure 2. Change Model for Two-Generation 2.0 Programs

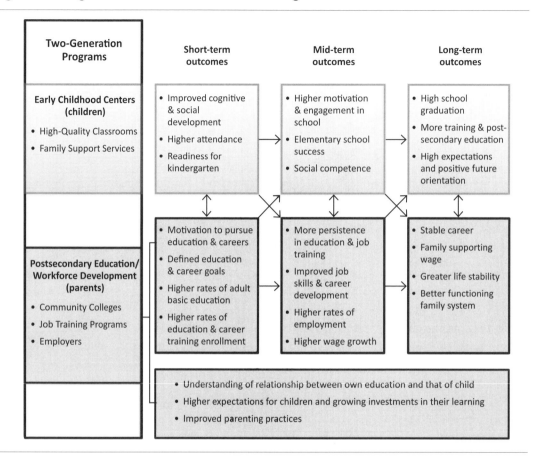

in the face of adversity. The most significant implication of risk and resilience theory for two-generation programs is that intensive interventions in more than one area of a child's life are essential.[21] "For young children facing cumulative and/or chronic risks," write Ann Masten and Abigail Gewirtz, "interventions need to be multi-level, individually tailored in intensity, targeting multiple domains of competence, and of sufficient length to promote lasting change."[22]

A Change Model for Two-Generation 2.0 Programs

Here we present a change model that illustrates how two-generation programs may strengthen child development (see figure 2).

In many respects, this model draws on the theoretical foundation of other articles in this issue, in addition to the three theories we've just described. For example, human resource and investment theories propose that successful learning, social development, and earning power across the lifespan depend on monetary and nonmonetary resources in the environment, an individual's inherent predispositions, and the interplay between the two.[23] These theories suggest that adequate resources and positive interactions produce more human and social capital, more social interaction, more cognitive stimulation, and better life opportunities. And family stress theory argues that the stress of living in a low-income environment harms children's development and causes psychological distress for parents, which in turn leads to inadequate parenting.[24]

As figure 2 shows, successful two-generation programs could influence parents to pursue more credentials, more education, and better jobs.[25] Better jobs mean increased income, improved financial stability, higher self-esteem, better mental health, less stress, and more effective parenting.[26] Improvements in children's development should follow, including school success and social competence.[27] Parents with more education and training may enrich the literacy and numeracy environments at home, and increase cognitive stimulation in other areas as well.[28] Better-educated parents may also serve as better academic role models, have higher educational expectations, and be better guides and advocates for their children's schooling, all of which may help children become more motivated, engaged, and successful.[29]

Our model also shows that the two-generation approach works in complex ways. For example, children's advances in learning might form a feedback loop, stimulating parents both to expand opportunities for their children and to get more education themselves.[30] In our model, the bidirectional arrows between parents' and children's trajectories illustrate these synergistic effects. Negative outcomes are also possible. For example, the simultaneous demands of employment, school, and childrearing might increase parents' stress and force them to spend too much time apart from their children, both of which are risk factors for family functioning, parenting, and children's development, especially for infants and toddlers.[31]

Building Blocks for Two-Generation 2.0 Programs

The building blocks for Two-Generation 2.0 programs are early childhood education for preschoolers and postsecondary education and workforce training for parents. What evidence from these areas encourages us to establish and expand two-generation programs today?

Early Childhood Education Programs

The design, implementation, and outcomes of early childhood education have been studied for more than 40 years, and we have compelling evidence that it can play a critical role in promoting positive life trajectories for low-income children.[32] We also have extensive evidence of what defines a high-quality early childhood program.[33] For example, when early childhood education classrooms are characterized by emotionally supportive teacher-child interactions, effective behavior management strategies, and classroom activities that promote student engagement and higher-order thinking, they are consistently linked to gains in children's learning.[34] Structural features of early childhood education programs can provide a foundation for teachers to interact effectively with children in ways that are cognitively stimulating and supportive; these include smaller class sizes, as well as ensuring that teachers have experience, strong educational qualifications, and training.[35] Effective early education programs also acknowledge and embrace diversity.[36]

The strongest, most rigorous short- and long-term findings about how early childhood education affects children come from two high-quality, pioneering model programs that were launched in the 1960s and 1970s: the Abecedarian Project and the Perry Preschool Project. Both programs offered enriched early childhood education to children (beginning in infancy and preschool, respectively), including well-developed curricula, experienced and trained teachers, and parent involvement.[37] Notably, both Abecedarian and Perry Preschool randomly assigned children to the experimental program or to a control group. The control group could access other early childhood programs that were available in nearby communities, but at that time in the U.S., such programs were rare.

In the short term, children in the two model programs showed higher levels of learning and social development than did children in the control group. In the long term—from elementary school through ages 21 to 27—children in the model programs were less likely to be placed in special education classes, to be held back a grade, to drop out of high school, to become pregnant as teenagers, or to participate in criminal activity; they also earned more as adults.[38] By age 30, adults from the Abecedarian program were much more likely than adults from the control group to have completed college.[39] The Perry Preschool and Abecedarian programs were expensive and small, involving 104 and 123 families, respectively. They were also limited to African-American families in two small cities.

The architects of Two-Generation 2.0 programs can also turn to research evidence from three additional sets of programs: (1) the Child-Parent Centers (CPC) Program; (2) Head Start; and (3) Universal Prekindergarten. CPC was launched in 1967 by the Chicago Public Schools, with funding from the federal government. It offered a multiyear enriched educational program from preschool through second grade to about 1,000 low-income children and their parents; a control group of about 550 children and

parents was drawn from randomly selected similar schools. For parents, the program emphasized significant engagement in activities at school or in field trips, and it offered a parent resource room staffed by a trained coordinator who was often another parent from the community. This parent resource room served as a space to make social connections and a site for workshops, speakers, and courses, including parenting, health, and GED courses.[40] A series of studies, which followed children from the program's end through age 28, shows that CPC participation was related to numerous positive outcomes. The CPC children were better prepared to enter school, and they performed better academically; they were more likely to complete high school and less likely to be involved with the criminal justice system; and they had better physical health.[41] However, these effects were not as large as those related to Abecedarian and Perry Preschool. But CPC was a much larger program than either Abecedarian or Perry Preschool, and it was successfully implemented in a large metropolis. It was also less expensive. Overall, it provides a well-researched example of the possibilities for creating contemporary two-generation programs. However, CPC was evaluated through what researchers call a quasi-experimental design—schools were randomly chosen for a comparison group of children, rather than randomly assigning individual children to treatment versus control groups. In addition, there were no assessments of children's development before the intervention, so we don't know whether the two groups of children and families differed from one another from the beginning.[42]

Head Start programs could also be a component of new two-generation programs. The nation's oldest and largest early childhood education program, Head Start was launched in 1965 as part of the War on Poverty. It provides comprehensive services that include early childhood education; medical, dental, and mental health care; nutrition counseling; and family support.[43] Although Head Start can be an important opportunity for low-income children and their families, its quality is uneven, and the program's intensity varies considerably around the country. For example, many centers are open only half a day during the school year and not at all in the summer.[44]

In 1998, Congress commissioned a randomized controlled trial to evaluate Head Start's impact on children's development, and an ambitious study of 4,667 children from 383 centers was launched in 2002. A central question for the study involved developmental timing: Do outcomes differ if children enter Head Start at age three versus age four? Three-year-olds and four-year-olds on a waiting list for the program were randomly assigned to Head Start or to the control group. Parents of the three-year-olds who were assigned to the control group were told that their children could attend Head Start the following year at age four. Children were assessed after one year of Head Start, and in the spring of kindergarten, first grade, and third grade. The Head Start Impact Study (HSIS) found that, no matter whether children entered at age three or age four, one year of Head Start led to modest improvements in children's language, literacy, and math skills, but did not affect their social development. However, these cognitive improvements faded by the end of kindergarten and stayed that way through the end of third grade.[45]

Head Start supporters were disappointed by these findings. However, it is important to recognize some problems in the evaluation design. First, a significant portion of the control group (40 percent) attended early childhood education centers in their communities, including Head Start. With widespread demand for early-childhood education in the twenty-first century, increasing requirements that preschool teachers be licensed, and the rapid expansion of state-funded and regulated prekindergarten programs, many early childhood programs in the United States have achieved at least a minimum level of quality. The question we should be asking, then, is whether we expect Head Start centers to be of higher quality than other centers and preschool programs. It follows that differences between children in Head Start and those in community or school-based early childhood programs might not be as large as they would be if the control group did not have access to early childhood programs at all.[46]

A second problem involves the three-year-old cohort and what their families decided when these children turned four. About 47 percent of the three-year-olds in the control group switched to Head Start at age four, and about 33 percent of the children who were randomly assigned to Head Start at age three did not attend Head Start the following year. These crossover patterns may have diluted the randomized design, and thus the study may have underestimated Head Start's impact on child development.

In addition to the Head Start Impact Study, nonexperimental studies (that is, studies that analyze longitudinal data sets, using sophisticated designs and statistical techniques in an effort to account for unmeasured biases) have provided evidence that Head Start has positive short- and long-term effects on a variety of child outcomes. These effects include higher levels of cognitive development and social competence, lower mortality later in childhood, higher rates of high school graduation and college attendance, better health, higher earnings, and less involvement with the criminal justice system.[47] This large body of research indicates that Head Start programs can indeed be part of a Two-Generation 2.0 strategy.

State-funded prekindergarten programs offer a third set of early childhood education opportunities for two-generation programs. At least 40 states now have their own prekindergarten programs, double the number in 1980.[48] These prekindergarten programs present the best evidence to date that early childhood education centers can be widely implemented, but like Head Start programs, their quality varies.[49] The results of research on how prekindergarten affects child outcomes are just emerging. Using sophisticated statistical techniques, two rigorous recent studies of prekindergarten programs— one of them conducted in Michigan, New Jersey, Oklahoma, South Carolina, and West Virginia, and the other conducted in Boston—reported some promising findings, although child outcomes varied significantly. In some cases, prekindergarten participation was linked to increases in prereading skills, early math skills, vocabulary, and executive functioning.[50] But these positive findings occurred in some states and not others, and variation in levels of state funding did not explain the pattern. The most promising findings for prekindergarten come from a series of studies of the universal prekindergarten program in the greater Tulsa, Oklahoma, metro area. Using a rigorous statistical approach similar to that of the five-state study, these investigations found that children in prekindergarten had significantly more short-term positive developmental outcomes than did children who had not experienced prekindergarten. The largest differences occurred in prereading skills, followed by spelling and math skills; at the end of the

program, prekindergarten children were performing five to nine months ahead of their same-aged peers who just missed the cutoff and started prekindergarten a year later.[51] Moreover, a later study found that participating in prekindergarten was linked to improved socioemotional development.[52] It is important to note that Oklahoma boasts one of the oldest and highest-quality prekindergarten programs in the country. Classes are small, and student-teacher ratios are low. All teachers have a B.A. and have been certified in early childhood education, and their salaries and benefits are commensurate with those of expert teachers in the Oklahoma K–12 system.

Clearly, a central feature of Two-Generation 2.0 human capital programs must be high-quality early childhood education. The studies we've described provide ample guidance for how to choose or design the early childhood education component. These early childhood programs also reflect tenets of the key theories we outlined above: (a) an intensive focus on enriching proximal environments for children; (b) timing during the early years; (c) promoting protective factors, such as social competence and positive relationships; and (d) sustained duration.

Education and Workforce Development Programs for Parents

In contrast to early childhood education, the 35-year history of education and workforce training programs for low-income parents has not been as encouraging.[53] However, many programs were developed and evaluated in the 1980s and '90s, and they offer key lessons for new two-generation programs. These ambitious education and job training programs began in response to concerns that too many teenagers were becoming parents and then relying on welfare. The first such program was Project Redirection, a complex, multisite program launched in 1980 by the Manpower Demonstration and Research Corporation (MDRC) and targeted toward socioeconomically disadvantaged teenage mothers. Participants had to be 17 or younger, pregnant or parenting, without a GED or high school degree, and on or eligible for welfare.[54] They received services for one year, including individual counseling; training in life management, parenting, and employability skills; referrals to health, education, and employment services in the community; and monthly stipends of $30 per month ($83 in 2013 dollars). They were also offered child care, though they largely relied on family members instead.[55] The program also included three significant innovations: individual participant plans, peer group sessions, and mentoring by older women in the community. Its goal was to increase adolescent mothers' human capital in a highly supportive environment. Although Project Redirection recognized the challenges and joys of early parenthood, it did not target children directly.

The quasi-experimental evaluation of Project Redirection compared about 300 participants with a control group of about 370 adolescent mothers from similar communities at four time points: before the program began, when the program ended one year later, and two and five years after participants enrolled. At the end of the program, Project Redirection participants were more likely to be enrolled in school and have job experience, and less likely to have become pregnant again. However, by two and five years after they joined the program, most of these advantages had disappeared. Mothers who had been through the program were somewhat less likely to be on welfare than mothers in the comparison group (49 percent versus 59 percent). But

they were more likely to have had another child, and there were no significant differences between the two groups in education, job training, and employment. In general, Project Redirection mothers were still quite disadvantaged at age 22.[56]

Clearly, a central feature of Two-Generation 2.0 human capital programs must be high-quality early childhood education.

On the other hand, children of program mothers were faring better at the five-year assessment than were children of comparison-group mothers. Project Redirection mothers reported better parenting skills and more breastfeeding, and they were more likely to have enrolled their children in Head Start. Children of program mothers also had larger vocabularies and fewer behavior problems, and the quality of their home environments was higher.[57] These findings represent the first indication that education and training programs for low-income teenage mothers, combined with intensive support services, can lead to long-term positive outcomes for children, even without evidence of continuing human capital improvements for parents.[58] However, the quasi-experimental nature of the study suggests that these findings should be interpreted with caution.

Project Redirection marked the beginning of a wave of similar large programs with randomized evaluation designs. Yet virtually none of them produced sizable, systematic effects on mothers' education and employment, and some had unintended negative effects. Three multisite programs operated in the late 1980s through the mid-1990s: the New Chance Demonstration and Ohio's Learning and Earning Program (LEAP) (both evaluated by MDRC), and the Teen Parent Demonstration (TPD), evaluated by Mathematica Policy Research. New Chance and TPD involved a wide range of services, including case management, life skills counseling, parenting classes, and education and workforce training, while LEAP required participants only to attend school. The programs' eligibility criteria were similar to those for Project Redirection, except that all participants were currently on welfare, and mothers in all three programs were 17 to 19 years old. New Chance was a voluntary program, while TPD and LEAP were mandatory for welfare recipients, linking school and work requirements to cash payments.[59]

The samples for the three randomized evaluations were sizable: 2,000 for New Chance, 4,000 for LEAP, and 5,000 for TPD. Program impacts were studied over time, and the final data were collected 3.5 years after the program began for New Chance, three and four years afterward for LEAP, and five and 6.5 years afterward for TPD.[60] Across the three programs, the impacts on young mothers' human capital were minimal. New Chance appeared to help some mothers earn a GED (possibly at the expense of earning a high school diploma), but the other programs did not produce such clear-cut educational advances. None of the programs consistently helped in other areas of the mothers' lives, such as earnings, employment, or welfare participation.

Rather than taking a two-generation approach, these three programs viewed child care as a support for mothers' education and work activities. TPD and LEAP offered several kinds of child care assistance, including referrals, subsidies, and free on-site child care. Yet most TPD and New Chance participants relied on relatives for child care, there are no data on the quality of the on-site child care programs, and we have no information about LEAP families' child care participation.[61]

New Chance and TPD also measured parenting and child outcomes. Neither program affected children's school readiness, vocabulary, or prosocial behavior. These findings are not surprising, given the programs' weak effects on mothers' education, employment, and income. Notably, New Chance mothers reported higher levels of parenting stress and more child behavior problems than did control-group mothers.[62] The program's evaluators speculated that because New Chance raised the hopes and expectations of its participants while urging them to engage in activities such as school or work that could increase stress, young mothers may have found these roles difficult to juggle, especially in the face of little clear personal progress.[63]

One more human capital initiative from the 1980s and '90s offers lessons for the new wave of two-generation programs. The Job Opportunity and Basic Skills (JOBS) program was created through welfare reform legislation, the Family Support Act of 1988.[64] (We do not review the most recent set of welfare-to-work programs, often referred to as Next Generation, because most did not involve education and training.) JOBS was implemented from 1988 to 1996, with 11 programs at seven sites, and it was evaluated by MDRC in a study called the National Evaluation of Welfare-to-Work Strategies (NEWWS).[65] The initiative tested two types of programs, in addition to one hybrid program. One set of JOBS programs was called Human

Capital Development (HCD); it focused on "education first" before fostering labor force participation. The second set, Labor Force Attachment (LFA), took a "work first" approach that emphasized searching for and quickly taking any type of job. The HCD programs primarily involved basic adult education (for example, remedial classes) and GED courses, and specifically did not promote postsecondary training. The hybrid program, in Portland, Oregon, combined a focus on employment with more advanced education and training, and it also counseled participants to seek higher-paying jobs even if that meant turning down a job offer with low wages.[66]

Like the programs discussed above, JOBS focused only on welfare participants, but the mothers' average age was 30. The full NEWWS study of JOBS involved about 40,000 mothers across all 11 sites, but many central findings of differences between the HCD and LFA programs come from just three sites—Atlanta, Georgia; Grand Rapids, Michigan; and Riverside, California. At each of those sites, mothers were randomly assigned to the HCD or LFA programs or to a control group. Mothers randomly assigned to the HCD programs were significantly more likely than control-group mothers to graduate from high school or earn a GED, though the proportion of mothers who achieved these things remained low (16.5 percent for participants versus 7.3 percent for the control group). This increase in education did not translate to higher levels of employment, and neither did participation in the LFA programs.

A recent reanalysis of the HCD programs, using a different statistical strategy, found that when mothers in the HCD programs increased their own education, their young children were likely to score higher on a school readiness test than children of control group mothers.[67] This association did not occur for the children whose parents were in the LFA group.

The hybrid program in Portland, Oregon, was an interesting outlier. Participants at this site achieved significantly higher levels of earnings over five years than control group mothers did, and they held on to jobs longer. The characteristics of Portland's program may have important implications for today's two-generation program designers. The program set employment in higher-paying jobs as its goal, and successfully conveyed this message to participants. Many participants were directed to the most appropriate mix of training programs, including GED classes and those that would lead to a certificate or trade license. The Portland site also collaborated with local community colleges from the outset; as a result, it was the only site where participants took postsecondary courses.[68]

Implications for Two-Generation 2.0 Programs

Although past experimental education and training programs for low-income mothers have generally had minimal effects, they offer a number of lessons for current two-generation programs. The first lesson involves the promise of comprehensive education and employment services, combined with extensive guidance and social support. Project Redirection pioneered these ideas, and other programs that target adults have moved these innovations forward. Program components such as peer support, mentors, coaches, and counselors have been shown to be effective for low-income students in general, although only a few studies have focused on low-income student-parents.[69] Similarly, there are hints from the NEWWS evaluation that programs can increase mothers' education and that this in turn is linked to improvements in children's learning. There are also hints from Project Redirection that when young mothers develop human capital, there may be long-term positive outcomes for children. However, the Project Redirection study did little to measure how parental behaviors changed at home, and we still have much to learn in this area.[70] Similarly, these programs presaged the central role of postsecondary education and credentialing to help low-income mothers succeed in the labor market; certainly, there is now extensive evidence for this in the broader population.[71]

The large-scale demonstration studies we've discussed also offer some cautionary lessons. In hindsight, targeting only adolescent mothers for education and workforce development seems very risky, given their immaturity.[72] Also, Two-Generation 1.0 programs set minimal goals for employment, and participants' monthly earnings were not sufficient to support a family. Today's emerging two-generation programs place a high priority on preparing parents for jobs that will lead to family-supporting wages. The studies also show how hard it is to combine multiple roles (worker, student, parent), and Two-Generation 2.0 programs should keep in mind the potential for too much stress, especially among young parents with infants and toddlers.

Two-Generation 2.0 Programs Emerge

In general, Two-Generation 1.0 programs were missing key elements, whether they were based in early childhood education or adult education and training. For instance, virtually no parent-oriented Two-Generation 1.0 program was consistently able to enroll participants' children in high-quality, on-site early childhood education. Similarly, the Two-Generation 1.0 programs based in early childhood education settings had little engagement with experts in adult learning, postsecondary education, and workforce development. This not only shows the extent to which parent-oriented and child-oriented programs have developed in separate silos, but also highlights the challenges to making two-generation programs work smoothly, seamlessly, and effectively. Based on the theories and evidence to date, we suggest that, in Two-Generation 2.0 programs, services for adults and children should be of equal intensity and quality. Research should examine how programs are implemented, how they balance adult and child elements, and the quality and intensity of their services.

Today's emerging two-generation programs place a high priority on preparing parents for jobs that will lead to family-supporting wages.

These issues are reflected in the findings of the one Two-Generation 2.0 program that has been implemented and experimentally evaluated—Enhanced Early Head Start, which operated from 2004 to 2007 as part of MDRC's multisite Enhanced Services for the Hard-to-Employ Demonstration and Evaluation Project. Enhanced Early Head Start added education and workforce components to Early Head Start programs (targeted to children from infancy to age three) in Kansas and Missouri.[73] An on-site staff specialist assessed parents' needs, gave them information and guidance about education and job-training programs in the community, and trained Early Head Start staff about these resources. About 600 families were randomly assigned to Enhanced Early Head Start or to a control group whose members could seek other local services.

A study of the outcomes three and a half years after random assignment revealed minimal impacts, with virtually no significant differences between the experimental and control groups for adults' employment, earnings, income, and parenting, or for their children's social and cognitive development. Moreover, parents in the experimental group reported higher levels of psychological distress.[74]

The evaluators offer a number of interpretations that have implications for Two-Generation 2.0 programs. First, the parent-focused services were difficult to implement in part because the front-line Early Head Start staff varied considerably in their expertise in, comfort with, and delivery of these services. Second, especially in rural areas where child care and transportation were not readily available, some parents expressed a strong interest in staying home with their young children rather than pursuing education and employment.[75] Another likely reason that Enhanced Early Head Start had little impact is that it offered referrals rather than education and job training itself, so the parental programming was not intensive.

Why Be Optimistic?

If past programs have had little effect on children's development and parents' human capital, why are we optimistic about a second wave of innovation, implementation, and evaluation of two-generation programs? First, designers of intensive education and training programs for parents have only just started to explore the positive repercussions of basing their programs in organizations "where the children are." It is a new idea to view high-quality early childhood education centers and prekindergarten programs as platforms for attracting parents into education and training.[76] Early childhood education centers promote social capital as parents and children participate regularly and get to know one another, program leaders, family support staff, and children's teachers.[77] These programs are likely to foster trusted, connected communities for parents and to be strong allies that share the hopes, expectations, and efforts to promote children's healthy development. Moreover, with the right combination of staff expertise, early childhood education centers could contribute strategically to helping parents stay in job training programs and enhancing their success. For example, as parents experience their young children thriving and learning at the center, they may be more motivated to improve their own education and economic standing.[78] Indeed, new findings from the Head Start Impact Study reveal that parents whose children were randomly assigned to Head Start were more likely to increase their own educational attainment (particularly at the postsecondary level) as well as employment over time than were parents of control group children.[79] Formalizing an education and job training program in an early childhood education organization could build upon this naturally occurring momentum. In other words, education and training programs for parents that emanate from their children's early childhood education centers may be more effective than those in separate silos.

Table 1. Characteristics of Current Two-Generation 2.0 Programs

Program	People served	Platform	Services	Background of group leaders	Assessment/ Evaluation
Adding adult programs to child programs					
Career*Advance* Community Action Project (CAP) of Tulsa, OK	Low-income parents and their children	Early Head Start and Head Start	Stackable training in nursing and health information technology at community colleges; incentives; career coaches; life skill training; peer support; center-based and home-based early childhood education	University faculty; antipoverty agency; workforce intermediary	Implementation and outcomes study
College Access and Success Program (CAASP); Educational Alliance	Low-income parents and their children	Early Head Start and Head Start programs	College and GED prep classes; ESL courses; case management; mental health counseling; financial supports; center-based and home-based early childhood education	Nonprofit organization; university and college faculty	Implementation and outcomes study
Adding child programs to adult programs					
Dual-Generation and Green Jobs, Los Angeles Alliance for a New Economy (LAANE)	Low-income parents and their children	Job training program and apprenticeships for existing jobs	Employment training in public utility for power and water; relevant courses in community colleges; online learning; peer supports; coaches; early childhood education	Antipoverty advocacy organization; coalitions of community organizers; labor union; government leaders; workforce intermediary	None

Second, the fields of education and workforce development have made considerable progress since the large-scale interventions for teenage mothers on welfare during the 1980s and '90s. One of the most significant advances is the emergence of workforce intermediaries, also called sectoral training, throughout the United States. Robert Giloth, a key leader in this area, writes that workforce intermediaries are "local partnerships that bring together employers and workers, private and public funding streams, and relevant partners to fashion and implement pathways to career advancement and family-supporting employment for low-skilled workers."[80] Giloth emphasizes that workforce intermediaries are effective with low-income adults because their central mission is to be "a trusted, valued partner serving the needs of both employers and less-skilled individuals."[81] Thus early childhood education centers have an untapped role—they can become key partners as workforce intermediaries. In several randomized trials, workforce intermediaries have had strong positive effects on the employment and earnings of low-income

Table 1 *(continued)*

Program	People served	Platform	Services	Background of group leaders	Assessment/ Evaluation
Adult and child programs merged within existing organizations or agencies					
Avance Parent-Child Education Program	Low-income families and their children, ages 0–3	Early education programs and elementary schools	Classes on parenting, toy making, and community resources; volunteer opportunities in early childhood classrooms; home visits; ESL courses, GED prep, and postsecondary education; early childhood education	Nonprofit organization; university graduate students and faculty; early education teachers	Outcomes study
The Annie E. Casey Foundation Atlanta Partnership	Low-income parents and their children	Early education programs and elementary schools	Workforce development; entrepreneurship opportunities; subsidized housing opportunities; asset-building programs; subsidized child care	Private foundation; elementary schools; neighborhood development agencies	Implementation and outcomes study
Garrett County Community Action Committee (GCCAC)	Low-income parents and their children	Head Start and child care services	Homeownership education; financial literacy classes; support for savings accounts; access to affordable rental units; case management; Head Start and child care	Nonprofit agency	Implementation and outcomes study
Adult and child programs as residential programs					
Keys to Degrees Program at Endicott College	Single parents and their children	Residential college	Housing in dorms; scholarships and financial support; courses toward a bachelor's degree; mentoring partnerships; life skills; Montessori early education	College president, faculty, and staff	None
Housing Opportunity and Services Together (HOST) at the Urban Institute	Head of household and their children	Housing authorities	Public or mixed-income housing; financial literacy; case management; self-sufficiency workshops; incentives; youth support groups and service projects; after-school programs	Housing authorities; research think tank	Implementation and outcomes study
Jeremiah Program in Minneapolis and St. Paul, MN	Single mothers and their children	Housing near community colleges	Housing in apartments; education and workforce training; life skills training; partnerships with employers; peer meetings; early childhood education	Community leaders and professionals	Designing a pilot study

youth and adults, but these studies haven't focused on parents *per se*.[82] However, the principles of workforce intermediary programs offer considerable promise for new two-generation programs. These principles include more direct links with employers and partnerships with community colleges, where effective program innovation involves peer support, coaching, and other enhanced student services.[83]

What Exists Now?

Table 1 summarizes the emerging Two-Generation 2.0 programs in the United States. We identified nine active human capital two-generation programs, with four types of structure: (1) adding education and job training programs for parents to early childhood education programs; (2) integrating early childhood education programs into education and workforce training programs; (3) merging parent and child programs that exist separately in umbrella organizations or agencies; and (4) establishing residentially based parent and child educational programming on or near college campuses or in public or mixed-income housing. Below, we present an example of each category.

Adding Adult Programs to Child Programs

CareerAdvance is a program of the Community Action Project (CAP) of Tulsa, a model antipoverty agency, directed by Steven Dow, that has received national recognition for innovation. The design of CareerAdvance was highly influenced by advances in the field of workforce development, and it is the first fully operating sectoral two-generation program in the United States.[84] CareerAdvance has taken a conservative approach—starting small with an intensive pilot and gradually expanding. Christopher King and Hirokazu

Yoshikawa developed CareerAdvance as an education and training program in the health care sector (nursing and medical technology) for parents of young children enrolled in CAP Tulsa's early childhood education centers. The program was piloted in 2009 after a market analysis identified the health care profession as a source of family-supporting wages in Tulsa. CareerAdvance offers a sequence of programs in partnership with community colleges so that participants can make concrete progress, exit at various points with certificates, but then return for further advancement. CAP Tulsa and King have developed and maintained partnerships with all the organizations that are essential components of a workforce intermediary, including community colleges, employers, public schools, GED and ESL programs, and the Tulsa Workforce Board. The program's innovations to enhance parents' success in school include contextualized GED preparation (that is, GED courses where reading and math lessons use health care terms and concepts), and a number of effective support components—career coaches, financial incentives, and peer group meetings.[85] The CareerAdvance program is expanding to include approximately 200 participants by 2015. It is tuition-free and covers all expenses (such as uniforms, stethoscopes, and textbooks) for participants who also receive an in-kind incentive of $300 for gas per semester for completing their coursework. Notably, family support staff in CAP Tulsa's early childhood education centers encourage parents to apply to the CareerAdvance program, and family support staff and CareerAdvance coaches work together to help families make progress. Thus this two-generation program at CAP Tulsa meets both of our guidelines for innovation: (1) the early childhood education component consists of Head Start centers with strong levels of quality, and (2) the education and workforce components are career-oriented, intensive, linked with employers and other partners, and offered in a highly supportive context.[86]

With other colleagues, we are conducting a quasi-experimental evaluation of Career*Advance*, called the CAP Family Life Study. It is a mixed-method, longitudinal study of participants in Career*Advance* and a matched comparison group of families where the children are enrolled in CAP Tulsa's early childhood education centers but the parents did not enroll in Career*Advance*. The study began in 2010 and will continue until 2015; it comprises about 400 parents and their children. King and colleagues are studying the program's implementation, and we are collecting data on parents, children, teachers, and schools at the start of the program and again each year for up to three years, using quantitative and qualitative methods. The variety of measurements in the CAP Family Life Study provides an unusual opportunity to understand the program's strengths and weaknesses, to test the hypothesis that parents' educational and career advances could lead to improved child development, and to examine a variety of mechanisms that might underlie the outcomes we observe.

Adding Child Programs to Adult Programs

This two-generation program's platform is job creation and employment-based training, and it is being implemented through the Los Angeles Alliance for a New Economy (LAANE), an antipoverty advocacy organization whose mission is to promote strong jobs, successful communities, and a healthy environment. LAANE has developed sustainable projects that foster employment among low-income families of color in low-income neighborhoods, while also improving the environment. LAANE's core activities involve community organizing, coalition building, policy advocacy, and communications. It has worked effectively with others in Los Angeles to convince the L.A. Department of Water and Power to offer many new jobs that involve energy conservation with built-in training. This successful initiative is called the Utility Pre-Craft Trainee Program (UPCT), and most trainees are men. Ellen Avis and Carol Zabin write that "the UPCT Program is a model of an entry-level training program that serves the needs of the utility employer and the worker-trainees, as well as furthering the goals of labor, community, and environmental stakeholders."[87] Its partners include the Department of Water and Power, the Los Angeles Trade Technical College, the Mayor's Office, the International Brotherhood of Electrical Workers, and the Southeast Los Angeles County WorkSource Center. The new two-generation program will promote a partnership between UPCT and two high-quality, mixed-income early childhood education centers to recruit cohorts of parents into the UPCT together. LAANE is also seeking to increase the number of women employees (currently 3 percent) in the Department of Water and Power. The Dual-Generation and Training for Green Jobs Program will include support services such as peer cohorts and career coaches. Because the starting wage for UPCT trainee/workers is $16 per hour, LAANE is not seeking partnerships with Head Start centers, because parents who earn that much would be ineligible for Head Start. A pilot program for 50 parents and their children began in 2013; no research study has yet been outlined.

Merging Adult and Child Programs

The Atlanta Partnership comprises the Annie E. Casey Foundation's Atlanta Civic Site, Sheltering Arms Early Learning and Resource Center, an elementary school, and the Center for Working Families. These individual programs have achieved national recognition and are located on the same campus in Atlanta. One of the closest links is that between Sheltering Arms and the adjacent Dunbar Elementary School, which ensures that children receive aligned, coordinated, high-quality education from infancy through age 10. The Center for Working Families has a longstanding record of promoting economic success for Atlanta's vulnerable children and families. The center provides a combination of comprehensive education and workforce development services, as well as coaching and leadership training, in one location so that residents can compete in the workforce. The two-generation program specifically targets parents of children in Sheltering Arms. In 2014, the program hopes to serve about 180 parents and children, combining early childhood education, workforce development, and other support services. An implementation study and a short-term outcomes study are in the works.

Residential Adult and Child Programs

The Jeremiah Program was established in Minneapolis, then expanded to St. Paul, in response to local civic and religious leaders' determination to reduce poverty for single mothers and their children. Although the founder is a priest and the program is named after a Bible passage, the Jeremiah Program does not have a religious affiliation and is funded by a wide range of philanthropies. The core program provides safe housing for low-income mothers and their children near community colleges, with on-site, high-quality early childhood education, beginning at six weeks through the preschool years. The Jeremiah Program's mission is to build mothers' and children's human capital in a supportive, goal-oriented context. Services include life-skills and personal-empowerment training, as well as guidance and coaching for success in postsecondary education followed by employment in a career. Jeremiah's Minneapolis and St. Paul sites have served more than 300 mothers and children, and the project plans to expand to Austin, Texas, and Fargo, North Dakota. The program's measured outcomes have been quite positive; mothers have achieved very high rates of associate's and bachelor's degrees, as well as stable employment with a family-supportive wage above $17 per hour, and their children frequently perform at or above grade level. However, no experimental evaluation has been conducted.

Annie E. Casey Programs

In addition to the programs listed in table 1, the Annie E. Casey Foundation has launched an initiative to strengthen programs that link family economic success with high-quality early childhood education for children.[88] The foundation's strategy is to identify barriers to the implementation of Two-Generation 2.0 programs, to work with promising programs to combine parent and child services, and to develop creative ways to improve implementation. The foundation has selected four sites (the Atlanta Partnership, CAP Tulsa, the Educational Alliance, and the Garrett County Community Action Committee) for funding to implement programs. A national evaluator will study challenges to and best practices in two-generation program implementation, as well as short-term parent and child indicators.

Conclusions and Challenges

Though Two-Generation 2.0 programs are in their infancy, they hold promise for increasing the human capital of low-income parents and children. They draw on lessons from the first wave of such programs in the 1980s and '90s, and they are building on numerous advances in programming for children and adults. We propose several considerations. Ideally, the Two-Generation 2.0 programs we have identified and others that emerge will undergo formal evaluation in the coming years. We need implementation studies that can tell program designers how best to serve parents and children together. Similarly, we need evaluation studies if we are to learn whether Two-Generation 2.0 programs are more effective than single-generation programs.

Second, we have yet to explore the question of how long programs for each generation should last. Moving undereducated mothers to a postsecondary track with appropriate workforce training takes many years. If an early childhood education center is the point of entry for adult programs as well, services for the child will end in a few years, and if the mother is in a cohort originating at the early childhood center, her daily interactions at that center will end as well. One solution has been to start the mothers' programming earlier, when their children are infants or toddlers. However, balancing employment, schooling, and parenting is difficult when children are so young. Another solution might be to coordinate parents' education and workforce programs with children's prekindergarten programs. If mothers' education and training programs start when children enroll in prekindergarten, then mothers and children could be integrated into a prekindergarten-to-third grade system, which could coordinate services for both generations over time.

Third, Two-Generation 2.0 programs should consider their target audience, and not just the age of the child. Which subgroups of mothers will benefit the most? Mothers with more education when they enter the program? Older mothers? Mothers with more experience in the workforce? Clearly, we must consider barriers to education and employment such as mental and physical health, substance use, family violence, and housing and transportation.

Finally, programs should be offered to fathers as well as mothers. Career*Advance* is serving a few fathers, and they may be an important subgroup in the LAANE program. We don't yet know how and why fathers might be similar to or different from mothers in their levels of participation and degree of success.

In sum, the dual goal of Two-Generation 2.0 human capital programs in the twenty-first century is to help parents advance their own education and achieve economic stability while their children become more prepared for school and more socially competent, thus expanding life opportunities for both generations over time. The time is ripe for innovation, experimentation, and further study.

ENDNOTES

1. Alice Boardman Smuts and Robert W. Smuts, *Science in the Service of Children, 1893-1935* (New Haven, CT: Yale University Press, 2006); Edward Zigler and Sally Styfco, *The Head Start Debates* (Baltimore: P.H. Brookes Publishing, 2004); P. Lindsay Chase-Lansdale, Jeanne Brooks-Gunn, and Roberta L. Paikoff, "Research and Programs for Adolescent Mothers: Missing Links and Future Promises," *Family Relations* 40 (1991): 396–404.

2. Sheila Smith, ed., *Two Generation Programs for Families in Poverty: A New Intervention Strategy* (Norwood, NJ: Ablex Publishing Corporation, 1995).

3. Jeanne Brooks-Gunn, Lisa J. Berlin, and Allison S. Fuligni, "Early Childhood Intervention Programs: What About the Family?" in *Handbook of Early Childhood Intervention*, ed. Jack P. Shonkoff and Samuel J. Meisels (New York: Cambridge University Press, 2000), 549–88; P. Lindsay Chase-Lansdale and Jeanne Brooks-Gunn, eds., *Escape from Poverty: What Makes a Difference for Children?* (New York: Cambridge University Press, 1995); Shelley Waters Boots, *Dual Generation: The Case for Linking CFES Strategies with Early Childhood Programs* (Baltimore: The Annie E. Casey Foundation, 2010).

4. Martha J. Zaslow et al., "Experimental Studies of Welfare Reform and Children," *The Future of Children* 12, no. 1 (2002): 79–95.

5. J. Lawrence Aber, Jeanne Brooks-Gunn, and Rebecca A. Maynard, "Effects of Welfare Reform on Teenage Parents and Their Children," *The Future of Children* 5, no. 2 (1995): 53–71; Robert C. Granger and Rachel Cytron, "Teenage Parent Programs: A Synthesis of the Long-Term Effects of the New Chance Demonstration, Ohio's Learning, Earning, and Parenting Program, and the Teenage Parent Demonstration," *Evaluation Review* 23 (1999): 107–45.

6. Kathleen M. Shaw et al., *Putting Poor People to Work: How the Work-First Idea Eroded College Access for the Poor* (New York: Russell Sage Foundation, 2006).

7. P. Lindsay Chase-Lansdale et al., "Mothers' Transitions from Welfare to Work and the Well-Being of Preschoolers and Adolescents," *Science* 299 (2003): 1548–52, doi: 10.1126/science.1076921; Ron Haskins, *Work Over Welfare: The Inside Story of the 1996 Welfare Reform Law* (Washington, DC: Brookings Institution Press, 2006).

8. Harry J. Holzer, "Good Workers for Good Jobs: Improving Education and Workforce Systems in the U.S.," *IZA Journal of Labor Policy* 1 (2012), article 5, doi: 10.1186/2193-9004-1-5; Paul Osterman, "Employment and Training Policies: New Directions for Less Skilled Adults," in *Reshaping the American Workforce in a Changing Economy*, ed. Harry J. Holzer and Demetra Smith Nightingale (Washington, DC: Urban Institute, 2007), 119–54.

9. Claudia Goldin and Lawrence F. Katz, *The Race between Education and Technology* (Cambridge, MA: The Belknap Press of Harvard University Press, 2008); Ron Haskins and Isabel Sawhill, *Creating an Opportunity Society* (Washington, DC: Brookings Institution Press, 2009).

10. Gordon Berlin, "Rewarding the Work of Individuals: A Counterintuitive Approach to Reducing Poverty and Strengthening Families," *The Future of Children* 17, no. 2 (2007): 17–42.

11. Greg J. Duncan and Richard J. Murnane, "Introduction: The American Dream, Then and Now," in *Whither Opportunity? Rising Inequality, Schools, and Children's Life Chances*, ed. Greg J. Duncan and Richard J. Murnane (New York: Russell Sage Foundation, 2011), 3–23.

12. Haskins and Sawhill, *Opportunity Society*.

13. Maureen Conway et al., *Sector Strategies for Low-Income Workers: Lessons from the Field* (Washington, DC: The Aspen Institute, 2007).

14. Avshalom Caspi, "The Child Is Father of the Man: Personality Continuities from Childhood to Adulthood," *Journal of Personality and Social Psychology* 78 (2000): 158–72; Arnold J. Sameroff and Katherine L. Rosenblum, "Psychosocial Constraints on the Development of Resilience," *Annals of the New York Academy of Sciences* 1094 (2006): 116–24.

15. Eric I. Knudsen et al., "Economic, Neurobiological, and Behavioral Perspectives on Building America's Future Workforce," *Proceedings of the National Academy of Sciences* 103 (2006): 10159.

16. Urie Bronfenbrenner, "Ecology of the Family as a Context for Human Development: Research Perspectives," *Developmental Psychology* 22 (1986): 723–42.

17. Jack P. Shonkoff and Deborah A. Phillips, eds., *From Neurons to Neighborhoods: The Science of Early Childhood Development* (Washington, DC: National Academy Press, 2000).

18. P. Lindsay Chase-Lansdale and L. D. Pittman, "Welfare Reform and Parenting: Reasonable Expectations," *The Future of Children* 16, no. 1 (2002): 167–83.

19. Ann S. Masten and Abigail H. Gewirtz, "Vulnerability and Resilience in Early Child Development," in *Handbook of Early Childhood Development*, ed. Kathleen McCartney and Deborah Phillips (Malden, MA: Blackwell, 2006), 22–43.

20. Ruth J. Friedman and P. Lindsay Chase-Lansdale, "Chronic Adversities," in *Child and Adolescent Psychiatry*, 4th ed., ed. Michael Rutter and Eric Taylor (London: Blackwell Publishing, 2000), 261–76.

21. P. Lindsay Chase-Lansdale and Elizabeth Votruba-Drzal, "Human Development and the Potential for Change from the Perspective of Multiple Disciplines: What Have We Learned?" in *Human Development across Lives and Generations: The Potential for Change*, ed. P. Lindsay Chase-Lansdale, Katherine Kiernan, and Ruth J. Friedman (New York: Cambridge University Press, 2004), 343–66.

22. Masten and Gewirtz, "Vulnerability and Resilience," 35.

23. Gary S. Becker, *A Treatise on the Family* (Cambridge, MA: Harvard University Press, 1991); Miriam R. Linver, Jeanne Brooks-Gunn, and Dafna E. Kohen, "Family Processes as Pathways from Income to Young Children's Development," *Developmental Psychology* 38 (2002): 719–34.

24. Rand Conger et al., "Family Economic Stress and Adjustment of Early Adolescent Girls," *Developmental Psychology* 29 (1993): 206–19; Vonnie C. McLoyd, "Socioeconomic Disadvantage and Child Development," *American Psychologist* 53 (1998): 185–204.

25. Chase-Lansdale and Votruba-Drzal, "What Have We Learned?"; Teresa Eckrich Sommer et al., "Early Childhood Education Centers and Mothers' Postsecondary Attainment: A New Conceptual Framework for a Dual-Generation Education Intervention," *Teachers College Record* 114 (2012): 1–40.

26. Carolyn J. Heinrich, "Parents' Employment and Children's Wellbeing," *The Future of Children* 24, no. 1 (2014): 121–46.

27. Greg J. Duncan, Kathleen M. Ziol Guest, and Ariel Kalil, "Early Childhood Poverty and Adult Attainment, Behavior, and Health," *Child Development* 81 (2010): 306–25; Greg J. Duncan, Katherine Magnuson, and Elizabeth Votruba-Drzal, " Boosting Family Income to Promote Child Development," *The Future of Children* 24, no. 1 (2014): 99–120.

28. Ariel Kalil, Rebecca Ryan, and Michael Corey, "Diverging Destinies: Maternal Education and the Developmental Gradient in Time with Children," *Demography* 49 (2012): 1361–83, doi: 10.1007/s13524-012-0129-5; Katherine A. Magnuson, "Maternal Education and Children's Academic Achievement during Middle Childhood," *Developmental Psychology* 43 (2007): 1497–1512; Ariel Kalil and Robert Crosnoe, "Two Generations of Educational Progress in Latin American Immigrant Families in the U.S.: A Conceptual Framework for a New Policy Context," in *Immigration, Diversity, and Education*, ed. Elena L. Grigorenko and Ruby Takanishi (New York: Routledge/Taylor and Francis, 2009), 188–204.

29. Pamela Klebanov and Jeanne Brooks-Gunn, "Cumulative, Human Capital, and Psychological Risk in the Context of Early Intervention: Links with IQ at Ages 3, 5, and 8," *Annals of the New York Academy of Sciences* 1094 (2006): 63–82.

30. Sommer et al., "Early Childhood Education Centers."

31. Jeanne Brooks-Gunn, Wen-Jui Han, and Jane Waldfogel, "First-Year Maternal Employment and Child Development in the First Seven Years," *Monographs of the Society for Research in Child Development* 75, no. 2 (2010): 50–8; Jane Waldfogel, *What Children Need* (Cambridge, MA: Harvard University Press, 2006).

32. W. Steven Barnett, "Effectiveness of Early Educational Intervention," *Science* 333 (2011): 975–78, doi: 10.1126/science.1204534; Jeanne Brooks-Gunn, "Early Childhood Education: The Likelihood of Sustained Effects," in *The Pre-K Debates: Current Controversies and Issues*, ed. Edward Zigler, Walter S. Gilliam, and W. Steven Barnett (Baltimore: Brookes Publishing, 2011); Haskins and Sawhill, *Opportunity Society*.

33. Barnett, "Effectiveness."

34. Andrew J. Mashburn et al., "Measures of Classroom Quality in Prekindergarten and Children's Development of Academic, Language, and Social Skills," *Child Development* 79 (2008): 732–49.

35. Raj Chetty, John N. Friedman, and Jonah E. Rockoff, "The Long-Term Impacts of Teachers: Teacher Value-Added and Student Outcomes in Adulthood" (working paper, National Bureau of Economic Research, Cambridge, MA, December 2011); Diane M. Early et al., "Teachers' Education, Classroom Quality, and Young Children's Academic Skills: Results from Seven Studies of Preschool Programs," *Child Development* 78 (2007): 558–80.

36. Eva Marie Shivers and Kay Sanders, "Measuring Culturally Responsive Early Care and Education," in *Quality Measurement in Early Childhood Settings*, ed. Martha Zaslow et al. (Baltimore: Brookes Publishing Co., 2011), 191–225.

37. Barnett, "Effectiveness"; Brooks-Gunn, "Likelihood of Sustained Effects."

38. W. Steven Barnett and Clive R. Belfield, "Early Childhood Development and Social Mobility," *The Future of Children* 16, no. 2 (2006): 73–98; Knudsen et al., "Economic, Neurobiological, and Behavioral Perspectives."

39. Frances A. Campbell et al., "Adult Outcomes as a Function of an Early Childhood Educational Program: An Abecedarian Project Follow-Up," *Developmental Psychology* 48 (2012): 1033–43.

40. Wendy T. Miedel and Arthur J. Reynolds, "Parent Involvement in Early Intervention for Disadvantaged Children: Does It Matter?" *Journal of School Psychology* 37 (2000): 379–402.

41. Arthur J. Reynolds et al., "School Based Early Childhood Education and Age-28 Well-Being: Effects by Timing, Dosage, and Subgroups," *Science* 333 (2011): 360–4, doi: 10.1126/science.1203618.

42. Jeanne Brooks-Gunn, "Intervention and Policy as Change Agents for Young Children," in Chase-Lansdale, Kiernan, and Friedman, *Human Development*, 293–340; Haskins and Sawhill, *Opportunity Society*.

43. Maris A. Vinovskis, *The Birth of Head Start: Preschool Education Policies in the Kennedy and Johnson Administrations* (Chicago: University of Chicago Press, 2005).

44. Waldfogel, *What Children Need*.

45. Michael Puma et al., *Head Start Impact Study: Final Report* (Washington, DC: U.S. Department of Health and Human Services, Administration for Children and Families, 2010).

46. Hilary M. Shager et al., "Can Research Design Explain Variation in Head Start Research Results? A Meta-Analysis of Cognitive and Achievement Outcomes," *Educational Evaluation and Policy Analysis* 35 (2013): 76–95, doi: 10.3102/0162373712462453; Fuhua Zhai, Jeanne Brooks-Gunn, and Jane Waldfogel, "Head Start and Urban Children's School Readiness: A Birth Cohort Study in 18 Cities," *Developmental Psychology* 47 (2011): 134–52.

47. David Deming, "Early Childhood Intervention and Life-Cycle Skill Development: Evidence from Head Start," *American Economic Journal: Applied Economics* 1, no. 3 (2009): 111–134, doi: 10.1257/app.1.3.111; Eliana Garces, Duncan Thomas, and Janet Currie, "Longer-Term Effects of Head Start," *American Economic Review* 92 (2002): 999–1012; Jens Ludwig and Doug L. Miller, "Does Head Start Improve Children's Life Chances? Evidence from a Regression Discontinuity Design," *Quarterly Journal of Economics* 122 (2007): 159–208; Zhai, Brooks-Gunn, and Waldfogel, "Birth Cohort Study"; Rae Lee et al., "Head Start Participation and School Readiness: Evidence from the Early Childhood Longitudinal Study-Birth Cohort," *Developmental Psychology*, published electronically March 25, 2013, doi:10.1037/a0032280.

48. Haskins and Sawhill, *Opportunity Society*; Vivian C. Wong et al., "An Effectiveness-Based Evaluation of Five State Pre-Kindergarten Programs," *Journal of Policy Analysis and Management* 27 (2008): 122–54, doi: 10.1002/pam.20310.

49. Mashburn et al., "Measures of Classroom Quality."

50. Wong et al., "An Effectiveness-Based Evaluation"; Christina Weiland and Hirokazu Yoshikawa, "Impacts of a Prekindergarten Program on Children's Mathematics, Language, Literacy, Executive Function, and Emotional Skills," online prepublication, *Child Development*, published electronically March 27, 2013, doi: 10.1111/cdev.12099.

51. William T. Gormley, Deborah Phillips, and Ted Gayer, "Preschool Programs Can Boost School Readiness," *Science* 320 (2008): 1723–24.

52. William Gormley et al., "Social-Emotional Effects of Early Childhood Education Programs in Tulsa," *Child Development* 82 (2011): 2095–109.

53. Sara Goldrick-Rab and Kia Sorensen, "Unmarried Parents in College," *The Future of Children* 20, no. 2 (2010): 179–203; Harry Holzer and Demetra Nightingale, *Workforce Policies for a Changing Economy* (Washington, DC: Urban Institute Press, 2007).

54. Denise F. Polit, "Effects of a Comprehensive Program for Teenage Parents: Five Years after Project Redirections," *Family Planning Perspectives* 21 (1989): 165–87.

55. Chase-Lansdale, Brooks-Gunn, and Paikoff, "Research and Programs."

56. Polit, "Effects."

57. Ibid.

58. Chase-Lansdale, Brooks-Gunn, and Paikoff, "Research and Programs."

59. Granger and Cytron, "Teenage Parent Programs."

60. Ibid.

61. Ibid.

62. Zaslow et al., "Experimental Studies."

63. Granger and Cytron, "Teenage Parent Programs."

64. P. Lindsay Chase-Lansdale and Maris A. Vinovskis, "Whose Responsibility? An Historical Analysis of the Changing Roles of Mothers, Fathers, and Society," in Chase-Lansdale and Brooks-Gunn, *Escape from Poverty*, 11–37.

65. Gayle Hamilton, *Moving People from Welfare to Work: Lessons from the National Evaluation of Welfare-to-Work Strategies* (New York: Manpower Demonstration Research Corporation, 2002).

66. Ibid.

67. Lisa A. Gennetian, Katherine A. Magnuson, and Pamela A. Morris, "From Statistical Association to Causation: What Developmentalists Can Learn from Instrumental Variables Techniques Coupled with Experimental Data," *Developmental Psychology* 44 (2008): 381–94.

68. Hamilton, *Moving People*.

69. Eric P. Bettinger and Rachel Baker, "The Effects of Student Coaching in College: An Evaluation of a Randomized Experiment in Student Mentoring" (working paper, National Bureau of Economic Research, Cambridge, MA, March 2011); Goldrick-Rab and Sorensen, "Unmarried Parents"; Ann E. Person, James E. Rosenbaum, and Regina Deil-Amen, "Student Planning and Information Problems in Different College Structures," *Teachers College Record* 108 (2006): 374–96.

70. Polit, "Effects."

71. Goldin and Katz, *The Race*.

72. Greg J. Duncan and Katherine A. Magnuson, "Individual and Parent-Based Intervention Strategies for Promoting Human Capital and Positive Behavior," in Chase-Lansdale, Kiernan, and Friedman, *Human Development*, 93–135; Mignon R. Moore and Jeanne Brooks-Gunn, "Adolescent Parenthood," in *Handbook of Parenting*, vol. 3, *Being and Becoming a Parent*, ed. Marc H. Bornstein (Mahwah, NJ: Lawrence Erlbaun, 2002), 173–214.

73. JoAnn Hsueh and Mary E. Farrell, *Enhanced Early Head Start with Employment Services: 42-Month Impacts from the Kansas and Missouri Sites of the Enhanced Services for the Hard-to-Employ Demonstration and Evaluation Project* (New York: Manpower Demonstration Research Corporation, 2012); John M. Love et al., eds., "What Makes a Difference? Early Head Start Evaluation Findings in a Developmental Context," *Monographs of the Society for Research in Child Development* 78, no. 1 (2013).

74. Hsueh and Farrell, *Enhanced Early Head Start*.

75. Ibid.

76. Sommer et al., "Early Childhood Education Centers."

77. Mario Small, *Unanticipated Gains: Origins of Network Inequality in Everyday Life* (New York: Oxford University Press, 2009).

78. Sommer et al., "Early Childhood Education Centers."

79. Terri J. Sabol and P. Lindsay Chase-Lansdale, "The Influence of Low-Income Children's Participation in Head Start on Parents' Educational Attainment" (paper presented at the Association for Public Policy Analysis and Management Conference, Baltimore, November, 2012).

80. Robert P. Giloth, ed., *Workforce Intermediaries for the Twenty-First Century* (Philadelphia: Temple University Press, 2005), 5.

81. Robert P. Giloth, "Introduction: A Case for Workforce Intermediaries," in Giloth, *Workforce Intermediaries*, 1–30.

82. Holzer, "Good Workers."

83. Chase-Lansdale and Brooks-Gunn, "Correlates"; Duncan and Magnuson, "Individual and Parent-Based Intervention Strategies"; Moore and Brooks-Gunn, "Adolescent Parenthood"; Thomas Brock, "Young Adults and Higher Education: Barriers and Breakthroughs to Success," *The Future of Children* 20, no. 1 (2010): 109–32; Christopher T. King et al., *The CareerAdvance® Pilot Project: Recommended Jobs Strategy for Families Served by the Community Action Project of Tulsa County* (Austin, TX: Ray Marshall Center, 2009).

84. King et al., "CareerAdvance®."

85. Brock, "Young Adults"; King et al., "CareerAdvance®."

86. Gormley, Phillips, and Gayer, "Preschool Programs."

87. Ellen Avis and Carol Zabin, *Training for the Future: Workforce Development for a 21st Century Utility* (Berkeley: Institute for Research on Labor and Employment, University of California, Berkeley, 2013), 14.

88. Karen Murrell, *Two Generation Approaches: Initial Observations and Reflections* (Baltimore: Annie E. Casey Foundation, 2012)

Stress and Child Development

Ross A. Thompson

Summary

Children's early social experiences shape their developing neurological and biological systems for good or for ill, writes Ross Thompson, and the kinds of stressful experiences that are endemic to families living in poverty can alter children's neurobiology in ways that undermine their health, their social competence, and their ability to succeed in school and in life. For example, when children are born into a world where resources are scarce and violence is a constant possibility, neurobiological changes may make them wary and vigilant, and they are likely to have a hard time controlling their emotions, focusing on tasks, and forming healthy relationships. Unfortunately, these adaptive responses to chronic stress serve them poorly in situations, such as school and work, where they must concentrate and cooperate to do well.

But thanks to the plasticity of the developing brain and other biological systems, the neurobiological response to chronic stress can be buffered and even reversed, Thompson writes, especially when we intervene early in children's lives. In particular, warm and nurturing relationships between children and adults can serve as a powerful bulwark against the neurobiological changes that accompany stress, and interventions that help build such relationships have shown particular promise. These programs have targeted biological parents, of course, but also foster parents, teachers and other caregivers, and more distant relatives, such as grandparents. For this reason, Thompson suggests that the concept of two-generation programs may need to be expanded, and that we should consider a "multigenerational" approach to helping children living in poverty cope and thrive in the face of chronic stress.

www.futureofchildren.org

Ross A. Thompson is a Distinguished Professor in the Department of Psychology and a research affiliate of the Center for Poverty Research at the University of California, Davis.

Ross A. Thompson

Children depend on the care of adults in the environment of relationships in which they live. This provides a compelling justification for two-generation efforts to support healthy growth. In this issue, other scholars draw attention to the ways that family resources—such as assets (including income), parents' education and health, and family assistance programs—can have both direct and indirect benefits for children.

This contribution is different from the others in several ways. First, I focus not only on resources but also on how family stress, and especially sources of stress that are common to at-risk children, can threaten healthy development. The children in the studies I discuss live in poverty, witness domestic violence or persistent marital conflict, live in foster care, are abused or neglected, have a depressed mother, or experience other kinds of significant chronic stress. Second, I focus on developing biological systems, although the studies I review also have considerable implications for behavioral development, socioemotional adjustment, and cognitive growth. Third, I try to understand how parenting quality and parent-child relationships affect children's biological functioning in ways that can have enduring behavioral consequences. My argument is that children are biologically designed to rely on early social experiences to guide the organization of their developing biological systems in ways that can be healthy or maladaptive. Those social experiences, especially in the family, can assist or undermine positive coping and adjustment, or in some cases alleviate the effects of prior stressful experiences. This is where the research I discuss has implications for early, multigenerational interventions.

The next section outlines a general portrayal of a child's developing biology, drawing on research into fetal programming, the neurobiology of stress and development, and how immunological systems function.[1] The picture is incomplete because these research fields are rapidly advancing, but we know enough already to draw conclusions about how early experience affects the developing organization of these biological systems. In the third section, I expand on the concept of "stress," drawing on research into the interaction of genes and the environment, to provide a more refined analysis of the kinds of experiences and conditions that pose immediate and longer-term risks to young children. The fourth section introduces the concept of developmental plasticity as a way to understand why early intervention is important, and what characteristics distinguish promising interventions to ameliorate children's stress. This section also profiles several examples of interventions that improve the stress neurobiology of children who live in difficult circumstances. The final section offers several provisional conclusions and implications of this work for thinking about multigenerational approaches to strengthening healthy development.

Developing Brain, Biology, and the Environment

Children are born into a world of unknowns. Newborns have no idea whether the environment into which they are born is rich or deficient in food, dangerous or secure, or populated by nurturing or abusive adults. Yet the ability to quickly adapt to environmental conditions is crucial to the newborn's immediate survival and to long-term development, especially if these conditions are likely to persist. Depending on which environmental conditions are detected, for example, the infant's developing metabolism might slow down to prepare for a world of deficient or inconsistent food resources, and its perceptual processes might become more or less vigilant for threats to its safety. Obviously, these adaptations are not made consciously. Rather, they reflect how young, developing biological systems organize themselves in response to environmental signals. The most important source of these signals is the quality of care that young children receive.

An illustration of how this occurs is early language learning.[2] Newborns cannot know whether they've been born in Paris, London, New York, Tokyo, or Kiev. Consequently, the young brain must develop the potential to learn any language, and studies show that six-month-olds can discriminate among a wide variety of human speech phonemes, many more than their parents can discern. Young infants are figuratively "citizens of the world."[3] But this universal perceptual ability is lost by age one as the child overhears the language (or languages) spoken in the home. This signals the brain to reorient speech perception to language-specific phonemes, making the child a more efficient language learner, and soon afterward an explosion in language learning occurs. Early experience instructs the brain about the language environment into which the child has been born.

There is every reason to believe that this biological sensitivity to environmental signals is not unique to language learning, nor does it begin at birth. In the uterus, the fetus is exposed to a variety of signals from the mother's diet, her emotions, and extra-uterine influences that can have potent effects on development. This was dramatically illustrated by longitudinal research (that is, research that follows people over time) on the Dutch famine of 1944. During World War II, the German military occupying the Netherlands blockaded food transports in reprisal for a strike by Dutch railway workers in support of the Allied invasion. As a result, official rations for the adult population fell abruptly to between 400 and 800 calories daily from December 1944 until April 1945, when the Allied liberation of the Netherlands began to succeed and adequate nutrition was quickly restored. The children born to the women who were pregnant during the Dutch famine have been followed into late adulthood. Although some of the immediate effects of maternal malnutrition (such as birth weight) did not significantly predict later outcomes, latent effects of malnutrition followed by food plenty had long-term consequences. In adulthood, these children were at significantly greater risk for a range of health and mental health problems, including obesity, heart disease, and schizophrenic disorders, compared with children, including same-sex siblings, whose gestation was not affected by the famine.[4] Investigators have concluded that these adult health problems may have resulted from fetal "programming" for nutritional deprivation followed by a lifetime of plentiful food for which these individuals were biologically unprepared.

Another illustration of how developing biology adapts to environmental signals concerns the neurobiology of stress. At birth, newborns have no idea whether they are living in the West Bank or the East Side, but adapting quickly to environmental conditions of threat or security is crucial to their survival. Considerable evidence suggests that the fetus is sensitive to hormonal and other physiological indicators of maternal stress, and that heightened exposure to stress in the womb is associated with greater reactivity to stress after birth, as well as longer-term problems with emotional and cognitive functioning.[5] In one longitudinal study, for example, mothers' depression during pregnancy was associated with heightened cortisol levels when infants were observed three months after birth as they underwent a moderately stressful procedure (cortisol is an important stress-related hormone).[6] In another longitudinal study, early exposure to maternal cortisol in the womb was associated with emotional difficulties and larger volume in the right amygdala (a brain structure that helps detect and respond to threat) in girls at age seven.[7] These findings are consistent with substantial research on animals that documents similar effects in the offspring of pregnant females that were subjected to stress.[8] In general, then, prenatal stress exposure makes children more reactive to challenge and threat.

After birth, a child's direct exposure to chronic stress alters developing stress neurobiology in comparable ways. A wealth of research with animals and humans has focused on the hypothalamic-pituitary-adrenocortical (HPA) axis, an important part of the neuroendocrine system (the body's regulatory system that integrates the nervous system with the endocrine system). The HPA axis matures significantly during the prenatal period and the early postnatal years.[9] When the brain detects threatening events and activates the HPA system, the consequences include production of cortisol that mobilizes energy, suppression of immune functioning, enhanced cardiovascular tone, and other critical components of the stress response. These responses have important psychological consequences, including greater focus on threat vigilance, heightened motivation for self-defense, and emotional arousal. In addition, basal levels of HPA functioning, which follow a circadian clock, are important to cortisol output, which helps to maintain our capacity to regulate our emotions and cope with stress.

Chronic stress, however, changes HPA functioning over time by altering the neurological circuitry that underlies the body's regulation of responses to stress. This occurs as repeated exposure to stressful events alters the sensitivity of the HPA system, in part through its effects on the limbic and cortical processes that regulate HPA activity.[10] The limbic system is central to motivation and memory; cortical processes influence thinking, reasoning, and emotional regulation. Owing to their effect on these systems that regulate HPA activity, stressful events can have far-reaching consequences for behavior and cognition.

The biological effects of stress undermine [children's] ability to concentrate, remember things, and control and focus their own thinking.

As the HPA system matures early in life, it is especially susceptible to the effects of chronic or severe stress. In a longitudinal study of children living in poverty, for example, environmental characteristics like poor housing quality, economic strain, and poor parenting were associated with disrupted HPA activity from seven months to age four.[11] Another study of poor children found that toddlers living in families characterized by violence between parents and mothers' "emotional unavailability" to the child also exhibited disruptions in normal HPA activity.[12] In older children, higher cortisol levels were associated with lower family socioeconomic status, and mothers of older children with higher cortisol levels were more likely to have symptoms of depression.[13]

The behaviors correlated with disrupted HPA activity are complex and depend in part on the nature of the stress that children experience. They include heightened vigilance and self-regulatory problems that may be manifested in poorer coping, cognitive and attention problems, poor emotional regulation, and difficulty in social functioning.[14] This constellation of behavioral problems, which arise from chronic activation of the HPA axis and the influence of stress hormones like cortisol on other biological systems (described below), have important implications for children's academic functioning as well as their capacity to develop constructive relationships with peers and adults. Stated differently, one of the reasons that children in stressful circumstances fall behind academically is that, in addition to the other disadvantages they experience, the biological effects of stress undermine their ability to concentrate, remember things, and control and focus their own thinking. And one of the reasons they experience social difficulties—with peers, for example—is that, in addition to the other disadvantages they experience, the biological effects of stress heighten emotional reactivity and undermine emotional self-regulation.

Early, chronic stress is associated with other biological challenges that also contribute to these behavioral consequences. Stress is associated with sharp increases in the autonomic nervous system's activity, including elevated blood pressure. As we've seen, stress hormones influence the functioning of cortical systems (such as the prefrontal cortex, which regulates many other neurobiological and cognitive processes) and limbic structures, including the amygdala, the hypothalamus (which is involved in motivational processes, including emotion), and the hippocampus (which contributes to the creation

of memories from current experience).[15] Chronic stress also suppresses the functioning of the immune system. Stress undermines the immune system's sensitivity to infectious challenges, increasing its response to cytokines (that is, inflammatory agents) and generally embedding "proinflammatory tendencies" into biological functioning.[16] In short, chronic and severe stress influences multiple biological systems, with diverse behavioral consequences; when this occurs early in life, the organization and functioning of these systems may be permanently altered.

Viewed from the perspective of biological adaptation, these developments are consistent with the young child's preparation for a life of adversity. If early experiences of family conflict, limited resources, and poor parenting are biological signals of the environmental conditions into which the child has been born, then it makes sense that the child develops biological systems that allocate mental resources to threat vigilance, foster quick and strong reactions to perceptions of danger, enable rapid mobilization of energy, and alter immunological functioning, yielding a behavioral pattern well suited to this kind of environment.

But there are several trade-offs. First, mental resources devoted to vigilance cannot as readily be devoted to learning, problem-solving, and other constructive pursuits. Second, although this behavioral pattern is adapted to conditions of adversity associated with family experience, it may be poorly suited to other social settings, such as at school and with peers, that require a different and more constructive set of behavioral skills. A social orientation toward detecting threats makes it hard to develop constructive relationships. Furthermore, the trouble these children have controlling their impulses and emotions limits their capacity to quickly adjust to the different requirements of other social settings. Because they respond to most situations in the way they have learned to respond at home, these children get into trouble.

A third trade-off of these biological adaptations to stress is that they are taxing. Chronic activation of the neuroendocrine, cardiovascular, and immunological systems extracts a cost. These systems are designed for short-term activation, and chronic arousal makes it more difficult to mobilize them and recover from their activation in the future. This principle is captured by the concept of "allostatic load," which refers to the progressive "wear and tear" on biological systems from the long-term effects of chronic stress. Considerable research documents that people with high allostatic load—or overload—are more susceptible to physical and mental health problems.[17]

Here is another way to consider the effects of chronic stress on developing biological systems. Human young have evolved to depend on their caregivers for protection, nurturance, and emotionally responsive care. When they receive these things, their developing neurological, neuroendocrine, immunological, and other biological systems organize to function appropriately, which also helps their developing cortical systems facilitate the growth of learning, problem-solving, and self-regulation. Stated simply, healthy biological and behavioral development depends on a supportive, responsive human environment. When children instead experience poverty, parental depression, family violence, or other circumstances, these biological systems and their interactions are disrupted. Such disruption may help children adapt to these conditions, but it also has immediate and long-term costs for healthy development.[18]

Defining Stress

Throughout this discussion, I have used the term stress, with qualifiers such as *chronic* or *severe*. But what exactly is stress?

Stress is a complex psychobiological process with biological, emotional, mental, and behavioral consequences, all of which influence one another.[19] It begins, of course, with the perception of threat or danger in the environment. Some threats are experienced in common by everyone (for example, the approach of a menacing stranger), and others are based more on individual experience (for example, the approach of a familiar person whom one fears). As I've noted, the biological processes associated with reactions to stress have psychological consequences for both children and adults.[20] Thus stress responses are accompanied by a mental orientation toward threat, mobilization of energy for self-defense, and emotional arousal. Stressful experiences vary significantly, however, in their severity, duration, and predictability. When children experience manageable stress, their developing biological systems are not disrupted. Indeed, children need such experiences to help these systems become adaptively self-regulating.[21] "Good" stress yields positive developmental and behavioral outcomes throughout life by helping individuals acquire coping skills.

What are the characteristics of good stress? Generally speaking, stressful experiences that are mild or moderate, predictable, and of short duration can be characterized as manageable and are likely to enhance biological functioning and promote mastery and competence. When stressful experiences are severe, chronic, compounding, and unpredictable, they are generally more likely to exceed an individual's self-regulatory capacities. For children, of course, another important factor in making stress manageable is the supportive presence of a caregiver. Considerable research with human and animal young shows that a parent's support buffers stressful events and helps children cope.[22] Although adults also rely on social support, for children the assistance of a caregiver is more fundamental in making stressful experiences manageable. When they experience a frightening injury or a routine immunization, the loss of a pet or a peer's rejection, children who have the support of caregivers manage more successfully than children who must rely on their own resources alone.

But this straightforward portrayal is complicated by individual differences in stress reactivity and coping. More resilient people may be able to manage amounts of stress that would undermine the coping of less resilient individuals. Research on how genes interact with the environment underscores how significantly individual characteristics moderate the effects of environmental events. In one widely publicized study, for example, a research team identified indicators of harsh or abusive parenting in the childhood histories of a large sample of men from Dunedin, New Zealand, who had been studied from birth through adulthood.[23] They also obtained information about the men's genetic characteristics—in particular, whether they were genetically prone to aggression and antisocial behavior. When the researchers sought to identify which adults would be most likely to exhibit antisocial behavior, they found that the combination of early harsh parenting and genetic vulnerability best foreshadowed behaviors like adolescent conduct disorder, criminal convictions for violent behavior, and antisocial personality disorder. Although genetic vulnerability and parenting history were each important, adults who had genetic vulnerability together with a history of harsh parenting were most likely to exhibit antisocial behavior.

Other studies have shown similar results. In one study, researchers observed mothers' sensitivity to their children when their infants were 10 months old, and measured externalizing behaviors (that is, acting-out behaviors such as conduct difficulties and aggression) when the children were 39 months old. Maternal insensitivity was significantly associated with later externalizing problems, but only for children with a genetic vulnerability to novelty-seeking and conduct problems. For children without this genetic factor, earlier maternal insensitivity did not predict later problems.[24] Taken together, therefore, the effects of stressful experiences depend significantly on a person's individual characteristics.

But here is a complication. Stressful experiences may actually alter the expression of genetic characteristics. The discovery that environmental experiences can alter how genes function is one of the signal achievements of the field of epigenetics. Epigenetics is concerned with influences on gene expression—that is, the activation, or "turning on and turning off," of genetic activity—that occur without changes in the DNA itself. These influences occur through changes in the biochemical regulatory systems surrounding the gene, which can be altered through the effects of environmental experiences.[25] As a result, a gene can remain the same but no longer be active. Epigenetic changes in gene expression can be short-term or enduring, and some can be transmitted across generations. Epigenetics has long been studied in plants and animals, but until recently we did not have the technology to study epigenetic influences in human behavior.

Epigenetic research on humans is still in its early stages, but it is already yielding important insights into how the environment influences gene expression. For example, early stress appears to produce changes in gene expression in children. One study examined children and adolescents born to mothers who said that they had experienced violence from their intimate partners while pregnant. The children exhibited epigenetic changes in the activation of the glucocorticoid receptor gene, which affects how the body reacts to stress. There was no evidence of epigenetic change in children whose mothers reported partner violence either before pregnancy or after the child's birth.[26] Looking at a more extreme situation, researchers found greater evidence for epigenetic changes in a group of children raised in orphanages than in a group raised by their biological parents, with changes evident in genes associated with brain development and functioning, stress reactivity, and immune function.[27] Indeed, there is some evidence that epigenetic changes in gene activation may help to account for some of the research findings discussed earlier in this article concerning the effects of early experience on developing stress reactivity. For example, the association between mothers' depression during pregnancy and greater cortisol reactivity in their children three months after birth was related to epigenetic changes in the activation of the glucocorticoid receptor gene.[28] Similarly, some of the adult health problems of people whose mothers were pregnant during the Dutch famine of 1944 may be related to a change in activation of the gene for insulin-like growth factor II (IGF2).[29] Thus epigenetics may be one reason that stress reactivity and other behaviors change in response to early adversity.

We don't know where the science of behavioral epigenetics will lead in understanding behavioral development. It is clear, however, that gene activity is part of a surprisingly dynamic constellation of biological influences on behavioral development. Equally consequential, early experience is an important influence on gene activity, and an important feature of early experience is stress.

These considerations are relevant to the concept of *toxic stress*, which was recently adopted by the American Academy of Pediatrics (AAP).[30] In a policy statement, the AAP alerted the pediatric community to sources of toxic stress that may affect children and urged them to work to reduce these harmful influences. The value of reducing chronic, severe stress in children is self-evident, and the AAP's effort to enlist the pediatric community is admirable. To the extent that we understand toxic stress solely as a characteristic of the experiences that befall children, however, we overlook the child's own characteristics as factors that exacerbate or buffer the impact of stressful events. Harm from stress, in other words, is not only in the nature of the experience but also in the nature of the child. In addition, the concept of toxic stress misses one of the most important factors that can make these experiences toxic: their epigenetic effects, which can render some children less capable of adapting to cope with stress over time.

There is another way that the concept of toxic stress may simplify the effects of stress on children. It contributes to the expectation that the effects of stressful experiences can accumulate to eventually overwhelm children's coping capacities and thus contribute to the breakdown of their health, consistent with the concept of allostatic load.

Accumulation and overload is indeed one way that stressful events have their detrimental impact. As we've seen, for example, infants and children in poverty, young children of chronically depressed mothers, and children who are abused show greater cortisol reactivity.[31] In this manner, heightened cortisol activity—combined with its neurobiological, cardiovascular, and immunological correlates—contributes to long-term health and mental health problems.

But there is a second way that stress can harm children. Rather than fostering hyperreactivity to stressful events, stress can make the body hyporesponsive; that is, it underrreacts to stress. One way this occurs is in children's responses to acute stress: rather than reacting to stressful events with heightened cortisol activity, they instead show a lower cortisol response than other children do. Another way this occurs is in basal levels of cortisol throughout the day: rather than exhibiting the normal diurnal pattern of elevated morning cortisol followed by a gradual decline, they instead show a flat cortisol response from morning through night. Hyporesponsiveness has been found among children who live in homes characterized by domestic violence and mothers' emotional unavailability, and among preschoolers who live in foster care.[32] This response pattern seems to reflect a stress system that shows signs of shutting down.

Hyperreactive and hyporesponsive stress responses are both disrupted patterns that arise from experiences of chronic stress with distinct risks to healthy development. Just as chronically high cortisol levels have many harmful consequences, including impaired immune function, chronically low cortisol levels can impair the body's ability to maintain appropriately high blood pressure and respond to stress with an increase in cardiovascular activity.[33] We don't know for certain why some children manifest one disrupted pattern rather than the other. But one hypothesis is that the hyperreactive pattern is associated with recurrent threat and danger, and hyporesponsiveness is associated with the deprivation or withdrawal of caregiver support.[34] We also don't know the distinct behavioral characteristics that are associated with each pattern of stress response. Much more remains to be understood about how chronic stress affects children's development.

From what we do know, however, it is clear that the effects of chronic, severe stress on children's development are more complicated than simple concepts like toxic stress suggest. We must consider the nature of the event, children's individual vulnerability or resiliency, the availability of support from caregivers, and the effects of prior experiences on children's coping capacities. As the AAP policy statement recognizes, this web of interrelated factors makes it important to view at-risk children in the context of their experiential history and their social ecology. Children who experience chronic, severe stress may be biologically and psychologically less able to adapt and cope with new stresses when they occur, contrary to the idea that regular stress toughens people and increases their resiliency. The social ecology is also important because children's coping capacities are significantly affected by the availability of social support from adults who can act as caregivers. Research on the Louisiana child victims of Hurricane Katrina indicates, for example, that children who showed the best long-term recovery from this tragedy were in the care of adults who could provide support, while children fared much worse either when they lost contact with their parents or when their parents were so traumatized that they could no longer function as caregivers.[35]

Studies like these, of course, are directly relevant to understanding multigenerational influences on child development. They illustrate how significantly children's ability to cope with stress relies on the support of caregivers. Unfortunately, they also illustrate how the stresses that affect children also have multigenerational impact, sometimes rendering the adults who could potentially provide support incapable of doing so. This is likely to be true not only when communities are beset by natural disasters, but also when they are economically impoverished, enmeshed in gang violence, or undermined in other ways. Indeed, when stressful events occur at the same time and compound one another—for example, when a family must cope with loss of income, parental depression, marital conflict, and moving to a different and more dangerous neighborhood in a short period of time—their impact is greater. These events affect not only children, but also the parents on whom children ordinarily rely for assistance, making the mobilization of two-generation efforts to support children much more challenging.

Plasticity

One reason that young organisms are more vulnerable to severe stress and other kinds of harm is the plasticity, or pliability, of their biological systems. Plasticity is the capacity of organisms to change with experience.[36] Biological and behavioral plasticity is greatest early in life, when the organism is developing most rapidly. It declines progressively with increasing age, as neural networks and behavioral patterns consolidate, although mature individuals retain some adaptive plasticity even at advanced ages. Early biological plasticity helps to explain why harmful experiences can have a more profound impact on the youngest children, whose immature systems are in their formative stages, than on

older children and adults, whose biological and behavioral systems have become consolidated. On the other hand, early plasticity also helps explain the remarkable pace of early-developing capacities, as the brain and other biological systems rapidly mature. Early biological plasticity, therefore, is a double-edged sword; it helps to explain why young children are affected so significantly by their experiences, for good or ill.

The early plasticity of the brain and other biological systems offers hope to those who aspire to help at-risk children. It suggests that even though early harm can undermine the organization of brain and behavioral systems, this disruption does not necessarily become immediately hard-wired to create dysfunction that cannot be changed. Because most of these systems remain relatively plastic (contrary to portrayals in the popular media of a fixed "brain architecture"), we may be able to intervene early in children's lives with experiences that help reorganize biological systems constructively. However, to capitalize on these opportunities, we must detect harm early. To be sure, we can intervene successfully at later ages. But later interventions are likely to require greater intensity (and cost) to overcome well-established neural networks or routinized behavior patterns that have consolidated over time. The fact that the plasticity of brain and behavioral functioning declines over time is one justification to focus on early experience, early screening, and early intervention when developmental problems are detected.

What kinds of rehabilitative interventions can have such effects? We can find clues in studies of interventions that have focused on at-risk children whose experiences of chronic adversity disrupted their biological stress systems. One such program, designed by psychologist Philip Fisher of the University of Oregon and his colleagues, aimed to reduce the stress associated with foster care by easing young children's transitions to new foster homes and enhancing continuity of care.[37] After their earlier foster-care placements, these children showed the profile of cortisol hyporesponsiveness described earlier. The intervention was designed to promote warm, responsive, and consistent relationships between children and their new foster parents in which positive behavior was encouraged, problem behavior was reduced, and caregiver stress was lowered. The program included individualized sessions with child therapists, weekly playgroup sessions, and other child-focused services. Foster parents completed intensive training before the children's placement, and they continued to receive support and supervision in daily phone contacts and weekly group meetings, and through on-call assistance. The children's biological or adoptive parents also received special assistance to establish consistency with the care provided by foster parents and to ease transitional adjustments. The program was thus a two-generation intervention involving multiple adults who functioned as caregivers for the child. Over six to 12 months of treatment, children in the intervention group progressively showed patterns of HPA reactivity that resembled the normal patterns of a community comparison group of children who had not experienced abuse; a control group of children assigned to regular foster-care placements did not show such improvement.[38] The recovery of the children in the treatment group was directly linked to reductions in the foster parents' stress levels.[39]

With a group of colleagues, Mary Dozier, a psychologist at the University of Delaware, designed another intervention to improve very young foster children's relationships and behavioral competence by helping foster parents better interpret and respond to infants' signals, enhance affectionate behavior, and provide more reliable support for infants' self-regulation. After 10 weeks of the home-based program, infants and toddlers in foster care showed more typical daily patterns of HPA activity and more moderated cortisol reactivity to a stressor compared with a group of foster-care infants in a different treatment program.[40]

Even though early harm can undermine the organization of brain and behavioral systems, this disruption does not necessarily become immediately hard-wired to create dysfunction that cannot be changed.

Nonexperimental studies of at-risk children paint a similar picture. In a study of families living in rural poverty, for example, another research group found that 24-month-old toddlers who had been exposed to chronic domestic violence were likely to have elevated cortisol reactions when presented with a challenging task. However, when mothers responded sensitively to their children—as recorded by the researchers when they observed the mothers and children together at seven, 15, and 24 months—this effect was buffered: children did not show such enhanced cortisol reactivity.[41] This finding is consistent with other research on humans and animals that documents the social buffering of children's responses to stress, primarily through support from parents.[42]

The experimental studies with children in foster care show that time-delimited interventions can help to normalize the biological disruptions that occur when children are exposed to stress early in their lives. Of course, we need more research to confirm and expand on these findings. In particular, we need long-term studies that follow children in the intervention and comparison groups as they grow older; we need to see whether other researchers can replicate the findings with different groups of people; and we need studies that measure a wider range of biological and behavioral outcomes.

We also need to understand the limits of biological and behavioral plasticity, even early in life. For example, one study of children adopted from Romanian orphanages, where they were profoundly deprived of normal human relationships, found that after six and a half years of supportive adoptive care, children who had been adopted after less than four months in the institution had basal cortisol levels that resembled those of comparison children raised in families. However, children who had lived at the orphanage for eight or more months did not show such a recovery. In fact, the longer the children had been in the institution's care, the more likely they were to show evidence of enduring cortisol disruption.[43]

These studies of children with adoptive and foster parents are promising, however, for at least two reasons. First, they expand the concept of two-generation interventions for at-risk children by targeting caregivers who are not biological parents. Such caregivers may also be important for other children in difficult circumstances whose parents are either not available or not capable of providing the stress-buffering support their children need, even with outside assistance. Indeed, parents may themselves be the primary source of children's stress. In such circumstances, it may be especially important for two-generation programs to mobilize other adults in children's lives, such as grandparents, child-care providers, and teachers.

Second, these programs demonstrate that well-designed early interventions can produce parallel advances in behavior and biology. Research in developmental biology underscores that the connection between biology and behavior is complex, and biological changes often occur without the expected behavioral correlates, or vice versa. In both the Dozier study and the Fisher study, however, alongside their biological measurements, the researchers obtained measures of behavioral change that can be viewed as further indicators of the programs' efficacy. In the Dozier intervention, infants and toddlers showed greater evidence of attachment to their foster parents. The Fisher intervention saw a similar gain in secure attachment behavior, and foster-care placements were more likely to succeed.[44] Because insecure attachment is associated with disturbed biological stress responses, the increases in secure attachment and the improved HPA reactivity in each study together indicate that the intervention was effective. In the end, researchers and practitioners should measure both behavioral and biological outcomes when they evaluate promising interventions to ameliorate the effects of early stress.

Even if they do not measure both behavioral and biological outcomes, evaluation researchers can focus on behaviors that are theoretically tied to the biological consequences of early stressful experiences. For example, one intervention for at-risk young children in poverty focused not on HPA reactivity (which, as we have seen, can contribute to self-regulatory problems for children experiencing stress), but on the difficulty in regulating their own behavior that at-risk young children in poverty commonly experience. At the beginning of the school year, the Chicago School Readiness Project gave Head Start teachers specialized training in classroom management strategies designed to help lower-income preschoolers better regulate their own behavior. When the school year ended, children in the treatment group showed fewer disruptive behaviors, less impulsiveness, and better preacademic performance than did children from classrooms where teachers underwent a different training regimen.[45] These findings are consistent with the results of other early intervention programs designed to help low-income preschool children with behavioral problems, especially the self-regulatory difficulties that can undermine academic success.[46] Significantly, these benefits for young children were obtained without parallel efforts to improve the quality of family functioning, which is sometimes the source of stress for at-risk young children. Once again, then, we see that two-generation programs can improve children's outcomes by targeting their relationships with adults who are not their biological parents.

Taken together, the studies I've discussed suggest ways to design two-generation interventions to ease the consequences of chronic stress for young children. In particular, they illustrate the value of an integrated biological-behavioral approach that considers children's needs from the standpoint of both stress neurobiology and behavioral competence. From a biological perspective, children exposed to chronic stress need rehabilitative experiences that minimize threat, maximize consistency and support, and strengthen self-regulatory skills. From a behavioral perspective, these biological remediations are further supported by an environment of relational warmth and responsiveness in which children can begin experiencing self-directed mastery. Aside from their focus on early intervention, the programs I've discussed are also distinguished by their emphasis on relationships between children and adults in which these various elements of support can be integrated. Whether two-generation programs target parents, preschool teachers, foster parents, or biological parents, focusing on relationships is likely to enhance their success.

The research on biological and behavioral plasticity has another implication for two-generation interventions designed to improve developmental outcomes. Interventions that seek to change parents' conduct in an effort to improve their children's wellbeing must confront the fact that adults' behavioral and biological plasticity is more limited than children's. In "risky families," parents as well as children experience chronic stress, and parents are likely to exhibit the same neuroendocrine, immunological, and cardiovascular correlates of persistent stress that their children do.[47] The difference is that persistent stress over time has caused the adults' biological and behavioral systems to become more consolidated and less flexible. Parents are also likely to have developed a network of personal beliefs—attributions, self-referential beliefs, and social schemas—and behavioral routines that reinforce their biological patterns of threat vigilance, quick stress reactivity and poor self-regulation. In short, the early plasticity of biological and behavioral systems benefits young children, and the decline of plasticity as we grow older can impede interventions for their parents. Adults who have lived with chronic stress for a long time are likely to have adapted to a life of challenge and adversity in ways that are not well-suited to sensitive, responsive parenting.

It is remarkable, therefore, that interventions to improve parenting behavior and thereby strengthen children's development can sometimes show such positive results. There is increasing evidence that carefully designed interventions, with goals suited to specific family needs, can promote changes in caregiver behavior that benefit young children.[48] Moreover, research is showing that preventive interventions to support the mental and emotional health of children in poverty are also yielding promising success.[49] By integrating our understanding of both the biological and behavioral consequences of chronic stress, we can carefully design interventions to better meet the needs of young children and their families. And we can conclude from these studies that young adult parents of at-risk children retain sufficient adaptive plasticity to promote beneficial change for the benefit of their offspring.

Conclusions

One theme of the articles in this issue of *Future of Children* is that adverse environments create stress that alters children's development. I have focused on the biological effects of stress on children to better understand how adversity "gets under the skin" to alter children's biological functioning and, partly as a consequence, their behavior. Of course, stress gets under the skin of parents and other caregivers, which is why two-generation interventions that strengthen child development are also important for adults. Because major sources of stress in young children's lives arise from family experience, and because the quality of parental care is children's major resource for buffering stress,

we must consider multigenerational interventions to address the multigenerational origins of children's stress. I use the term "multigenerational" deliberately. At times, three-generation interventions may be necessary, for example, to enlist a grandparent to help a parent provide the kind of sensitive care that young children need for healthy growth.

Because major sources of stress in young children's lives arise from family experience, and because the quality of parental care is children's major resource for buffering stress, we must consider multigenerational interventions to address the multigenerational origins of children's stress.

What are the benefits of taking biology into account when we examine how stress affects early development? What does a biological approach contribute that an exclusive focus on behavioral development does not? Biological markers of disturbance from adverse early experiences are important because they provide a multilevel analysis of how stress affects children in which behavioral disruption and biological disruption mutually underlie young children's adaptive difficulties. Looking at biology and behavior together, we can better understand the causes and consequences of stress, the benefits and costs of behavioral plasticity, and, most of all, the potential avenues for early intervention and remediation.

For this reason, one important avenue for future research is to look more deeply into the biological consequences of promising interventions to benefit at-risk young children. The intervention studies discussed in this article provide encouraging leads. But we need to expand the range of behavioral and biological markers that could tell us whether an intervention is achieving the desired developmental outcomes, so that we can use biological as well as behavioral indices in field studies of interventions for at-risk children and families. As one illustration, a pair of researchers showed that after three and a half years of participation in a conditional cash-transfer antipoverty program in Mexico, preschool children showed lower basal cortisol levels, and children of the most depressed mothers showed the greatest benefit.[50]
In another instance, using data from the National Health and Nutrition Examination Survey to study mothers with two or more children, two economists showed that, over time, the 1993 expansion of the Earned Income Tax Credit significantly reduced the levels of multiple biological indicators that reflect allostatic stress and inflammation.[51] In yet another example, a group of researchers reported that an intervention program for at-risk four-year-olds was effective in improving cortisol reactivity, and this led to reductions in aggression by the follow-up assessment.[52]
Studies like these are important not because biological outcomes are more important than behavioral ones (indeed, biological markers can be difficult to interpret without corresponding behavioral data), but because they give us added insight into the developmental processes that can make an intervention more or less effective.

The research discussed in this article also underscores that relationships are crucial to normalizing at-risk children's biological and behavioral systems. The Fisher and Dozier studies both emphasize strengthening young children's security in relationships by improving caregivers' responsiveness and reducing their stress. Nonexperimental studies also show the importance of secure relationships early in life. We've seen, for example, that sensitivity on the part of adults buffers the effects of young children's exposure to domestic violence, that negative relationship influences (such as mothers' "emotional unavailability" or fighting between parents) contributes to HPA hyperreactivity, and that harsh parenting produces epigenetic changes in gene expression that are related to conduct problems. Taken together, young children's early relationships seem to be the most important context for shaping individual differences in stress reactivity and coping. These early relationships can affect young children in many ways: solicitude and support may be reliable or unreliable; they may feel protected from or exposed to threats; adults may or may not respond to their specific needs; and they may or may not feel a generalized sense of security.[53] Unpacking these diverse relational influences can help us develop better theories, and strengthening the security and responsiveness of young children's early relationships seems to be a promising way to make interventions more effective.

If young children are born into a world of unknowns, they quickly begin to understand the characteristics of those who care for them. Those characteristics guide them biologically and behaviorally to prepare for a life of security or adversity. This is the foundation of two-generation interventions for young children.

ENDNOTES

1. For a more detailed overview of these topics, consult Ross A. Thompson, "Relationships, Regulation, and Early Development," in *Handbook of Child Psychology and Developmental Science,* 7th ed., ed. Richard M. Lerner, vol. 3, *Social and Emotional Development,* ed. Michael E. Lamb, and Cynthia Garcia-Coll (New York: Wiley, forthcoming).

2. Patricia K. Kuhl, "Is Speech Learning 'Gated' by the Social Brain?" *Developmental Science* 10 (2007): 110–20, doi: 10.1098/rstb.2007.2154; Patricia K. Kuhl et al., "Phonetic Learning as a Pathway to Language: New Data and Native Language Magnet Theory Expanded (NLM-e)," *Philosophical Transactions of the Royal Society London B: Biological Sciences* 363 (2008): 979–1000.

3. Janet F. Werker, "Baby Steps to Learning Language," *Journal of Pediatrics* 143 (2003): doi: 10.1067/S0022-3476(03)00403-7.

4. For an introduction to this extensive literature, consult L. H. Lumey et al., "Cohort Profile: The Dutch Hunger Winter Families Study," *International Journal of Epidemiology* 36 (2007): 1196–1204, doi: 10.1093/ije/dym126.

5. Curt A. Sandman et al., "Exposure to Prenatal Psychobiological Stress Exerts Programming Influences on the Mother and Her Fetus," *Neuroendocrinology* 95 (2012): 7–21, doi: 10.1159/000327017.

6. Tim F. Oberlander et al., "Prenatal Exposure to Maternal Depression, Neonatal Methylation of Human Glucocorticoid Receptor Gene (NR3C1), and Infant Cortisol Stress Responses," *Epigenetics* 3 (2008): 97–106, doi: 10.4161/epi.3.2.6034

7. Claudia Buss et al., "Maternal Cortisol over the Course of Pregnancy and Subsequent Child Amygdala and Hippocampus Volumes and Affective Problems," *Proceedings of the National Academy of Sciences* 109 (2012): E1312–19, doi: 10.1073/pnas.1201295109.

8. Marta Weinstock, "The Long-Term Behavioural Consequences of Prenatal Stress," *Neuroscience and Biobehavioral Reviews* 32 (2008): 1073–86, doi: 10.1016/j.neubiorev.2008.03.002.

9. Sonia J. Lupien et al., "Effects of Stress Throughout the Lifespan on the Brain, Behaviour, and Cognition," *Nature Reviews Neuroscience* 10 (2009): 434–45, doi: 10.1038/nrn2639.

10. Yvonne M. Ulrich-Lai and James P. Herman, "Neural Regulation of Endocrine and Autonomic Stress Responses," *Nature Reviews Neuroscience* 10 (2009): 397–409, doi: 10.1038/nrn2647.

11. Clancy Blair et al., "Allostasis and Allostatic Load in the Context of Poverty in Early Childhood," *Development and Psychopathology* 23 (2011): 845–57, doi: 10.1017/S0954579411000344.

12. Melissa Sturge-Apple et al., "Interparental Violence, Maternal Emotional Unavailability, and Children's Cortisol Functioning in Family Contexts," *Developmental Psychology* 48 (2012): 237–49, doi: 10.1037/a0025419.

13. Sonia J. Lupien et al., "Child's Stress Hormone Levels Correlate with Mother's Socioeconomic Status and Depressive State," *Biological Psychiatry* 48 (2000): 976–80, doi: 10.1016/S0006-3223(00)00965-3.

14. Clancy Blair and C. Cybele Raver, "Child Development in the Context of Adversity: Experiential Canalization of Brain and Behavior," *American Psychologist* 67 (2012): 309–18, doi: 10.1037/a0027493; Gary W. Evans and Pilyoung Kim, "Childhood Poverty, Chronic Stress, Self-Regulation, and Coping," *Child Development Perspectives* 7 (2013): 43–8, doi: 10.1111/cdep.12013.

15. Ulrich-Lai and Herman, "Neural Regulation."

16. Gregory E. Miller, Edith Chen, and Karen J. Parker, "Psychological Stress in Childhood and Susceptibility to the Chronic Diseases of Aging: Moving toward a Model of Behavioral and Biological Mechanisms," *Psychological Bulletin* 137 (2011): 959–97, doi: 10.1037/a0024768.

17. Andrea Danese and Bruce S. McEwen, "Adverse Childhood Experiences, Allostasis, Allostatic Load, and Age-Related Disease," *Physiology & Behavior* 106 (2012): 29–39, doi: 10.1016/j.physbeh.2011.08.019.

18. Camelia E. Hostinar and Megan Gunnar, "The Developmental Effects of Early Life Stress: An Overview of Current Theoretical Frameworks," *Current Directions in Psychological Science* 22 (2013): 400–6, doi: 10.1177/0963721413488889.

19. Megan Gunnar and Karina Quevedo, "The Neurobiology of Stress and Development," *Annual Review of Psychology* 58 (2007): 145–73, doi: 10.1146/annurev.psych.58.110405.085605.

20. Lupien et al., "Effects of Stress."

21. Richard A. Dienstbier, "Arousal and Physiological Toughness: Implications for Mental and Physical Health," *Psychological Review* 96 (1989): 84–100, doi: 10.1037/0033-295X.96.1.84.

22. Camelia E. Hostinar, Regina M. Sullivan, and Megan R. Gunnar, "Psychobiological Mechanisms Underlying the Social Buffering of the Hypothalamic-Pituitary-Adrenocortical Axis: A Review of Animal Models and Human Studies across Development," *Psychological Bulletin* 140 (2014): 256–282, doi: 10.1037/a0032671.

23. Avshalom Caspi et al., "Role of Genotype in the Cycle of Violence in Maltreated Children," *Science* 297 (2002): 851–4, doi: 10.1126/science.1072290.

24. Marian J. Bakermans-Kranenburg and Marinus H. van Ijzendoorn, "Gene-Environment Interaction of the Dopamine D4 Receptor (DRD4) and Observed Maternal Insensitivity Predicting Externalizing Behavior in Preschoolers," *Developmental Psychobiology* 48 (2006): 406–9, doi: 10.1002/dev.20152.

25. For a helpful introduction to this field, consult Michael J. Meaney, "Epigenetics and the Biological Definition of Gene x Environment Interactions," *Child Development* 81 (2010): 41–79, doi: 10.1111/j.1467-8624.2009.01381.x.

26. Karl M. Radtke et al., "Transgenerational Impact of Intimate Partner Violence on Methylation in the Promoter of the Glucocorticoid Receptor," *Translational Psychiatry* 1: e21, doi: 10.1038/tp.2011.21.

27. Oksana Yu. Naumova et al., "Differential Patterns of Whole-Genome DNA Methylation in Institutionalized Children and Children Raised by Their Biological Parents," *Development and Psychopathology* 24 (2012): 143–55, doi: 10.1017/S0954579411000605.

28. Oberlander et al., "Prenatal Exposure."

29. Lumey et al., "Cohort Profile."

30. Andrew S. Garner et al., "Early Childhood Adversity, Toxic Stress, and the Role of the Pediatrician: Translating Developmental Science into Lifelong Health," *Pediatrics* 129 (2012): e224–31, doi: 10.1542/peds.2011-2662.

31. Dante Cicchetti and Fred A. Rogosch, "The Impact of Child Maltreatment and Psychopathology on Neuroendocrine Functioning," *Development and Psychopathology* 13 (2001): 783–804.

32. Sturge-Apple et al.,"Interparental Violence"; Philip A. Fisher, Mark J. Van Ryzin, and Megan R. Gunnar, "Mitigating HPA Axis Dysregulation Associated with Placement Changes in Foster Care," *Psychoneuroendocrinology* 36 (2011): 531–9, doi: 10.1016/j.psyneuen.2010.08.007; Mary Dozier et al., "Foster Children's Diurnal Production of Cortisol: An Exploratory Study," *Child Maltreatment* 11 (2006): 189–97, doi: 10.1177/1077559505285779.

33. Jacqueline Bruce et al., "Early Adverse Care, Stress Neurobiology, and Prevention Science: Lessons Learned," *Prevention Science* 14 (2013): 247–56, doi: 10.1007/s11121-012-0354-6.

34. Ibid.

35. Mindy E. Kronenberg et al., "Children of Katrina: Lessons Learned about Postdisaster Symptoms and Recovery Patterns," *Child Development* 81 (2010): 1241–59, doi: 10.1111/j.1467-8624.2010.01465.x.

36. Brian Kolb, Robbin Gibb, and Terry E. Robinson, "Brain Plasticity and Behavior," *Current Directions in Psychological Science* 12 (2003): 1–5, doi: 10.1111/1467-8721.01210.

37. Fisher et al., "Mitigating HPA Axis Dysregulation"; Philip A. Fisher et al., "Effects of a Therapeutic Intervention for Foster Preschoolers on Diurnal Cortisol Activity," *Psychoneuroendocrinology* 32 (2007): 892–905, doi: 10.1016/j.psyneuen.2007.06.008.

38. Ibid.

39. Philip A. Fisher and Mike Stoolmiller, "Intervention Effects on Foster Parent Stress: Associations with Child Cortisol Levels," *Development and Psychopathology* 20 (2008): 1003–21, doi: 10.1017/S0954579408000473.

40. Mary Dozier et al., "Effects of an Attachment-Based Intervention on the Cortisol Production of Infants and Toddlers in Foster Care," *Development and Psychopathology* 20 (2008): 845–59, doi: 10.1017/S0954579408000400; Mary Dozier et al., "Developing Evidence-Based Interventions for Foster Children: An Example of a Randomized Clinical Trial with Infants and Toddlers," *Journal of Social Issues* 62 (2006): 767–85, doi: 10.1111/j.1540-4560.2006.00486.x.

41. Leah C. Hibel et al., "Maternal Sensitivity Buffers the Adrenocortical Implications of Intimate Partner Violence Exposure During Early Childhood," *Development and Psychopathology* 23 (2011): 689–701, doi: 10.1017/S0954579411000010.

42. Megan R. Gunnar and Bonny Donzella, "Social Regulation of the Cortisol Levels in Early Human Development," *Psychoneuroendocrinology* 27 (2002): 199–200, doi: 10.1016/S0306-4530(01)00045-2.

43. Megan R. Gunnar et al., "Salivary Cortisol Levels in Children Adopted from Romanian Orphanages," *Development and Psychopathology* 13 (2001): 611–28, doi: 10.1017/S095457940100311X.

44. Mary Dozier et al., "Effects of a Foster Parent Training Program on Young Children's Attachment Behaviors: Preliminary Evidence from a Randomized Clinical Trial," *Child and Adolescent Social Work Journal* 26 (2009): 321–32, doi: 10.1007/s10560-009-0165-1; Philip A. Fisher and Hyoun K. Kim, "Intervention Effects on Foster Preschoolers' Attachment-Related Behaviors from a Randomized Trial," *Prevention Science* 8 (2007): 161–70, doi: 10.1007/s11121-007-0066-5; Philip A. Fisher, Bert Burraston, and Katherine Pears, "The Early Intervention Foster Care Program: Permanent Placement Outcomes from a Randomized Trial," *Child Maltreatment* 10 (2005): 61–71, doi: 10.1177/1077559504271561.

45. C. Cybele Raver et al., "Targeting Children's Behavior Problems in Preschool Classrooms: A Cluster-Randomized Controlled Trial," *Journal of Consulting and Clinical Psychology* 77 (2009): 302–16, doi: 10.1037/a0015302; C. Cybele Raver et al., "CSRP's Impact on Low-Income Preschoolers' Preacademic Skills: Self-Regulation as a Mediating Mechanism," *Child Development* 82 (2011): 362–78, doi: 10.1111/j.1467-8624.2010.01561.x.

46. Karen L. Bierman et al., "Executive Functions and School Readiness Intervention: Impact, Moderation, and Mediation in the Head Start REDI Program," *Development and Psychopathology* 20 (2008): 821–43, doi: 10.1017/S0954579408000394.

47. Rena L. Repetti, Shelley E. Taylor, and Teresa E. Seeman, "Risky Families: Family Social Environments and the Mental and Physical Health of Offspring," *Psychological Bulletin* 128 (2002): 330–66, doi: 10.1037//0033-2909.128.2.330.

48. See review in Blair and Raver, "Child Development in the Context of Adversity."

49. Hirokazu Yoshikawa, J. Lawrence Aber, and William R. Beardslee, "The Effects of Poverty on the Mental, Emotional, and Behavioral Health of Children and Youth," *American Psychologist* 67 (2012): 272–84, doi: 10.1037/a0028015.

50. Lia C. H. Fernald and Megan R. Gunnar, "Poverty-Alleviation Program Participation and Salivary Cortisol in Very Low-Income Children," *Social Science & Medicine* 68 (2009): 2180–9, doi: 10.1016/j.socscimed.2009.03.032.

51. William N. Evans and Craig L. Garthwaite, "Giving Mom a Break: The Impact of Higher EITC Payments on Maternal Health" (working paper, National Bureau of Economic Research, Cambridge, MA, 2010), http://www.nber.org/papers/w16296.pdf.

52. Colleen R. O'Neal et al., "Understanding Relations among Early Family Environment, Cortisol Response, and Child Aggression via a Prevention Experiment," *Child Development* 81 (2010): 290–305, doi: 10.1111/j.1467-8624.2009.01395.x.

53. Thompson, "Relationships, Regulation."

Intergenerational Payoffs of Education

Neeraj Kaushal

Summary

Better-educated parents generally have children who are themselves better educated, healthier, wealthier, and better off in almost every way than the children of the less educated. But this simple correlation does not prove that the relationship is causal. Neeraj Kaushal sifts through the evidence from economics and public policy and reviews large national and international studies to conclude that, indeed, education has large intergenerational payoffs in many areas of children's lives, and that these payoffs persist over time.

Kaushal shows that, if anything, traditional measures of returns to education—which focus on income and productivity—almost certainly underestimate the beneficial effects that parents' education has on their children. She reports causal positive effects not only on children's test scores, health, and behavior, but also on mothers' behaviors that can affect their children's wellbeing, such as teenage childbearing and substance use. Her findings suggest that, as a component of two-generation programs, helping parents extend their education could go a long way toward reducing inequality across generations and promoting children's healthy development.

Thus the rationale for two-generation programs that boost parents' education is compelling. However, Kaushal cautions, the U.S. education system reinforces socioeconomic inequality across generations by spending more money on educating richer children than on educating poorer children. By themselves, then, two-generation programs will not necessarily ameliorate the structural factors that perpetuate inequality in this country.

www.futureofchildren.org

Neeraj Kaushal is an associate professor of social work at Columbia University, a research associate at the National Bureau of Economic Research, and a research fellow at the Institute for the Study of Labor (IZA) in Bonn, Germany.

I n 1848, in a report to the Massachusetts State Board of Education, the American educational reformer Horace Mann wrote, "Education then, beyond all other devices of human origin, is a great equalizer of the conditions of men,—the balance wheel of the social machinery." Over the next 160 years, research across disciplines, countries, and time periods has documented that parents' education is highly correlated with the education, earnings, and health of their children. If this relationship is causal, education could be a "great equalizer" not just of the conditions of men (and women), but also of their children.

Education influences not only economic and noneconomic opportunities, but also lifestyle choices, for example, decisions about marriage, sex, and fertility.

Parents' education affects the wellbeing of their children through a multitude of channels. Perhaps the most obvious is family income. Researchers have established a strong causal relationship between education and earnings.[1] On average, each additional year of schooling raises a person's earnings by 10 percent.[2] Better-educated parents thus have higher incomes, an important determinant of wellbeing across all stages of life.

Parents with higher incomes simply have more resources to invest in their children. Children who grow up in families with fewer financial constraints are better nourished.

They live in more prosperous neighborhoods that have better schools and other amenities, as well as physical environments that are conducive to positive psychosocial development.[3] They are healthier, and, more importantly, their families have the resources to deal with chronic health conditions that can have a cumulative impact on health in adulthood. Indeed, many of the investments in children that a higher family income makes possible bring dividends in the form of a healthy and prosperous adulthood.

Family income, however, is just one of the many ways that better-educated parents contribute to the lives of their children. Better-educated parents invest more efficiently in the education and wellbeing of their children. Arguably, they are better able to understand and use health information for themselves and their children. Further, expectations of higher income and better health make better-educated parents more future oriented, which may influence their life choices and the choices they make for their children.

Education basically augments an individual's stock of knowledge. This augmented knowledge affects numerous decisions, ranging from everyday questions of nutrition, health, and entertainment to less frequently made choices such as how much money to save every month, whether to invest in stocks or bonds, and so on. Further, children learn from the attitudes and behaviors of their parents, which are often informed by knowledge acquired through education. Thus education influences not only economic and noneconomic opportunities, but also lifestyle choices, for example, decisions about marriage, sex, and fertility.

Hundreds of studies document correlations that support these channels of intergenerational transmission.[4] Social scientists, however, have been cautious about drawing inferences from the simple correlations between parents' education and the education, health, income, and overall development of their children. In this article, I review the evidence from the fields of economics and public policy about whether these associations are causal, and discuss the policy implications.

Broadly, the studies I review show that education has high intergenerational payoffs in multiple areas of life. But they also document that the U.S. education system reinforces socioeconomic inequality across generations. This is not for lack of investment in education. The Organisation for Economic Co-operation and Development (OECD) calculated in 2012 that the United States spends 7.3 percent of its GDP on education, which is higher than the average of 6.2 percent among the OECD's 34 member nations. Yet the odds that the children of parents without a secondary education will go to college are much lower in the United States than in other countries—29 percent, versus the OECD average of 44 percent.[5]

In the United States, a large number of young adults who do not yet have a college education have children. Many of them adjust to parenthood by forgoing further investments in their own skills and education, but some enroll in two- or four-year undergraduate institutions. In 2011, nearly a quarter of U.S. college students were parents with dependent children.[6] Programs that help these families invest both in the parents' education and skills and in their children's development should reduce intergenerational transmission of socioeconomic inequality and enhance children's life chances.

Theoretical Issues

To study intergenerational mobility, economists have generally followed what is commonly referred to as the Human Capital Model, which is based on the works of Gary Becker and Nigel Tomes.[7] This model allows for biological or genetic transmission across generations, but it also assumes that economic factors—such as parents' investments in their own education and skills, family income, and wealth—play an important role.[8] It predicts that intergenerational transmission happens in two ways: first, better-educated parents invest more or more efficiently in their children's human capital (that is, their skills, knowledge, and health); second, health and ability are transmitted from parents to children biologically or genetically.

The Human Capital Model thus helps explain why intergenerational inequalities persist. The policy question is whether government policies and programs can reduce these inequalities. Gary Solon has expanded the Becker and Tomes model by allowing for governmental investment in education.[9] Solon assumes that intergenerational transmission due to genetic and biological factors is the same across countries. Thus, in Solon's model, differences in intergenerational transmission from country to country could arise either from income inequalities or from differences in governments' investments in education or social policies that support the education of low-income parents. Solon's model predicts that intergenerational perpetuation of inequalities should be lower in countries with less inequality and greater public support for programs that help low-income families enhance their education.[10] Cross-national research supports these predictions.

One study of 42 countries, for instance, estimated that the correlation between parents' and their children's years of schooling is the strongest in countries with more inequality and low investment in public education, and the weakest in countries with high investment in public education.[11] The United States was somewhere in the middle. These simple correlations, however, do not establish causality. Indeed, it is challenging to estimate the causal effect of parents' level of schooling on their children's education without controlling for the abilities or health that children inherit from their parents genetically. Further, people who are more future oriented may invest more not only in their own education and health, but in the health and education of their children as well.[12] Thus a spurious third factor (genetic endowments, or future orientation of parents) may be behind the correlation between parents' education and their children's education, or other measures of their children's wellbeing. In the next few sections, I review studies that have systematically investigated the causal association between parental education and the wellbeing of their children.

Intergenerational Mobility in Education

To estimate the effect of parents' education on their children's education, researchers have used innovative approaches to at least partially control for unmeasured heritable ability. These studies can be divided in two groups:

- studies that compare siblings, studies that compare twins, or studies that compare adoptees and biological children to control for family characteristics and genetic endowments, and;

- studies of natural or quasi-natural experiments—for example, changes in laws of compulsory years of schooling, or random assignment into educational programs—to see whether an increase in parents' education triggered by such an event influences the education of their children.

Studies of Siblings, Twins, and Adoptees

In one of the first studies to control for unmeasured abilities or endowments, researchers compared test scores of siblings, aged 5 to 8, whose teenage mothers received additional schooling between the siblings' births. They found that standardized achievement test scores of children born after the mother acquired a high school degree were 5 percent higher than the test scores of children born before the degree.[13] Further, continuing schooling after childbirth did not impede the intellectual development of the child who was born before the mother acquired additional schooling. These findings suggest that programs that encourage teenage women to postpone having children (for example, Temporary Assistance to Needy Families) or policies that encourage teenage mothers to remain in school after childbirth (for example, welfare-to-work and education-first programs) may have the added benefit of helping their children succeed in school. But a caveat is in order: birth order could also explain the study's results. More experienced mothers may be more skilled at raising children, meaning that the younger siblings' higher test scores could be attributed, at least in part, to the fact that they were born to a mother who already had child-rearing experience.

In one ambitious effort to control for genetic factors, researchers studied differences in years of formal schooling among the children of identical twins in the Minnesota Twin Registry.[14] They assumed that variations in schooling between the identical twins themselves were random. Breaking the sets of twins down by gender, the researchers found that the fathers' schooling level had a positive and significant effect on their children's education. The mothers' level of education had a positive but statistically insignificant effect in some models, and a negative but significant effect in other models. The assumption that variations in schooling between the twins were random, however, was criticized by several scholars, who argued that educational differences in twins indicated that there were other unmeasured differences between them, and that such differences likely increased bias due to measurement error.[15]

Researchers have also studied the differences between adopted and biological children to tease out the effect of genetics in measuring the intergenerational benefits of parental education.[16] Unfortunately, these studies are based on two somewhat implausible assumptions. First, they assume that the adoptees are randomly assigned to the adopting families. Second, they assume that parents treat their adopted and biological children in the same manner. If these assumptions were valid, however, the effect of genetics on children's education could be estimated by comparing the correlations between parents' schooling and the schooling of their biological children, on the one hand, and between the same parents' schooling and the schooling of their adopted children, on the other. Keeping in mind that their core assumptions must be valid for the results to be accurate, these studies suggest that genetic factors have a larger influence on children's education than parents' level of schooling does, although parents' schooling has a statistically significant and nontrivial effect.

The correlation between parents' and their children's years of schooling is the strongest in countries with more inequality and low investment in public education, and the weakest in countries with high investment in public education.

Policy Experiments

During the 20th century, many countries, developing as well as industrialized, passed laws that either imposed or raised mandatory minimum years of schooling. Researchers have exploited the increases in education that followed to study how parents' education affects their children's educational attainment. This empirical technique is known as the Instrumental Variables method; in this case, it estimates the effect on children's educational success of an increase in their parents' schooling that was imposed by law and was thus not related to unobserved characteristics of the parents, such as heritable ability.

One group of researchers took advantage of differences in mandatory years of schooling among U.S. states.[17] Between 1915 and 1970, states increased the number of years of compulsory schooling for children by different amounts. The researchers found that a one-year increase in the education of either parent lowered the probability that 7- to 15-year-old children would repeat a grade by two to seven percentage points, and lowered the probability that 15- to 16-year-old children who lived at home would drop out of school by two to four percentage points.

Another study exploited variation in fathers' education resulting from the World War II GI Bill. Among veterans born between 1923 and 1926, the bill increased postsecondary education levels by 20 percent.[18] Using the increase in education that the G.I. Bill produced across cohorts of fathers, this study found that a one-year increase in fathers' education reduced the probability that their 8- to 15-year-old children would repeat a grade by about two to three percentage points. However, this study could be thrown off by an obvious confounding factor: the fathers' military service.

Studies based on changes in mandatory years of schooling in other countries have produced modest results. A study of such changes in Norway, for example, generally found weak and statistically insignificant evidence of a causal relationship between parental education and children's educational attainment. However, the causal effect was statistically significant when the samples were restricted to less-educated mothers.[19] Another study exploited the U.K. Education Act of 1972, which increased the minimum school-leaving age from 15 to 16. It found that mothers' schooling, but not fathers' schooling, had a positive effect on children's educational attainment.[20]

In the United States, researchers have also applied data from evaluation studies of programs or policies designed for low-income parents (for example, welfare-to-work programs), but evidence of an effect on children's educational attainment is weak. The National Evaluation of Welfare-to-Work

Strategies Child Outcomes Study, for example, randomly assigned welfare recipients with young children to either an education-first or a job-first program. The evaluation also included a control group assigned to neither program. Examining data from this evaluation, researchers found that mothers' education was positively associated with children's readiness for school, and negatively associated with mothers' reports of children's academic problems.[21] But the study found that mother's education had no effect on children's problem behaviors such as lying, bullying, and cheating, or on social behaviors such as getting along and cooperating with others. Further, there was only weak evidence that the observed effects persisted in later years.

Does mothers' education bring greater intergenerational returns than fathers' education? As we've seen, the empirical evidence is mixed. An extensive review of the research concludes that despite a decade of work on the subject, "we have a wide range of findings about whether it is mother's or father's education that matters more for offspring."[22] The question is an important one, both because mothers are the primary caregivers for many young children and because of a persistent education gender gap in many countries. An increase in a mother's human capital would increase her bargaining power, which she might use to steer family resources toward investments that enhance her children's wellbeing. Education also increases the value of parents' time, and it may affect the amount of time parents spend with their children as well as the productivity of the time they spend in child-enhancing activities.[23] Some have argued that a mother's schooling and employment could compete with her child-rearing activities and thus adversely affect her children's wellbeing.[24] On the other hand, better-educated mothers also tend to have fewer children. The increased time they spend in school and at work thus does not necessarily mean that they spend less time per child than the less educated do. Indeed, research based on the American Time Use Survey concludes that better-educated mothers spend more time on average with their children.[25]

To sum up, this short review of intergenerational persistence of educational inequality leads to four main conclusions:

- Simple correlations grossly overstate the association between parents' educational attainment and that of their children because of confounding factors (for example, heritable ability).

- Parents' education has a positive effect on the education of their offspring, and the effect is somewhat higher for less-educated or low-income parents, lending support to policies that target less-educated parents.

- The jury is still out on whether mothers' or fathers' schooling produces greater intergenerational transmission of education.

- There is at best only weak evidence that programs designed to educate or train less-educated mothers can improve their children's educational attainment, though the lack of stronger evidence could be the result of poor study design or implementation.

The Role of Family Income

Better-educated parents earn higher wages and are less likely to experience unemployment. Research into the causal effect of education on earnings has concluded that an additional year of schooling raises earnings by an average of 10 percent.[26] Further, recent studies show that education is a more important determinant of earnings now than

it was a quarter-century ago.[27] Scholars at the Brookings Institution's Hamilton Project have estimated that, for someone starting college in 2010 and going on to earn a degree, lifetime earnings would be $450,000 more than those of someone with a high school degree—an earnings gap 75 percent larger than the gap three decades earlier (that is, for someone who started college in 1980).[28]

Better-educated parents thus simply have more resources for raising their children. Hundreds of studies have documented a positive association between family income and children's health, educational attainment, and behavior.[29] Compared with more affluent parents, low-income parents are less able to invest in education-related items and activities for their children.[30] Low-income parents also have less of their own time to invest in their children because they are more likely to be single parents, to work nonstandard hours, and to have inflexible work schedules.[31] Children from high-income families are more likely than poorer children to enroll in college and to persist through graduation when they do, and these gaps have widened in recent decades. For example, children from low-income families who were born around 1980 finished college at a rate only four percentage points higher than did low-income children born in early 1960s. Among children from high-income families, the corresponding increase was 18 percentage points.[32]

However, these simple associations between family income and children's education do not establish causality, and only a few studies have been able to make a persuasive case for it.[33] Critics of the idea that the relationship is causal argue that household income depends on parental characteristics. Many such characteristics can be observed by researchers, and thus they can be controlled for in statistical analyses. But some characteristics cannot be observed and could have a confounding effect. For example, children inherit many of their parents' characteristics. The mere fact that children from high-income families have more education and higher earnings as adults thus tells us little about causation; the correlation could simply reflect transmission due to genetic factors rather than the effect of income.

But some researchers have taken advantage of policies and programs that give families additional income to investigate income's influence on children's wellbeing, and they have concluded that family income has positive and sometimes large effects. A number of studies have used information from experiments with a negative income tax that were conducted during the 1970s. One found that elementary school children in the experimental group (whose families gained $2,000 per year, an increase in income of about 50 percent) did better in school and had better attendance records.[34] Another study concluded that the income gains from these experiments increased adolescents' attendance and high-school completion rates, but not their test scores.[35]

Another common technique to control for unmeasured factors such as parents' abilities and mental health is to compare siblings. One study compared the educational outcomes of younger and older siblings when they were of the same age to study the effect of different levels of income in the same family over time and found that economic conditions in early childhood are important determinants of years of completed schooling. [36] (It is likely that higher income improved parents' mental health and increased their nonmonetary investments in children; if so, this study may be seeing both direct and indirect effects of

income on children's education.) Similarly, recent studies of experimental welfare reform, antipoverty policies, and the expansion of the Earned Income Tax Credit have consistently found that increases in family income have positive effects on children's academic achievement.[37]

Knowledge spurs parents to adopt healthy lifestyles and behaviors themselves and to inculcate the same in their children.

One innovative study collected longitudinal data about children in 11 counties of western North Carolina and compared data on children in Native American families who benefited from casino profits with data on nonnative families who did not receive any benefit. The study found that an increase in income led to higher levels of education and a lower incidence of criminality among children.[38] Further, the effects were larger in poorer families; an additional $4,000 per year for the poorest households increased children's educational attainment by one year by the time they reached age 21, and reduced the chances that 16- and 17-year-old children would commit a minor crime by 22 percent.

Most research on how parents' income affects their children's development has investigated the effect of current income, which is often measured with a considerable degree of error. Economists, following Milton Friedman, often argue that families base their consumption decisions on what they consider their permanent incomes, or average income over a considerable period of time, and not their current incomes.[39] One study that distinguished between permanent income (which the study defined as average income over the 13 years from 1979 to 1991) and current income (income in any single year) found that while current family income had a modest and often statistically insignificant effect on children's cognitive, social, and emotional development, permanent income had a somewhat larger and statistically significant effect.[40]

To sum up, substantial research on how parents' income affects children's outcomes suggests that inferences drawn on the basis of simple correlations of family income and child wellbeing overstate the role that family income plays. Studies that meticulously control for unobserved confounding factors find that income has a positive effect on children's development, but that the effect is not large. Thus researchers have concluded that government programs to boost income have a more modest role in promoting upward economic mobility than correlational studies would suggest.

Parents' Education and Children's Health

Epidemiologists consider socioeconomic status (SES) to be the key determinant of health, and education is widely acknowledged as the most basic component of SES, not least because it shapes future SES, for example, through occupational and earning opportunities.[41] Economists argue that better-educated people are more efficient at keeping themselves healthy. Arguably, better-educated parents are also more efficient at helping their children stay healthy: knowledge helps parents make informed decisions about their children's nutrition

and health care. Because parental education boosts family income, education also helps provide resources for timely health care. And education influences behaviors (for example, it reduces smoking, drug abuse, binge drinking) and lifestyles (it increases physical exercise) that account for about half of premature mortality in the United States. Knowledge spurs parents to adopt healthy lifestyles and behaviors themselves and to inculcate the same in their children.[42]

Most empirical research on how parents' education affects the health of their offspring has focused on young children. Researchers commonly study children's health status as reported by parents, birth weight, and anthropometric measures such as stunting, wasting, being underweight, neonatal mortality, infant mortality, and child mortality. But because health in childhood has a cumulative effect on adult health, parents' investment in their children's health is likely to be more visible in adulthood. Thus studies based on children's health are likely to underestimate the overall effect of family income on health. Unfortunately, most nationally representative data sets do not have information that allows researchers to compare parents' education with the health of their adult children.

The evidence of an association between parents' education and children's health is extensive.[43] But because genetic endowments are the most important determinant of children's health, it is challenging to provide convincing evidence that this association is causal. One way to control for the effect of genetics is to compare the children of adoptive versus biological parents. Using a number of nationally representative U.S. data sets, a study that took this approach concluded that the relationship between parents' education and children's health is not due simply to the genetic link.

The same researchers also found not only that children's health is positively related to their parents' schooling, but that this relationship becomes more pronounced as children grow older. Further, they found that the children of better-educated parents are more likely to recover from chronic childhood health conditions. For children in low-income families, adverse health shocks accumulate, and, as a result, children in low-income families reach adulthood with poorer health. Low-income children also tend to reach adulthood with less education, and both poor health and less education are likely to affect their earning ability and therefore their general health throughout adulthood. Others have arrived at similar findings using data from Canada.[44]

In considering the relationship between parents' education and their children's health, one caveat is in order: most studies have found that the effect of parents' education is reduced or largely eliminated after controlling for income, suggesting that parents' education affects children's health primarily through its economic benefits.

Education, Marriage, and Fertility

Education may also reduce early marriage and teen parenthood, both of which adversely affect mothers' and children's health.[45] In traditional societies, women's low level of empowerment and dependency may cause them to marry early and have children in adolescence. Education, on the other hand, may increase their empowerment and lower their dependency. Because mothers are often the primary caregivers for infants and young children, their empowerment is likely to channel family resources toward mothers' and children's wellbeing. In Western societies too, teenage pregnancy often limits young mothers' options and interrupts their

schooling. But in this context, teen fertility may be affecting schooling, rather than the other way around.[46]

Here again, researchers have used "natural experiments" to determine the direction of causality between education and marriage and education and teenage fertility. For example, one study, looking at the five decades from 1940 to 1990, used the opening of colleges in the county where a woman lived when she was 17 years old to predict mothers' level of education. The researchers showed that the supply of nearby colleges was closely correlated with residents' levels of education, and using this measure allowed them to control for potentially unobserved individual confounding factors such as family background or "forward-looking" behavior. (For instance, women with a forward outlook might decide to acquire a college education and postpone childbearing.) The study found that mothers' education had a positive influence on marriage, infant health, use of prenatal care, and rate of smoking.[47] Another study exploited the Universal Primary Education Program introduced in Nigeria in 1976, and exposure to this program by age and region, to study the effect of women's education on their fertility. It found that increasing female education by one year reduced early fertility, defined as the number of children born before age 25, by 0.26 births.[48]

In the United States, researchers have found that better-educated couples have more knowledge and make more efficient use of contraceptive methods.[49] Similar findings have been reported in other countries.[50] A recent study based on increases in women's education in Turkey, which were triggered by education reforms, found that schooling improved women's knowledge of their ovulation cycle, increased their use of contraceptives, increased their age at first marriage and first birth, lowered the number of children they had, and reduced child mortality.[51]

To sum up, studies conducted in the U.S. and other Western societies, as well as in developing countries, suggest that better-educated mothers are more likely to use contraceptives and have fewer children, and there is some evidence that their infants are healthier as well.

The Cost Conundrum

Governments—local, state, and federal—almost universally subsidize education to bring private investments in education close to the social optimum. Despite these subsidies, experts largely concur that the U.S. education system falls short of delivering on its promise of being a "great equalizer."[52] Michael Haut and Alexander Janus attribute half the correlation between young adults' education and those of their parents' to the American patterns of residential and school segregation.[53] They estimate that eliminating segregation and making education completely homogeneous across secondary schools would lower the intergenerational correlation in education by 40 to 50 percent.

A critical factor in postsecondary education is affordability. Over the past four decades, the cost of postsecondary education in the United States has increased faster than the median family income. In the 1970s, the annual tuition at a public university was 4 percent of the median family income; at a private university, it was 20 percent. By 2009, the figures were 10 percent and 45 percent, respectively.[54] In 2012–13, the inflation-adjusted cost of tuition and fees at four-year

public colleges and universities was three and a half times what it was three decades ago; at two-year public and four-year private institutions, it was nearly three times higher.[55] And as higher education becomes less affordable, the returns to education are rising. An exhaustive study of U.S. inequality concluded that 60 percent of the rise in wage inequality from 1973 to 2005 was due to the growing difference in the wages of highly educated and less-educated people.[56]

Detailed investigations have found that financial aid, tuition, and fees affect people's decisions about whether to enroll.[57] One study, which exploited the elimination of the Social Security Student Benefit Program in 1982 to investigate how financial aid affects college enrollment and educational attainment, found that, for any given recipient, a $1,000 increase in annual grant aid (in 1998 dollars) increased educational attainment by 0.16 years and the probability of attending college by four percentage points.[58] Other studies have found that tuition subsidies have similar effects on enrollment.[59]

Traditionally, state governments have supported postsecondary education by providing universal subsidies in the form of low tuition and fees at public universities and colleges. But fiscal constraints and rising enrollment rates in recent years have compelled state governments to lower these subsidies. As a result, federal financial aid, channeled through a complex set of programs, has become the largest source of funding for postsecondary education.[60] In 2006, a commission appointed by the U.S. Department of Education called the financial aid system "confusing, complex, inefficient, [and] duplicative," adding that it "frequently does not direct aid to students who truly need it."[61]

Research suggests that the college enrollment and graduation rates of low-income adults are sensitive to tuition costs, and thus targeted tuition subsidies could make college education more affordable for low-income families. At the federal level, although education grants are almost entirely targeted to support low-income families, tax deductions for college education almost exclusively benefit families higher on the income scale. In fact, according to the OECD, the United States is one of only three rich countries that spend less on the education of poorer children than on that of richer children.[62] The U.S. system of institutional funding for postsecondary education thus perpetuates educational inequality.

As a nation, we spend big bucks on higher education. In 2011–12, the combined fiscal support for postsecondary education from state governments added up to $72 billion; federal grants and aid and federal loans, from private, state, and institutional sources, amounted to $245 billion. New college loans in constant dollars have doubled over the past decade, with outstanding student debt mounting to $956 billion in 2012.[63] Policy makers, therefore, should be asking: Are these funds well targeted and spent efficiently? Can these expenses be sustained? My review of the research on intergenerational payoffs of education shows that investment in education is an important instrument of intergenerational mobility. However, the rising cost of postsecondary education is likely to discourage low-income families from investing in it, a scenario that does not augur well for economic mobility.

Two-Generation Education Programs

Most policy interventions to improve children's wellbeing focus on children themselves.

The proven intergenerational benefits of parents' education, however, suggest that investments in parents are likely to have a lasting effect on children's health and development and increase their wellbeing as adults.

In many low-income families, family obligations and lack of resources keep young parents from attaining a college education or upgrading their skills. They have unstable jobs with low wages, with negative consequences for their children's wellbeing. In the past, several two-generation programs have been designed with the explicit aim to invest in parents' education and training as well as in the early education of their children. Examples of these programs include the Child Family Resource Program, funded from 1973 to 1983 by the U.S. Department of Health and Human Services (DHHS), which provided a large number of social and educational services to 1,000 families per year; the Comprehensive Child Development Program, also funded by DHHS, which supported 4,000 families in 1994 by providing them with social, health, and education services; and New Chance, supported by public and private funds, which aimed to provide comprehensive services to about 1,500 families consisting of disadvantaged young mothers and their children.

One review of the short-term effects of six two-generation programs that were implemented between 1970 and the early 1990s concluded that these programs had small short-term positive effects on children's cognitive ability, behavior, and health, and a large effect on whether parents attained a GED, but no effect on adult literacy or parents' income or employment.[64] In general, they found that two-generation programs increased the participation rates of children and their parents in social and educational services relevant to their needs. However, comparing the funds allocated to the two-generation programs they evaluated and the combined investments in high-quality programs for child development programs and high-quality programs for adult education and parenting, the researchers concluded that a high-quality two-generation program would require a greater commitment of public funds—about 50 to 100 percent more per family—than was allocated to the programs their study evaluated.

In many low-income families, family obligations and lack of resources keep young parents from attaining a college education or upgrading their skills.

Another issue relates to the quality of services that two-generation programs provide. The study of six two-generation programs found that the intensity of child-focused services delivered under the two-generation programs they evaluated was less than that of the services delivered by high-quality early childhood programs such as the Infant Health and Development Program. As a result, the positive effects of the two-generation programs on children's cognitive development were small. Similarly, if two-generation programs are to have large effects on parental employment and income, these programs need to match the educational and training services for parents to their current skills, interests, and aptitudes, with an eye toward the economic opportunities that these services would create.

Recent years have seen renewed interest in two-generation programs, many of which are discussed in detail elsewhere in this issue. These programs are relatively new, and it is perhaps too soon to evaluate their performance. The theoretical basis for these programs is strong and compelling, but their success rests on their design and implementation.

Conclusions

This article has reviewed research in the fields of economics and public policy and presents evidence from national and international studies that increasing the education of parents generates large two-generation benefits across multiple domains. I focused on research that investigated the causal effects of parental education on a range of child wellbeing measures, including test scores, school attendance, educational attainment, health, and behavior, as well as effects on mothers that could impact child wellbeing, such as teenage childbearing, unhealthy behaviors, and knowledge and use of contraceptives. The combined evidence tells us that education has large and persistent intergenerational payoffs. These benefits are not fully captured in the traditional measures of returns to education, namely, income and productivity. Findings from these studies thus suggest that the conventional measures of returns to parental education underestimate its overall impact.

This article also shows that although the United States spends more on education as a proportion of its GDP than other rich nations do, our education system perpetuates intergenerational educational inequality by spending more on educating richer children than poorer children.

Neeraj Kaushal

In a large number of low-income families, the adults and children alike have needs, and programs that cater to both sets of needs—by investing in parents' education and skills at the same time as they invest in children's development—would go a long way toward reducing intergenerational inequality and promoting child development. There is not enough research evidence, however, to say whether two-generation education programs, narrowly defined as those with programmatic elements for both generations, are the most cost effective and efficient way to lower inter-generational inequality. Evaluations of two-generation programs implemented during the 1980s and 1990s suggest that these programs lacked both the intensity of child-focused ser-vices that high-quality early childhood pro-grams provided and the funding commitment that successful child education and adult parenting and education programs enjoyed. Beyond the question of two-generation pro-grams per se, the two-generation mechanism discussed in this article—that is, improving children's lives by helping their parents get more education—has two broad implications for understanding and ameliorating social and economic inequalities. First, the causes of educational and income inequality transcend generations. Second, any policy initiative to reduce such inequality can potentially work to reduce inequality across generations.

ENDNOTES

1. For a detailed review of this literature, see David Card, "The Causal Effect of Education on Earnings," in Orley Ashenfelter and David E. Card, eds., *Handbook of Labor Economics*, vol. 3A (Amsterdam: Elsevier, 1999): 1801–63.

2. David Card, "Estimating the Return to Schooling: Progress on Some Persistent Econometric Problems," *Econometrica* 69 (2001): 1127–60.

3. Greg J. Duncan and Jeanne Brooks-Gunn, eds., *Consequences of Growing Up Poor* (New York: Russell Sage Foundation, 1997); Robert Haveman and Barbara Wolfe, *Succeeding Generations: On the Effects of Investment in Children* (New York: Russell Sage Foundation, 1994).

4. Duncan and Brooks-Gunn, *Consequences*; Greg J. Duncan and Richard J. Murnane, eds., *Whither Opportunity? Rising Inequality, Schools, and Children's Life Chances* (New York: Russell Sage Foundation, 2011); John Ermisch, Markus Jäntti, and Timothy M. Smeeding, eds., *From Parents to Children: The Intergenerational Transmission of Advantage* (New York: Russell Sage Foundation, 2012); Michael Grossman, "Education and Nonmarket Outcomes," in Eric Hanushek and Finis Welch, eds., *Handbook of the Economics of Education*, vol. 1 (Amsterdam: North-Holland, 2006): 577–633.

5. Organisation for Economic Co-operation and Development (OECD), *Education at a Glance 2012: Highlights* (Paris: OECD Publishing, 2012), doi: 10.1787/eag_highlights-2012-en.

6. Center for Law and Social Policy, *Yesterday's Nontraditional Student Is Today's Traditional Student* (2011), http://www.clasp.org/admin/site/publications/files/Nontraditional-Students-Facts-2011.pdf.

7. Gary S. Becker and H. Gregg Lewis, "On the Interaction between the Quantity and Quality of Children," *Journal of Political Economy* 81 (1973): S279–88; Gary S. Becker and Nigel Tomes, "An Equilibrium Theory of the Distribution of Income and Intergenerational Mobility," *Journal of Political Economy* 87 (1979): 1153–89.

8. Casey B. Mulligan, *Parental Priorities and Economic Inequality* (Chicago: University of Chicago Press, 1997).

9. Gary Solon, "Intergenerational Mobility in the Labor Market," in Ashenfelter and Card, *Handbook of Labor Economics*, vol. 3A, 1761–1800.

10. Sandra E. Black and Paul J. Devereux, "Recent Developments in Intergenerational Mobility," in Orley Ashenfelter and David Card, eds., *Handbook of Labor Economics*, vol. 4B (Amsterdam: North-Holland, 2011): 1487–1542.

11. Tom Hertz et al., "The Inheritance of Educational Inequality: International Comparisons and Fifty-Year Trends," *B.E. Journal of Economic Analysis & Policy* 7, no. 2 (2008): 1–42.

12. Victor R. Fuchs, "Time Preference and Health: An Exploratory Study," in Victor R. Fuchs, ed., *Economic Aspects of Health* (Chicago: University of Chicago Press, 1982): 93–120.

13. Mark R. Rosenzweig and Kenneth I. Wolpin, "Are There Increasing Returns to the Intergenerational Production of Human Capital? Maternal Schooling and Child Intellectual Achievement," *Journal of Human Resources* 29 (1994): 670–93.

14. Jere R. Behrman and Mark R. Rosenzweig, "Does Increasing Women's Schooling Raise the Schooling of the Next Generation?" *American Economic Review* 92 (2002): 323–34.

15. See Zvi Griliches, "Sibling Models and Data in Economics: Beginnings of a Survey," *Journal of Political Economy* 87 (1979): S37–64; John Bound and Gary Solon, "Double Trouble: On the Value of Twins-Based Estimation of the Return to Schooling," *Economics of Education Review* 18 (1999): 169–82.

16. Bruce Sacerdote, "How Large Are the Effects from Changes in Family Environment? A Study of Korean American Adoptees," *Quarterly Journal of Economics* 122 (2007): 119–57, doi: 10.1162/qjec.122.1.119; Anders Björklund, Mikael Lindahl, and Erik Plug, "The Origins of Intergenerational Associations: Lessons from Swedish Adoption Data," *Quarterly Journal of Economics* 121 (2006): 999–1028, doi: 10.1162/qjec.121.3.999.

17. Philip Oreopoulos, Marianne E. Page, and Anne Huff Stevens, "The Intergenerational Effects of Compulsory Schooling," *Journal of Labor Economic* 24 (2006): 729–60.

18. Marianne E. Page, "Fathers' Education and Children's Human Capital: Evidence from the World War II G.I. Bill" (working paper, University of California, Department of Economics, 2006).

19. Sandra E. Black, Paul J. Devereux, and Kjell G. Salvanes, "Why the Apple Doesn't Fall Far: Understanding Intergenerational Transmission of Human Capital," *American Economic Review* 95 (2005): 437–49.

20. Arnaud Chevalier, *Parental Education and Child's Education: A Natural Experiment* (discussion paper, Institute for the Study of Labor [IZA], Bonn, Germany, 2004), http://ftp.iza.org/dp1153.pdf.

21. Katherine Magnuson, *The Effect of Increases in Welfare Mothers' Education on Their Young Children's Academic and Behavioral Outcomes: Evidence from the National Evaluation of Welfare-to-Work Strategies Child Outcomes Study* (discussion paper, University of Wisconsin, Institute for Research on Poverty, 2003), http://www.irp.wisc.edu/publications/dps/pdfs/dp127403.pdf.

22. Black and Devereux, "Recent Developments."

23. Ibid.

24. Behrman and Rosenzweig, "Increasing Women's Schooling."

25. Jonathan Guryan, Erik Hurst, and Melissa Kearney, "Parental Education and Parental Time with Children," *Journal of Economic Perspectives* 22, no. 3 (2008): 23–46.

26. Card, "Estimating the Return."

27. Claudia Goldin and Lawrence F. Katz, "The Future of Inequality: The Other Reason Education Matters So Much," *Milken Institute Review* (July 2009): 26–33, http://www.milkeninstitute.org/publications/review/2009_7/26-33mr43.pdf; Michael Hout, "Social and Economic Returns to College Education in the United States," *Annual Review of Sociology* 38 (2012): 379–400, doi: 10.1146/annurev.soc.012809.102503.

28. Michael Greenstone and Adam Looney, "Regardless of the Cost, College Still Matters," *Brookings on Job Numbers* (blog), October 5, 2012, http://www.brookings.edu/blogs/jobs/posts/2012/10/05-jobs-greenstone-looney.

29. See Duncan and Brooks-Gunn, *Consequences*.

30. Ariel Kalil and Thomas DeLeire, eds., *Family Investments in Children's Potential: Resources and Parenting Behaviors That Predict Children's Success* (Mahwah, NJ: Lawrence Erlbaum Associates, 2004); Neeraj Kaushal, Katherine Magnuson, and Jane Waldfogel, "How Is Family Income Related to Investments in Children's Learning?" in Duncan and Murnane, *Whither Opportunity*, 187–206.

31. Eugene Smolensky and Jennifer Appleton Gootman, eds., *Working Families and Growing Kids: Caring for Children and Adolescents* (Washington, DC: National Academies Press, 2003).

32. Martha J. Bailey and Susan M. Dynarski, "Inequality in Post-Secondary Education," in Duncan and Murnane, *Whither Opportunity*, 117–32.

33. Susan Mayer, *What Money Can't Buy: The Effect of Parental Income on Children's Outcomes* (Cambridge, MA: Harvard University Press, 1997).

34. Rebecca Maynard and Richard J. Murnane, "The Effects of a Negative Income Tax on School Performance: Results of an Experiment," *Journal of Human Resources* 14 (1979): 463–76.

35. Neil J. Salkind and Ron Haskins, "Negative Income Tax: The Impact on Children from Low-Income Families," *Journal of Family Issues* 3 (1982): 165–80, doi: 10.1177/019251382003002003.

36. Greg J. Duncan et al., "How Much Does Childhood Poverty Affect the Life Chances of Children?" *American Sociological Review* 63 (1998): 406–23.

37. Greg J. Duncan, Pamela A. Morris, and Chris Rodrigues, "Does Money Really Matter? Estimating Impacts of Family Income on Young Children's Achievement with Data from Random-Assignment Experiments," *Developmental Psychology* 47 (2011): 1263–79, doi: 10.1037/a0023875; Gordon Dahl and Lance Lochner, "The Impact of Family Income on Child Achievement: Evidence from the Earned Income Tax Credit," *American Economic Review* 102 (2012): 1927–56, doi: 10.1257/aer.102.5.1927.

38. Randall Akee et al., "Parent's Incomes and Children's Outcomes: A Quasi-Experiment Using Transfer Payments from Casino Profits," *American Economics Journal: Applied Economics 2 (2010)*: 86–115, doi: 10.1257/app.2.1.86.

39. Milton Friedman, *A Theory of the Consumption Function* (Princeton: Princeton University Press, 1957).

40. David M. Blau, "The Effect of Income on Child Development," *Review of Economics and Statistics* 81 (1999): 261–76, doi: 10.1162/003465399558067.

41. Nancy E. Adler and Katherine Newman, "Socioeconomic Disparities in Health: Pathways and Policies," *Health Affairs* 21, no. 2 (2002): 60–76.

42. J. Michael McGinnis and William H. Foege, "Actual Causes of Death in the United States," *JAMA: The Journal of the American Medical Association* 270 (1993): 2207–12.

43. Grossman, "Education and Nonmarket Outcomes."

44. Janet Currie and Mark Stabile, "Socioeconomic Status and Health: Why Is the Relationship Stronger for Older Children?" *American Economics Review* 93 (2003): 1813–23.

45. World Health Organization, *The World Health Report 1995—Bridging the Gaps* (Geneva: World Health Organization, 1995), http://www.who.int/whr/1995/en/whr95_en.pdf.

46. Joshua D. Angrist and William N. Evans, "Children and Their Parents' Labor Supply: Evidence from Exogenous Variation in Family Size," *American Economic Review* 88 (1998): 450–77.

47. Janet Currie and Enrico Moretti, "Mother's Education and the Intergenerational Transmission of Human Capital: Evidence from College Openings," *Quarterly Journal of Economics* 118 (2003): 1495–1532, doi: 10.1162/003355303322552856.

48. Una Okonkwo Osili and Bridget Terry Long, "Does Female Schooling Reduce Fertility? Evidence from Nigeria," *Journal of Development Economics* 87 (2008): 57–75, doi: 10.1016/j.jdeveco.2007.10.003.

49. Mark Rosenzweig and Paul Schultz, "Schooling, Information and Nonmarket Productivity: Contraceptive Use and Its Effectiveness," *International Economic Review* 30 (1989): 457–77.

50. T. Paul Schultz, "Why Governments Should Invest More to Educate Girls," *World Development* 30 (2002): 207–25.

51. Mehmet A.Dincer, Neeraj Kaushal, and Michael Grossman, "Mother's Education, Fertility and Child Health: Evidence from a Natural Experiment in Turkey" (working paper, Columbia University, 2013).

52. Ron Haskins, Harry Holzer, and Robert Lerman, *Promoting Economic Mobility by Increasing Postsecondary Education* (Washington, DC: Economic Mobility Project, Pew Charitable Trusts, 2009), http://www.pewtrusts.org/uploadedFiles/wwwpewtrustsorg/Reports/Economic_Mobility/PEW_EM_Haskins%207.pdf; Isabel Sawhill, "Opportunity in America: The Role of Education," *Future of Children* policy brief (Fall 2006), http://futureofchildren.org/futureofchildren/publications/docs/16_02_PolicyBrief.pdf.

53. Michael Haut and Alexander Janus, "Educational Mobility in the United States since the 1930s," in Duncan and Murnane, *Whither Opportunity*, 165–86.

54. "The Rich and the Rest: American Inequality Is a Tale of Two Countries," *The Economist*, October 13, 2012, http://www.economist.com/node/21564418.

55. National Center for Education Statistics (NCES), "Fast Facts: Tuition Costs of Colleges and Universities," accessed August 8, 2013, http://nces.ed.gov/fastfacts/display.asp?id=76.

56. Goldin and Katz, "The Future of Inequality."

57. Thomas J. Kane, "Evaluating the Impact of the DC Tuition Assistance Grant Program," *Journal of Human Resources* 42 (2007): 555–82.

58. Susan M. Dynarski, "Does Aid Matter? Measuring the Effect of Student Aid on College Attendance and Completion," *American Economic Review* 93 (2003): 279–88.

59. Neeraj Kaushal, "In State Tuition for the Undocumented: Education Effects on Mexican Young Adults," *Journal of Policy Analysis and Management* 27 (2008): 771–92, doi: 10.1002/pam.20366; Kane, "Evaluating the Impact."

60. Haskins, Holzer, and Lerman, *Promoting Economic Mobility*.

61. Spellings Commission on Higher Education, *A Test of Leadership: Charting the Future of U.S. Higher Education* (Washington, DC: U.S. Department of Education, 2006).

62. OECD, *Education at a Glance 2012*.

63. Sandy Baum and Kathleen Payea, *Trends in Students Aid 2012* (New York: College Board Advocacy and Policy Center, 2012); Federal Reserve Bank of New York, "Household Credit," http://www.newyorkfed.org/regional/householdcredit.html.

64. Robert Pierre, Jean I. Layzer, and Helen V. Barnes, "Two-Generation Programs: Design, Cost, and Short-Term Effectiveness," *Future of Children* 5 (1995): 76–93.

Two-Generation Programs and Health

Sherry Glied and Don Oellerich

Summary

Parents' health and children's health are closely intertwined—healthier parents have healthier children, and vice versa. Genetics accounts for some of this relationship, but much of it can be traced to environment and behavior, and the environmental and behavioral risk factors for poor health disproportionately affect families living in poverty. Unhealthy children are likely to become unhealthy adults, and poor health drags down both their educational attainment and their income.

Because of the close connection between parents' and children's health, write Sherry Glied and Don Oellerich, we have every reason to believe that programs to improve parents' health will improve their children's health as well. Yet few programs aim to work this way, except for a narrow category of programs that target pregnant women, newborns, and very young children. Glied and Oellerich assess these programs, discuss why there are so few of them, and suggest ways to expand them. Their chief conclusion is that structural barriers in the U.S. health-care system stand in the way of such programs. Some of these barriers have to do with health insurance, access to care, and benefits, but the biggest one is the fact that physicians typically specialize in treating either children or adults, rather than families as a whole. The Affordable Care Act has begun to break down some of these barriers, the authors write, but much remains to be done.

www.futureofchildren.org

Sherry Glied is the dean and a professor of public service at New York University's Robert F. Wagner Graduate School of Public Service. Don Oellerich is the deputy chief economist in the Office of the Assistant Secretary for Planning and Evaluation at the U.S. Department of Health and Human Services.

Sherry Glied and Don Oellerich

The health of children and the health of their parents are strongly linked. Health depends on genes, environments, and behaviors; parents and children share all of these. Specialized providers—hospitals, doctors, and clinics—provide services to children and parents that contribute to their health. Well-established and expanding government programs, including Medicaid and the Children's Health Insurance Program (CHIP), as well as employer-sponsored coverage and subsidized coverage in health marketplaces, help to finance this care. In short, we have both the rationale and the financing basis for two-generation approaches to health. Yet relatively few two-generation interventions aim to improve health, except for a narrow category of programs that target pregnant women, newborns, and very young children.

In this article, we assess these programs, discuss why there are so few of them, and suggest ways to expand them. We conclude that the health-care system incorporates several structural barriers that make it hard to develop and expand such programs. These barriers include the way health insurance is made available, what benefits are covered, how people gain access to care, and, particularly, the nature of physician practice and specialization.

The Patient Protection and Affordable Care Act (ACA) made important strides toward overcoming these barriers by building on the foundation of publicly and privately provided insurance. The ACA makes more low-income parents eligible for public health insurance; provides subsidized family coverage through health insurance marketplaces; requires that all insurance plans in the marketplaces offer a minimum essential benefits package, including coverage of mental health and substance-use treatment services on a basis equal to coverage of other medical benefits; supports innovative service-delivery systems such as medical care homes; and, building on programs in the states, establishes the Maternal, Infant, and Early Childhood Home Visiting (MIECHV) Program.[1] Despite this step forward, significant gaps remain in the financing and service delivery systems, creating new opportunities to improve health through two-generation programs. By building on the ACA and related legislation, we could encourage the spread of evidence-based two-generation approaches.

Children's and Parents' Health

Improving children's health can help with two problems. First, although most children are healthy, nearly a quarter (23.3 percent) have a chronic health condition. Table 1 describes the most common chronic health conditions in children under 18. About 9 percent of children have asthma, the most common condition. Mental health and behavioral health conditions, including attention deficit hyperactivity disorder (ADHD), anxiety, conduct disorder, and depression, are also fairly prevalent.

Second, unhealthy children become unhealthy adults. For example, chronic conditions that persist through age 16 are related to poor adult health at age 42.[2] Poor health in childhood has other long-term repercussions: it contributes to lower educational attainment and income in adulthood.[3]

Almost all diseases result from complex interactions among genes, environmental agents, and behaviors. Parents are the source of children's genetic endowments;

Table 1. Percentage of U.S. Children 0–18 with Chronic Health Conditions

Chronic condition	Prevalence
Asthma	9.0%
Learning disabilities	7.8%
Attention deficit hyperactivity disorder	6.4%
Speech problems	3.7%
Oppositional defiant disorder or conduct disorder	3.3%
Developmental delay	3.2%
Anxiety problems	2.9%
Bone, joint, or muscle problems	2.2%
Depression	2.0%
Hearing problems	1.4%
Vision problems	1.3%
Autism spectrum disorder	1.1%
Epilepsy or seizure disorder	0.6%
Diabetes	0.4%
Brain injury or concussion	0.3%
Tourette Syndrome	0.1%

Source: National Survey of Children's Health 2007.

parents and children share living environments; and parents play a critical role in shaping children's behavior.[4] It is not surprising, then, that parents' health and children's health are highly correlated. The National Survey of Children's Health indicates that 93.2 percent of the children of mothers who were reported to be in excellent or very good health were themselves in excellent or very good health. But only 64.9 percent of the children of mothers who were reported to be in good, fair, or poor health were in excellent or very good health.[5] The converse is also true. When children are unhealthy, parents' wellbeing suffers.[6]

Many studies document the connections between parents' and children's health. At one extreme, the connections across generations are physical. A mother's health, nutrition, behaviors, and exposure to various negative experiences during pregnancy not only affect her, they also affect her baby's birth weight, wellbeing, and health. A pregnant or breast-feeding mother's intake of nutrients likewise affects both her own health and her infant's.[7] Shared genetic endowments can also raise the risk of poor health in both parents and children. For example, genetics can explain more than half of a person's risk for obesity. Family food preferences and eating habits likewise affect both children's and adults' obesity rates.[8] Environmental exposure constitutes a third category of shared risks. For example, living in a community with limited access to healthy and affordable food choices may affect the health of both parents and their children. Finally, a health condition or behavior in one generation can affect other aspects of health in a different generation. For example, parents who smoke are more likely to get lung cancer and suffer from cardiovascular disease, and their children are more likely to have low birth weight.

Table 2. Prevalence of Health Risk Factors among U.S. Children

Risk factor or health condition	Prevalence
Underweight births	8%
Preterm births	12%
Children 0–6 living with someone who smokes regularly	6%
Children under 18 living with at least one parent who smokes regularly	22%
Children under 18 in families with income below 138% of the federal poverty level living with a parent who smokes regularly	31%
Obesity (children 2–19)	17%
Children under 18 living with at least one parent who is obese	43%
Children living with at least one parent who had major depression in the past year	21%
Children living with at least one parent who abuses alcohol or drugs	9%
Children with one or more chronic health condition	24%
Families that include a child with a disability	4%

Sources: Centers for Disease Control and Prevention; Federal Interagency Forum on Child and Family Statistics; Medical Expenditure Panel Survey; Child Welfare Information Gateway; National Survey of Children's Health; Qi Wang, *Disability and American Families, 2000* (Washington, DC: U.S. Census Bureau, 2005).

Table 2 shows the prevalence of intergenerational risk factors. Exposure to smoke, parental alcohol or drug use, and preterm birth and low birth weight each affect about 10 percent of American children. Two to three times as many children are affected by parental depression and obesity. Next, we discuss these risk factors and their effects on children's and adults' health.

Risk Factors in Pregnancy and the Neonatal Period

Low birth weight and preterm birth are risk factors for many types of poor health in childhood.[9] The prenatal environment may also affect children's health, and their health as adults, in ways that are independent of birth weight.[10] Most of the factors that lead to a poor prenatal environment (including mothers' high blood pressure, smoking, infections, and poor nutrition) also directly affect mothers' health.

Tobacco Exposure. Smoking is the leading cause of preventable illness and death among adults in the United States. Most of the deaths associated with tobacco use occur among smokers themselves, but exposure to environmental tobacco smoke also causes deaths, accounting for an estimated 3,000 U.S. lung cancer deaths per year. For children, most exposure to tobacco smoke occurs at home. Newborns who are exposed to environmental tobacco smoke have a higher risk of sudden infant death syndrome, and environmental tobacco smoke is associated with several other health problems in children, including middle ear infections, asthma, and lower respiratory tract infections.[11]

As table 1 shows, asthma is the most common chronic condition among children. Exposure to tobacco smoke makes asthma symptoms worse, and children with asthma visit the doctor for their symptoms more often if they live in a home with a smoker.[12] Asthma symptoms can disrupt children's and parents' lives in many ways; for example, children with asthma symptoms are more likely to miss school.[13] The incidence of childhood asthma has been increasing rapidly (notwithstanding declines in tobacco use).

In addition to its direct effect on children's health, parents' smoking may indirectly affect their children by increasing the likelihood that the children will take up smoking themselves, even more so if both parents are current smokers. Children of past smokers (that is, people who have quit) are no more likely to start smoking than are children of people who have never smoked.[14]

Obesity. Obesity in adults raises the risk of many chronic diseases, including diabetes, high blood pressure, heart disease, arthritis, and certain cancers.[15] Its complications in children are similar, and include an increased risk of type 2 diabetes. Obese children are also more likely to become obese adults, and some evidence suggests that obese children have worse health in adulthood even if they lose the excess weight as adults.[16]

Parental obesity is the strongest single risk factor for childhood obesity.[17] Parents and children share both genetic predispositions to obesity and environmental risk factors. Parents' influence on childhood obesity begins during pregnancy. Both a mother's malnutrition and excessive weight gain during pregnancy are associated with a higher risk of childhood obesity. On a more subtle level, what a mother eats while she is pregnant influences her child's food and flavor preferences. Breastfeeding may reduce the risk of childhood obesity, while certain ideas about how and how much to feed infants, including the perception that "a chubby baby is a healthy baby," may contribute to overfeeding. Parents have considerable control over their children's eating throughout early childhood as they purchase and prepare food and model eating behaviors for their children.[18]

Parental Depression. Depression is relatively common. By definition, it reduces wellbeing. Its presence can make other illnesses worse, and it can hurt parents in the labor market. The National Research Council estimates that at least 15 million children live with a parent who is depressed. New mothers are more likely than other people to be depressed; about 13 percent of all new mothers experience depression. Women who are socially disadvantaged have particularly higher rates of depression both during pregnancy and after a child is born.[19]

Parents' depression harms children's wellbeing. Postpartum depression is related to poor parenting; for children, a mother's postpartum depression can lead to delays in development, weaker cognitive skills, attention disorders, and a much greater likelihood of behavioral problems.[20] The way parents' depression affects children's development appears to have both a genetic and a behavioral basis. Epidemiologists estimate that children whose mothers were depressed are as much as six times as likely to suffer from depression as adults, compared with children whose mothers were not depressed. On average, depressed mothers give their children less positive reinforcement and adopt less consistent disciplinary practices. Maternal depression detracts from nurturing and supportive parenting; in parent-child interactions, depressed mothers have been described as disengaged, less responsive to children's cues, and less warm than mothers who do not meet the criteria for depressive symptoms. Children's wellbeing may also be indirectly harmed through maternal depression's effects on marriage and family functioning.[21]

Toxic Stress. Exposure to prolonged adverse experiences can alter children's developmental trajectories, with lifelong implications for physical and mental health.[22] Such experiences include extreme poverty, recurrent physical or emotional maltreatment or neglect, severe maternal depression, parental substance abuse or incarceration, and exposure to chronic violence.[23] Some scholars and clinicians, including those at the Center on the Developing Child at Harvard University, define the physical and mental health effects that follow these prolonged adverse experiences as a response to "toxic stress." In this issue of *Future of Children,* Ross Thompson argues that the concept of toxic stress may not capture how a child's own vulnerabilities and resilience can mediate the long-term response to external sources of severe stress.[24] There is no disagreement, however, that robust and accumulating scientific evidence documents that physical health and mental health share a common foundation with learning and behavior in the earliest years, and that there are long-term advantages to addressing these domains of development early and in ways that affect both adults and children.[25]

Substance Abuse. Drug and alcohol abuse together account for about 4.2 percent of deaths in the United States. A mother's substance abuse during pregnancy can have consequences for children that include low birth weight, withdrawal symptoms, impaired development, and infant mortality. And parents' substance abuse continues to have harmful effects throughout childhood, most prominently through much higher rates of child abuse and neglect.[26]

Chronic Conditions of Childhood. Most of the literature on health effects across generations focuses on how parents' health affects their children. Children's health, however, also has direct and indirect effects on parents' wellbeing. Parents of chronically ill children have a higher risk of mental health problems.[27] Children's chronic illnesses may also hurt parents' careers, both because parents need to miss work to care for their sick children and because parents may pass up promising opportunities because they need to keep their health insurance, a problem known as "job lock."

Common Risk Factors. All the risk factors described above are more common among families living in poverty, who are more likely to be poorly educated, have children early, experience chronic violence, and have short intervals between pregnancies.[28] These conditions harm adults and, the evidence suggests, affect children's physical health and mental health, as well as their learning and behavior, in the earliest years.[29] Prenatal stress and low birth weight are more common among lower-income mothers.[30] A baby born within 12 months of a previous child who was born prematurely or had low birth weight is highly likely to also be premature or have low birth weight.[31] Parents with less education are more likely to smoke than are those with more education.[32] Mothers who have low social support and experience more adverse life events are more likely to suffer from postpartum depression.[33] Alcohol and drug addiction are more common among socially disadvantaged people.[34] The high rates of overlap among these risk factors, and between these risk factors and socioeconomic status, are persistent challenges in designing and evaluating programs that seek to ameliorate them.

Two-Generation Interventions

The most common two-generation health programs are those that tackle conditions where there is a direct physical connection between generations. The most prevalent of these is prenatal care, which is nearly universally available. Some 70 percent of pregnant women use prenatal care starting in the first trimester, and approximately 95 percent of pregnant women receive some prenatal care over the course of their pregnancy. Since 1981, federal legislation has gradually expanded Medicaid eligibility for pregnant women, providing care during pregnancy, at birth, and for 60 days after birth. In 1988, states were allowed to set Medicaid eligibility for pregnant women at up to 185 percent of the federal poverty level; today, states can extend coverage above 185 percent of the poverty level. Congress expanded eligibility on explicitly two-generation grounds, reasoning that by providing care for pregnant women, Medicaid could save money on the treatment and care of newborns. Today, 40 percent of U.S. births are financed through Medicaid.

The Special Supplemental Nutrition Program for Women, Infants, and Children (WIC), sponsored by the Department of Agriculture, also focuses on pregnancy and the immediate postnatal period, providing nutritious foods, nutrition counseling and health-care referrals both to low-income pregnant and postpartum women and to their children up to age five. In 2012, WIC served an estimated 9 million people, including 900,000 pregnant women and 6.7 million infants and children.

Medicaid and WIC serve a very large group of low-income women. A more targeted program, Healthy Start, begun by the U.S. Health Services Administration in 1991, aims to reduce infant mortality in high-risk communities. In 2010, 104 federally funded Healthy Start projects in 38 states served almost 39,000 pregnant women and nearly 40,000 infants and children, providing prenatal and postnatal medical care and nutrition for high-risk parents and their newborns, as well as family planning and women's health services.

Most recently, the Maternal, Infant, and Early Childhood Home Visiting (MIECHV) program, authorized under the ACA, seeks to improve mothers' and children's health, children's development, and families' economic self-sufficiency by supporting and educating families with infants, toddlers, and young children. MIECHV targets families in high-risk communities who have been difficult to reach with other programs.

The MIECHV program builds on decades of experience. Home visitation has roots in the 1960s, when public health nurses and social workers began going to families' homes to promote positive parenting and prevent child maltreatment.[35] By 2009, almost all states had home-visiting programs that assessed families' risks and supported parents. States have improved these services by making it easier to refer parents to community resources and by introducing evidence-based practices. By 2008, the Children's Bureau of the Administration for Children and Families was administering and funding 17 cooperative agreements in 15 states to develop the infrastructure to scale up high-quality home visiting programs to prevent child maltreatment and promote children's and families' wellbeing. An evaluation of these programs is under way.

States are also trying and evaluating a number of enhancements to home visitation that explicitly target intergenerational health. Some of these enhancements focus on maternal depression. Mothers who are enrolled in home visitation programs are more likely than other mothers to have symptoms of depression, in part because they have experienced higher rates of violent trauma.[36] Home visitation was not designed to treat maternal depression, and most home visitors do not have the clinical training to do so. Instead, home visitors in some programs have begun working collaboratively with mental health professionals to offer in-home cognitive behavioral therapy to depressed mothers in conjunction with home visitation. The preliminary results are promising—not only have mothers' depressive symptoms decreased, but home visitation itself has become more effective.

Some child development programs also include health-focused components, although most of these are aimed directly at children rather than taking a two-generation approach. For example, Early Head Start (EHS)—a federal program started in 1995 for low-income, pregnant women and their children up to age three—includes home visitation, case management, parent education, child care, child development, health care and referrals, and family support among its services, which are offered beginning with pregnancy. The program is administered at the local level through direct federal grants to providers and is subject to federal regulations and monitoring. Like Head Start, the corresponding program for preschool children, at least 90 percent of children enrolled in EHS must be from families whose income is at or below the federal poverty level, and 10 percent of the enrolled children must be children with disabilities. During the 2011–12 program year, Early Head Start served more than 170,000 children at more than 900 sites nationwide. However, because of funding limitations, EHS serves only about 4 percent of eligible infants, toddlers, and their families.

Program statistics show that more than 90 percent of Head Start and EHS children have health insurance, are up to date on their immunizations, and are receiving basic health and dental services. Moreover, most of their mothers have health insurance and receive both prenatal and postnatal health care and education.[37] However, these children and their parents still have tremendous needs, particularly in the areas of developmental delays, disabilities, and mental health. For example, more than 50 percent of new EHS mothers report depressive symptoms, a rate that is four to five times greater than that of the general population of new mothers. A 2007 study of EHS reported that among EHS mothers who participated in a national program evaluation, those who were depressed when their child entered EHS were significantly less likely to be depressed by the time their children were five (two years after the program ended).[38]

Programs That Target Shared Risk Factors

Policy makers, program officials, and community leaders have grown interested in two-generation models that target environmental risk factors that affect both parents and children, particularly risk factors that influence obesity and smoking.[39] The U.S. Centers for Disease Control and Prevention is helping 50 communities implement the Communities Putting Prevention to Work initiative. These communities are committed to making environmental changes that will have significant, measureable effects on adults' and children's health by encouraging healthy behaviors related to weight, nutrition, physical activity, and smoking. The approach includes offering resources for quitting smoking, maintaining safe places for physical activity, and making fresh fruits and vegetables available.[40]

Targeting Conditions That Affect Children and Parents Differently

The least developed or widespread programs are those that target children beyond the early years and focus on risk factors that have different effects on children and parents. For example, pediatricians who treat children with mental health conditions rarely assess and even less frequently do anything about parents' mental health conditions that may contribute to the children's problems.[41] Likewise, surprisingly, pediatricians often do not ask about parents' smoking when they treat an asthmatic child, and they very rarely intervene to help change parents' smoking behavior.[42]

Programs to address toxic stress are in their infancy. In 2011, the U.S. Department of Health and Human Services awarded $12 million to researchers at six universities to collaborate with Early Head Start programs to improve basic parent-child interactions in the highest-risk EHS families.[43] The American Academy of Pediatrics, in a 2012 policy statement, envisions that pediatric medical homes (a model of care that we discuss in the final section of this article) can play a key role in identifying and treating toxic stress.[44]

Effects of Two-Generation Interventions on Health

We've shown that parents' health affects children's health, and vice versa, and we've described where two-generation programs are most and least likely to be found. But do these programs work, and, if so, for whom do they work best? Next we examine the evidence for two-generation programs, focusing on each of the risk factors described above.

Pediatricians who treat children with mental health conditions rarely assess and even less frequently do anything about parents' mental health.

Programs that Target Risk Factors in Pregnancy

The most common programs that target risk factors in pregnancy are those that offer prenatal care. Prenatal care is strongly associated with improvements in mothers' health, up to and including a lower risk of death during pregnancy and childbirth.[45] The strength of the relationship between prenatal care and infants' wellbeing is less clear-cut, and it is difficult to assess because mothers who seek and obtain prenatal care differ from those who do not. Recent analyses of survey data suggest that prenatal care beginning in the first three months of pregnancy has very modest effects on children's birth weight and other measures of children's health; for example, it increases average birth weight by only about 20 grams (less than three-quarters of an ounce).[46] Earlier medical studies have likewise found that prenatal care has ambiguous effects on birth weight.[47] Several analyses of policies that extended Medicaid eligibility to low-income pregnant women or reduced the barriers to Medicaid enrollment, thus enhancing access to prenatal care, have shown improvements in birth weight.[48] Yet even in these studies, the impact of prenatal care is modest, reducing the rate of low birth weight (defined as birth weight less than 5.5 pounds) by less than 1 percentage point in the target population.

A second type of intervention during the prenatal period is embodied by the WIC program, which seeks to improve mothers' nutrition and healthy behaviors during pregnancy and breast-feeding. Multiple studies that compare WIC participants with other, similar women, as well as econometric analyses, have shown that WIC participants have fewer low-birth weight babies and longer gestations, and are less likely to experience a preterm birth.[49]

Two-Generation Programs that Target Smoking

We have considerable evidence about the efficacy of programs and policies to reduce smoking, but there is no conclusive evidence about which interventions are most effective in decreasing parents' smoking specifically.[50] Indeed, at least one study suggests that policies to promote smoke-free workplaces and public spaces may actually increase children's exposure to tobacco smoke, because parents smoke at home rather than at work.[51]

The most compelling evidence of two-generation effects in programs that help people quit smoking comes from those that focus on smoking during pregnancy. A comprehensive review of randomized studies of such programs found that smoking rates among pregnant women fell by an average of six percentage points. The review found no significant differences in the efficacy of most alternative approaches (such as cognitive behavioral therapy, nicotine replacement therapy, or feedback in the form of advice or counseling), although programs that offered incentives for quitting, such as packages of gum or a monetary reward, had slightly greater effects. These interventions also led to reductions in low birth weight and pre-term births. Soon after their children were

born, women who had participated in smoking cessation programs during pregnancy remained significantly less likely to smoke than nonparticipants, although differences between the two groups became insignificant by several months after delivery.[52]

Two-Generation Programs to Prevent Obesity

Because mothers' weight gain and diet during pregnancy can increase childhood obesity, some interventions aim to prevent excessive gestational weight gain and encourage healthy nutrition.[53] Other two-generation programs that target obesity focus on preschool and school-aged children.

Evaluations of these programs have generally looked only at short-term effects, and they have shown weak, though generally positive, results.[54] There is some encouraging evidence that parental engagement can help prevent obesity in the youngest children by shaping their eating and physical activity habits.[55] No evaluations have examined how two-generation interventions affect obesity or weight gain in children as they grow to adulthood.

Parents' Mental Health and Substance Use

A variety of drugs and psychotherapies can ameliorate major depression in parents. Using these interventions appears to produce better outcomes for children, including reduced emotional and behavioral distress and higher educational attainment.[56] Given the strong link between mothers' depression and depression in children and adolescents, a few studies have examined programs that intervene with both depressed mothers and their children. Some of these interventions have been shown to reduce the development of psychopathology in children, though others have not.[57]

Several studies have shown that substance-use treatment programs for mothers lead to better outcomes for their children. Programs that integrate substance-use services with child care or with other child-related services work better than those that target only mothers.[58]

Two-Generation Programs for Children with Chronic Conditions

There are effective interventions for many chronic conditions that occur in children. Assessments of these interventions sometimes examine their effects on parents, and some of these assessments show that reducing children's symptoms improves parents' health.[59] In most cases, however, these interventions do not directly target the consequences for parents of children's chronic health conditions.

Barriers to Two-Generation Approaches

Well-developed, broadly disseminated two-generation programs that aim to improve health share one characteristic: they focus on the period when the connection between mother and child is physical. From an organizational and structural point of view, pregnancy and breast-feeding are periods when treating just one person, the mother, can affect the health of both mother and child. Fewer interventions target health problems that occur after that physical bond has ended, and few that do so have been broadly disseminated.

Two-generation programs face two sets of barriers. First, and most readily amenable to policy, is the system of financing care

for children and adults. Today, thanks to expansions of Medicaid and CHIP, low-income children are more likely to have health insurance than are their parents. Recently, some states have expanded Medicaid and CHIP coverage to parents. The evidence indicates that when parents can enroll, eligible children are more likely to be enrolled as well. Children are also more likely to have a regular source of care and to use preventive services.[60]

But the income eligibility standards for Medicaid and CHIP are different for children and adults. And employee contributions for employer-sponsored health insurance are also substantially higher for workers who cover their families than for those who cover only themselves. For these reasons, even when parents and children all have health insurance, the coverage may come from different sources. In most higher-income families, parents and children are all covered by private, employer-sponsored insurance. In many lower-income families, however, parents are covered by employer-sponsored insurance and children are covered by Medicaid or CHIP. For example, parents and children all carry Medicaid coverage in only 46 percent of families with incomes below 138 percent of the federal poverty level. Insurers, whether public or private, are not required to pay for services provided to household members who are not themselves covered by a policy. Thus, differences in insurance coverage within a family diminish the incentives for any payer to invest in two-generation health programs that serve both covered and non-covered family members.

The ACA will not entirely erase the disconnect between parents' and children's sources of health insurance coverage. For families with incomes below 138 percent of the federal poverty level, new access to Medicaid coverage under the ACA (in states that choose to expand Medicaid) may let parents and children be covered by the same health plan. In many low-income families whose incomes are above 138 percent of the poverty line, however, children will continue to be eligible for CHIP but parents will not, and parents will be enrolled in plans in the new health insurance marketplaces. Without a change in policy, these parents and children will remain in different plans.

> *Parallel financing and delivery systems for children's and adults' health services may be the biggest factor limiting the development and spread of two-generation programs in health.*

The second barrier to two-generation programs is the structure of the health-care delivery system itself. Once babies are born, they go to pediatricians for their care. Pediatricians constitute a specialized system of health-care delivery that is quite separate from health care for adults. Over 60 percent of physician visits by children 15 and under are to pediatricians and pediatric specialists. By contrast, nearly 95 percent of physician visits by adults 19–44 are to nonpediatric physicians. Put differently, pediatricians and pediatric specialists see almost no adults (adults constitute less than 2 percent of the caseload of pediatricians and pediatric

specialists), and fewer than 5 percent of visits to adult generalist and specialist physicians are from children. In most cases, a pediatrician who sees a child with an emotional disorder has little contact with the child's mother. Even if the pediatrician recognizes that the child's mother is depressed, she is unlikely to consider treating the mother directly to be within the scope of her practice (and she might not know where to make a referral for adult depression). If she does treat the mother, she will be not be able to bill the visit to the child's insurance, and she might not participate in the mother's insurance plan's network.

Expanded coverage under the ACA will not solve this problem, even if parents and children have the same insurance. Existing two-generation programs have largely avoided the divide between adults' and children's health care by bypassing the health-care delivery system through nonmedical approaches. Ironically, the existence of well-established and parallel financing and delivery systems for children's and adults' health services may be the biggest factor limiting the development and spread of two-generation programs in health.

Conclusions and Opportunities to Expand Two-Generation Programs

As we've seen, home visiting and other effective, evidence-based two-generation programs to reduce children's health risks exist. But most of them focus on the prenatal and postnatal periods. The ACA expands some of these programs, but their reach remains limited. By further expanding these programs, we could further improve children's health.

We found no effective programs in widespread use that apply two-generation approaches to target children's health problems after these problems have actually begun. At that point, a child's care is usually under the direction of a pediatrician and is paid for by the child's health insurance. Pediatricians have not traditionally considered parents' health in their practice, and they are rarely family focused. Moreover, they face financial disincentives to consider parents' health because parents of low-income children are often uninsured or are covered through different health plans than their children's.

The ACA, which will expand coverage to millions of lower-income parents, particularly in states that choose to participate in the Medicaid expansion, is a necessary step for tackling children's health problems through two-generation approaches. But to have a significant effect on two-generation treatment practices, state policy makers must take at least two further steps. Fortunately, the ACA provides some opportunities for them to do so.

First, in most states, previous expansions of insurance have meant that children became eligible for Medicaid or CHIP while, in many cases, their parents remained uninsured. Under the ACA, the parents of Medicaid- or CHIP-eligible children will be able to get health insurance through either Medicaid or the new health insurance marketplaces. In many such cases, particularly among families with incomes over 138 percent of the federal poverty level, parents and children will be covered by different health plans unless the states take further action. The Centers for Medicare and Medicaid Services has offered the states some options to help families avoid splitting their coverage. States may offer a so-called Bridge plan—a Medicaid/CHIP managed-care plan that could also be sold

in the health insurance marketplaces to families with children enrolled in the plan, as well as to families who are transitioning from Medicaid/CHIP into the private market.[61] States could achieve similar results by using Medicaid premium assistance payments, an option under ACA, to purchase family health insurance coverage in the marketplace that includes parents and their children. Finally, the Basic Health Program, a provision of the ACA to be implemented in 2014, may give states additional opportunities to design programs for low-income people that span Medicaid and the health insurance marketplaces. Modeled after a program in Washington state, the Basic Health Program would offer continuity of care for a population that is likely to gain and lose Medicaid eligibility because of small fluctuations in income. It will give states the flexibility to offer publicly funded insurance to those whose income is too high to be eligible for Medicaid.

Financing health insurance for parents and their children through the same managed-care plan will give the plans' administrators financial incentives to encourage the development of two-generation health programs. Plan-level incentives, however, may not be enough. A key second step is to give providers incentives to generate meaningful changes in their practices. One way to generate such incentives is the patient-centered medical home model. Medical homes make additional payments to providers who coordinate their services with those of other medical and social service providers. The Medicaid Health Home, a variant of the medical home model, targets Medicaid patients with chronic health conditions, including mental health problems. Health homes have yet to develop two-generation models, but their structure offers financial incentives and opportunities to do so, particularly if parents' and children's coverage is also coordinated.[62]

The rationale for two-generation programs that target both children's and parents' health problems is strong. Many children's health problems are linked to the family's environment and behaviors. Effective two-generation programs that address these problems exist. Structural factors have limited their dissemination in the past, but the ACA offers new opportunities to develop and implement such programs.

ENDNOTES

1. Kirsten Beronio et al., "Affordable Care Act Will Expand Mental Health and Substance Use Disorder Benefits and Parity Protections for 62 Million Americans" (research brief, Office of the Assistant Secretary for Planning and Evaluation, U.S. Department of Health and Human Services, Washington, DC, February 2013), http://aspe.hhs.gov/health/reports/2013/mental/rb_mental.pdf.

2. Anne Case, Angela Fertig, and Christina Paxson, "The Lasting Impact of Childhood Health and Circumstance," *Journal of Health Economics* 24 (2005), 365–89.

3. Anne Case, Darren Lubotsky, and Christina Paxson, "Economic Status and Health in Childhood: The Origins of the Gradient," *American Economic Review* 92 (2002), 1308–34; Janet Currie and Mark Stabile, "Child Mental Health and Human Capital Accumulation: The Case of ADHD," *Journal of Health Economics* 25 (2006), 1094–1118, doi: 10.1016/j.jhealeco.2006.03.001.

4. Katherine M. Kitzmann and Bettina M. Beech, "Family-Based Interventions for Pediatric Obesity: Methodological and Conceptual Challenges from Family Psychology," *Couple and Family Psychology: Research and Practice* 1 (2011), 45–62.

5. Maternal and Child Health Bureau, *"The Health and Well-Being of Children: A Portrait of States and the Nation 2007"* (Rockville, MD: U.S. Department of Health and Human Services, 2009), http://mchb.hrsa.gov/nsch/07main/moreinfo/pdf/nsch07.pdf.

6. Hope Corman, Kelly Noonan, and Nancy E. Reichman, "Mothers' Labor Supply in Fragile Families: The Role of Child Health," *Eastern Economic Journal* 31 (2005), 601–16.

7. Douglas Almond and Janet Currie, "Human Capital Development before Age Five," in Orley Ashenfelter and David Card, eds., *Handbook of Labor Economics*, vol. 4B (Amsterdam: North-Holland, 2011), 1315–1486.

8. Jennifer Bishop et al., "Childhood Obesity" (Washington, DC: Office of the Assistant Secretary for Planning and Evaluation, U.S. Department of Health and Human Services, 2005), accessed October 23, 2013, http://aspe.hhs.gov/health/reports/child_obesity/index.cfm.

9. Almond and Currie, "Human Capital Development."

10. Almond and Currie, "Human Capital Development"; Kelly Noonan et al., "Effects of Prenatal Care on Child Health at Age 5," *Maternal and Child Health Journal* 17 (2013), 189–99, doi: 10.1007/s10995-012-0966-2.

11. David P. Hopkins et al., "Reviews of Evidence Regarding Interventions to Reduce Tobacco Use and Exposure to Environmental Tobacco Smoke," *American Journal of Preventive Medicine* 20, no. 2S (2001), 16–66; Naomi Priest et al., "Family and Carer Smoking Control Programmes for Reducing Children's Exposure to Environmental Tobacco Smoke," *Cochrane Database of Systematic Reviews*, issue 4 (2008), article CD001746, doi: 10.1002/14651858.CD001746.pub2.

12. Tina Neogi, Jon O. Neher, and Sarah Safranek, "Clinical Inquiry: How Does Smoking in the Home Affect Children with Asthma?" *Journal of Family Practice* 61 (2012), 292–93.

13. Sheniz A. Moonie et al., "Asthma Status and Severity Affects Missed School Days," *Journal of School Health* 76 (2006), 18–24; Yorke Janelle, Sharon L. Fleming, and Caroline Shuldham, "Psychological Interventions for Children with Asthma," *Cochrane Database of Systematic Reviews*, issue 4 (2005), article CD003272, doi: 10.1002/14651858.CD003272.pub2.

14. Stephen E. Gilman et al., "Parental Smoking and Adolescent Smoking Initiation: An Intergenerational Perspective on Tobacco Control," *Pediatrics* 123 (2009), e274–81, doi: 10.1542/peds.2008-2251.

15. Stephen D. H. Malnick and Hilla Knobler, "The Medical Complications of Obesity," *Quarterly Journal of Medicine* 99 (2006), 565–79, doi: 10.1093/qjmed/hcl085.

16. Richard J. Deckelbaum and Christine L. Williams, "Childhood Obesity: The Health Issue," *Obesity Research* 9 (2001), 239S–43S, doi: 10.1038/oby.2001.125.

17. Leonard H. Epstein et al., "Ten-Year Follow-up of Behavioral, Family-Based Treatment for Obese Children," *Journal of the American Medical Association* 264 (1990), 2519–23; Gavitt A. Woodard et al., "Halo Effect for Bariatric Surgery: Collateral Weight Loss in Patients' Family Members," *Archives of Surgery* 146 (2011), 1185–90, doi: 10.1001/archsurg.2011.244.

18. Stephanie L. Anzman, Brandi Y. Rollins, and Leann L. Birch, "Parental Influence on Children's Early Eating Environments and Obesity Risk: Implications for Prevention," *International Journal of Obesity* 34 (2010), 1116–24, doi: 10.1038/ijo.2010.43.

19. National Research Council and Institute of Medicine, *Depression in Parents, Parenting, and Children: Opportunities to Improve Identification, Treatment, and Prevention* (Washington, DC: National Academies Press, 2009); Cindy Lee Dennis and Ellen Hodnett, "Psychosocial and Psychological Interventions for Treating Postpartum Depression," *Cochrane Database of Systematic Reviews*, issue 4 (2007), article CD006116, doi: 10.1002/14651858.CD006116.pub2; Stevan E. Hobfoll et al., "Depression Prevalence and Incidence among Inner-City Pregnant and Postpartum Women," *Journal of Consulting and Clinical Psychology* 63 (1995), 445–53.

20. Dennis and Hodnett, "Psychosocial and Psychological Interventions."

21. Carrie W. Rishel, "Pathways to Prevention for Children of Depressed Mothers: A Review of the Literature and Recommendations for Practice," *Depression Research and Treatment* (2012), article 313689, doi: 10.1155/2012/313689; Olivia Golden and Karina Fortuny, *Improving the Lives of Young Children: Meeting Parents' Health and Mental Health Needs through Medicaid and CHIP so Children Can Thrive* (Washington, DC: Urban Institute, 2011), http://www.urban.org/UploadedPDF/412315-Meeting-Parents-Health.pdf; M. Christine Lovejoy et al., "Maternal Depression and Parenting Behavior: A Meta-Analytic Review," *Clinical Psychology Review* 20 (2000), 561–92.

22. "Toxic Stress: The Facts," Center on the Developing Child, Harvard University, accessed October 23, 2013, http://developingchild.harvard.edu/topics/science_of_early_childhood/toxic_stress_response.

23. Jack P. Shonkoff, "Building a New Biodevelopmental Framework to Guide the Future of Early Childhood Policy," *Child Development* 81 (2010), 357–67, doi: 10.1111/j.1467-8624.2009.01399.x.

24. Ross A. Thompson, "Stress and Child Development," *Future of Children* 24, no. 1 (2014): 41–60.

25. Jack P. Shonkoff et al., "The Lifelong Effects of Early Childhood Adversity and Toxic Stress," *Pediatrics* 129 (2012), e232–46; Jennifer S. Middlebrooks and Natalie C. Audage, *The Effects of Childhood Stress on Health across the Lifespan* (Atlanta: Centers for Disease Control and Prevention, National Center for Injury Prevention and Control, 2008), http://www.cdc.gov/ncipc/pub-res/pdf/childhood_stress.pdf; M. Ann Easterbrooks, Kenneth Ginsburg, and Richard M. Lerner (2013) "Resilience among Military Youth," *Future of Children* 23, no. 2 (2013), 99–120.

26. Ali H. Mokdad et al., "Actual Causes of Death in the United States, 2000," *Journal of the American Medical Association* 291 (2004), 1238–45; Catherine Turnbull and David A. Osborn, "Home Visits During Pregnancy and after Birth for Women with an Alcohol or Drug Problem," *Cochrane Database of Systematic Reviews*, issue 1 (2012), article CD004456, doi: 10.1002/14651858.CD004456.pub3; Richard P. Barth, "Preventing Child Abuse and Neglect with Parent Training: Evidence and Opportunities," *Future of Children* 19 (2009), 95–118.

27. Janelle Yorke and Caroline Shuldham, "Family Therapy for Asthma in Children," *Cochrane Database of Sysematic Reviews*, issue 2 (2005), article CD000089, doi: 10.1002/14651858.CD000089.pub2; Richard P. Hastings and Alexandra Beck, "Practitioner Review: Stress Intervention for Parents of Children with Intellectual Disabilities," *Journal of Child Psychology and Psychiatry*, 45 (2004), 1338–49.

28. Jack P. Shonkoff, "Building a New Biodevelopmental Framework to Guide the Future of Early Childhood Policy," *Child Development* 81 (2010), 357–67, doi: 10.1111/j.1467-8624.2009.01399.x.

29. Jack P. Shonkoff et al., "The Lifelong Effects of Early Childhood Adversity and Toxic Stress," *Pediatrics* 129 (2012), e232–46, doi: 10.1542/peds.2011-2663; Middlebrooks and Audage, *Effects of Childhood Stress*; "Toxic Stress: The Facts."

30. Nancy E. Reichman et al., "Effects of Prenatal Care on Maternal Postpartum Behaviors," *Review of the Economics of the Household* 8 (2010), 171–97, doi: 0.1007/s11150-009-9074-5.

31. Szu-Fu Chen et al., "The Impact of Interpregnancy Interval and Previous Preterm Birth on the Subsequent Risk of Preterm Birth," *Journal of the Society for Gynecologic Investigation* 12 (2005), 202–7.

32. Hopkins et al., "Reviews of Evidence."

33. Dennis and Hodnett, "Psychosocial and Psychological Interventions."

34. Turnbull and Osborn, "Home Visits."

35. Diane Paulsell et al., *Home Visiting Evidence of Effectiveness Review: Executive Summary* (Washington, DC: Office of Planning, Research and Evaluation, Administration for Children and Families, U.S. Department of Health and Human Services, 2011), http://www.acf.hhs.gov/sites/default/files/opre/homvee_executivesummary_rev10_15_2011.pdf.

36. Michael W. O'Hara and Annette M. Swain, "Rates and Risk of Postpartum Depression—A Meta-Analysis," *International Review of Psychiatry*, 8 (1996), 37–54; Jack Stevens et al., "Depression and Trauma History in First Time Mothers Receiving Home Visitation," *Journal of Community Psychology* 30 (2002), 551–64, doi: 0.1002/jcop.10017; Robert T. Ammerman et al., "Treatment of Depressed Mothers in Home Visiting: Impact on Psychological Distress and Social Functioning," *Child Abuse & Neglect* (2013), doi: 10.1016/j.chiabu.2013.03.003; Robert T. Ammerman et al., "Changes in Depressive Symptoms in First Time Mothers in Home Visitation," *Child Abuse & Neglect* 33 (2009), 127–38, doi: 10.1016/j.chiabu.2008.09.005.

37. Advisory Committee on Head Start Research and Evaluation, *Advisory Committee on Head Start Research and Evaluation: Final Report* (Washington, DC: U.S. Department of Health and Human Services, 2012), http://www.acf.hhs.gov/sites/default/files/opre/eval_final.pdf; Office of Head Start, "Program Information Report (PIR) 2011 Summary Report," (U.S. Department of Health and Human Services, 2011).

38. Ammerman et al., "Treatment of Depressed Mothers."

39. Kitzmann and Beech, "Family-Based Interventions."

40. "Communities Putting Prevention to Work," Centers for Disease Control and Prevention, accessed October 23, 2013, http://www.cdc.gov/CommunitiesPuttingPreventiontoWork/index.htm.

41. Ardis L. Olson et al., "Primary Care Pediatricians' Roles and Perceived Responsibilities in the Identification and Management of Maternal Depression," *Pediatrics* 110 (2002), 1169–76; Amy M. Heneghan et al., "Do Pediatricians Recognize Mothers with Depressive Symptoms?" *Pediatrics* 106 (2000), 1367–73; Kathi J. Kemper and Kelly J. Kelleher, "Rationale for Family Psychosocial Screening," *Ambulatory Child Health* 1 (1996), 311–24.

42. Jonathan P. Winickoff et al., "Addressing Parental Smoking in Pediatrics and Family Practice: A National Survey of Parents," *Pediatrics* 112 (2003), 1146–51; Jonathan P. Winickoff et al., "Child Health Care Clinicians' Use of Medications to Help Parents Quit Smoking: A National Parent Survey," *Pediatrics* 115 (2005), 1013–17.

43. "Early Head Start University Partnership Grants: Buffering Children from Toxic Stress, 2011–2016," Office of Planning, Research and Evaluation, Administration for Children and Families, U.S. Department of Health and Human Services, accessed October 23, 2013, http://www.acf.hhs.gov/programs/opre/research/project/early-head-start-university-partnership-grants-buffering-children-from.

44. Andrew S. Garner et al., "Early Childhood Adversity, Toxic Stress, and the Role of the Pediatrician: Translating Developmental Science Into Lifelong Health," *Pediatrics* 129 (2012), e224–31.

45. Jeani Chang et al., "Pregnancy-Related Mortality Surveillance—United States, 1991–1999," *Morbidity and Mortality Weekly Report* 52 (2003), 1–8; Noonan, et al., "Effects of Prenatal Care."

46. Reichman et al., "Effects of Prenatal Care."

47 Kevin Fiscella, "Does Prenatal Care Improve Birth Outcomes? A Critical Review," *Obstetrics & Gynecology* 85 (1995), 468–79.

48. Almond and Currie, "Human Capital Development."

49. Janet Currie, "U.S. Food and Nutrition Programs," in Robert A. Moffitt, ed., *Means-Tested Transfer Programs in the United States* (Chicago: University of Chicago Press, 2003), 199–290.

50. Hopkins et al., "Reviews of Evidence"; Priest at al., "Smoking Control Programmes."

51. Adda Jérôme and Francesca Cornaglia, "The Effect of Bans and Taxes on Passive Smoking," *American Economic Journal: Applied Economics* 2 (2010), 1–32, doi: 10.1257/app.2.1.1.

52. Judith Lumley et al., "Interventions for Promoting Smoking Cessation During Pregnancy," *Cochrane Database of Systematic Reviews*, issue 3 (2009), article CD001055, doi: 10.1002/14651858.CD001055.pub3.

53. Anzman, Rollins, and Birch, "Parental Influence."

54. Helen Skouteris et al., "Parental Influence and Obesity Prevention in Pre-Schoolers: A Systematic Review of Interventions," *Obesity Reviews* 12 (2011), 315–28, doi: 10.1111/j.1467-789X.2010.00751.x.

55. Elizabeth Waters et al., "Interventions for Preventing Obesity in Children," *Cochrane Database of Systematic Reviews*, issue 12 (2011), article CD001871, doi: 10.1002/14651858.CD001871.pub3.

56. Meredith L. Gunlicks and Myrna M. Weissman, "Change in Child Psychopathology with Improvement in Parental Depression: A Systematic Review," *Journal of the American Academy of Child & Adolescent Psychiatry* 47 (2008), 379–89.

57. Rishel, "Pathways to Prevention."

58. Olivia Silber Ashley, Mary Ellen Marsden, and Thomas M. Brady, "Effectiveness of Substance Abuse Treatment Programming for Women: A Review," *American Journal of Drug and Alcohol Abuse* 29 (2003): 19–53, doi: 10.1081/ADA-120018838; Alison Niccols et al., "Integrated Programs for Mothers with Substance Abuse Issues and Their Children: A Systematic Review of Studies Reporting on Child Outcomes," *Child Abuse and Neglect* 36 (2012): 308–22, doi: 10.1016/j.chiabu.2011.10.007.

59. Hastings and Beck, "Stress Intervention."

60. U.S. Government Accountability Office, *Medicaid and CHIP: Given the Association between Parent and Child Insurance Status, New Expansions May Benefit Families* (Washington, DC: U.S. Government Accountability Office, 2011); Sara Rosenbaum and Ramona Perez Trevino Whittington, "Parental Health Insurance Coverage as Child Health Policy: Evidence from the Literature," research brief, First Focus, George Washington University School of Public Health and Health Services, 2007, http://www.firstfocus.net/sites/default/files/r.2007-6.25.rosenbaum.pdf.

61. Centers for Medicare and Medicaid Services, "Frequently Asked Questions on Exchanges, Market Reforms, and Medicaid," Baltimore, MD, 2012, http://www.cms.gov/CCIIO/Resources/Files/Downloads/exchanges-faqs-12-10-2012.pdf.

62. Embry M. Howell, Olivia Golden, and William Beardslee, *Emerging Opportunities for Addressing Maternal Depression under Medicaid* (Washington: Urban Institute, 2013), http://www.urban.org/UploadedPDF/412758-Emerging-Opportunities-for-Addressing-Maternal-Depression-under-Medicaid.pdf.

Boosting Family Income to Promote Child Development

Greg J. Duncan, Katherine Magnuson, and
Elizabeth Votruba-Drzal

Summary

Families who live in poverty face disadvantages that can hinder their children's development in many ways, write Greg Duncan, Katherine Magnuson, and Elizabeth Votruba-Drzal. As they struggle to get by economically, and as they cope with substandard housing, unsafe neighborhoods, and inadequate schools, poor families experience more stress in their daily lives than more affluent families do, with a host of psychological and developmental consequences. Poor families also lack the resources to invest in things like high-quality child care and enriched learning experiences that give more affluent children a leg up. Often, poor parents also lack the time that wealthier parents have to invest in their children, because poor parents are more likely to be raising children alone or to work nonstandard hours and have inflexible work schedules.

Can increasing poor parents' incomes, independent of any other sort of assistance, help their children succeed in school and in life? The theoretical case is strong, and Duncan, Magnuson, and Votruba-Drzal find solid evidence that the answer is yes—children from poor families that see a boost in income do better in school and complete more years of schooling, for example. But if boosting poor parents' incomes can help their children, a crucial question remains: Does it matter when in a child's life the additional income appears? Developmental neurobiology strongly suggests that increased income should have the greatest effect during children's early years, when their brains and other systems are developing rapidly, though we need more evidence to prove this conclusively.

The authors offer examples of how policy makers could incorporate the findings they present to create more effective programs for families living in poverty. And they conclude with a warning: if a boost in income can help poor children, then a drop in income—for example, through cuts to social safety net programs like food stamps—can surely harm them.

www.futureofchildren.org

Greg J. Duncan is a Distinguished Professor in the School of Education at the University of California, Irvine. Katherine Magnuson is an associate professor in the School of Social Work at the University of Wisconsin–Madison. Elizabeth Votruba-Drzal is an associate professor in the Department of Psychology at the University of Pittsburgh. Portions of this article were drawn from a review chapter on socioeconomic status by Duncan, Magnuson, and Votruba-Drzal in the forthcoming *Handbook of Child Psychology and Developmental Science*. The authors are grateful for support from the National Institute for Child Health and Human Development through grant P01HD065704.

Greg J. Duncan, Katherine Magnuson, and Elizabeth Votruba-Drzal

Using a poverty line of about $23,000 for a family of four, the U.S. Census Bureau counted more than 16 million U.S. children—more than one in five—living in poor families in 2012.[1] Poor children begin school well behind their more affluent peers and may lose even more ground during the school years. On average, poor U.S. children have lower levels of kindergarten reading and math skills than their more fortunate peers (figure 1). Moreover, when compared with people whose families had incomes of at least twice the poverty line during their early childhood, adults who were poor as children completed two fewer years of schooling and, by the time they reached their 30s, earned less than half as much, worked far fewer hours per year, received more in food stamps, and were nearly three times as likely to report poor overall health (table 1).[2] Poor boys were more than twice as likely to be arrested later in life, and poor girls were five times as likely to bear a child out of wedlock before age 21.

Poverty is associated with a cluster of disadvantages that may be harmful to children, including low levels of parental education and living with a single parent. To determine whether children would be helped by a policy that is designed to increase family incomes and nothing else, we focus on distinguishing the effects of family income from those of other sources of disadvantage. In policy terms, this approach lets us answer the following question: To what extent would children's development be affected by policies that give low-income parents more income, but do not directly target other characteristics of parents or family environments? In other words, would increasing family income through policies such as the Earned Income Tax Credit, food stamps, or the Child Tax Credit lead to better child outcomes? If the benefits are larger than the costs, income-support programs for parents might constitute a wise two-generation investment.

If income is beneficial for children, we also need to know at what point in children's lives an income-support program for parents would be most effective. But few studies of poverty's effects have been able to focus on the timing of economic hardship in children's lives, partly because such studies rarely include children at a variety of childhood stages. Recent research in neuroscience and developmental psychology suggests that poverty early in a child's life may be particularly harmful. Not only does the astonishingly rapid development of their brains leave young children sensitive and vulnerable to environmental conditions, but the family (as opposed to school or peers) dominates their everyday lives. Where we can, as we summarize the evidence for income's effects on children, we pay attention to the timing of economic deprivation. After reviewing both experimental and other evidence of the ways poverty may affect children, we highlight emerging research based on newly available data that include measures of poverty recorded as early as the prenatal year alongside adult outcomes measured in the fourth decade of life.

The strongest evidence, drawn from social experiments, has linked increases in family income to increased school achievement in middle childhood and greater school attainment (for example, high school completion) in adolescence and early adulthood. Although we have virtually no experimental evidence of how economic deprivation affects children in the first several years of life, other kinds of evidence suggest that poverty early in childhood may reduce adult earnings and work hours.

Figure 1. Rates of Kindergarten Proficiencies for Poor, Near Poor, and Middle-Class Children

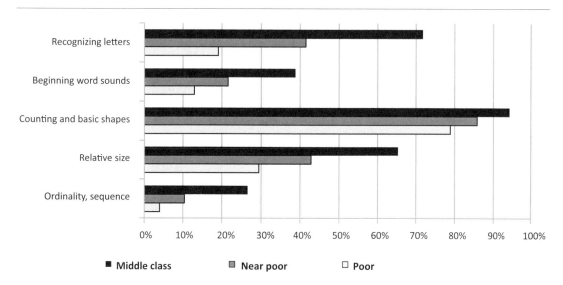

Source: Authors' calculations from the Early Childhood Longitudinal Study, Kindergarten Class of 1998–99.

Note: "Poor" is defined as income below the official U.S. poverty threshold. "Near poor" is defined as income between one and two times that poverty line. "Middle class" is defined as income above twice the poverty line.

We conclude with our thoughts about how social policy makers might focus attention on poverty occurring across childhood. The weight of the evidence indicates that increased income does indeed give children a better chance to develop successfully, although the likely impact of changes to the family incomes of low-income children appears to vary depending on the children's age and the form (cash versus in-kind) of the income change.

People who advocate for income-support policies often emphasize the potential benefits of increasing the incomes of low-income families, and they point to studies of policy changes that increased income support. But evidence from these studies can suggest what to expect not only from policies that increase the generosity of programs such as the Earned Income Tax Credit and food stamps, but also from those that reduce income or in-kind supports.

Why Poverty May Hinder Healthy Development

We use the terms "poverty" and "low income" synonymously. The official U.S. poverty thresholds designate a set of income levels below which families are considered "poor" and above which they are not. These thresholds let us consistently track poverty rates over time and serve to determine who is eligible for various programs. But there is no evidence that these particular dollar thresholds meaningfully differentiate families' economic needs. Indeed, evidence indicates that improving the incomes of families both just below and just above the poverty line will have similarly positive effects. But from studies that consider links between income and children's development across a larger spectrum of the income distribution, it is also clear that income changes have larger effects for low-income children than for children from wealthier families.[3] Accordingly, we focus on evidence of how variations in income

Table 1. Adult Outcomes (Age 30–37) by Income between the Prenatal Year and Age Five

	Income below the official U.S. poverty line	Income between one and two times the poverty line	Income more than twice the poverty line
Completed schooling (mean)	11.8 years	12.7 years	14.0 years
Annual earnings (mean)	$17,900	$26,800	$39,700
Annual work hours (mean)	1,512	1,839	1,963
Annual food stamps (mean)	$896	$337	$70
Poor health	13%	13%	5%
Arrested (men only)	26%	21%	13%
Nonmarital birth (women only)	50%	28%	9%

Source: Greg J. Duncan, Kathleen M. Ziol-Guest, and Ariel Kalil, "Early Childhood Poverty and Adult Attainment, Behavior, and Health," *Child Development* 81 (2010): 306–25.

Note: Earnings and food stamp values are in 2005 dollars.

affect children in poor families, rather than on how such variations affect middle-class or wealthy families.

What are the consequences of growing up in a poor household? Economists, sociologists, developmental psychologists, and neuroscientists emphasize different ways that poverty may influence children's development. Three main theoretical frameworks describe these processes: family and environmental stress, resources and investment, and culture. Each framework is grounded in a different scholarly discipline, and they differ in the extent to which they focus on socioeconomic status (SES) in general rather than on income, poverty, or any other particular component of SES (for example, parents' education or occupational prestige). Nevertheless, these frameworks overlap and are complementary.

Family and Environmental Stress

As Ross Thompson explains in this issue of *Future of Children*, economically disadvantaged families experience more stress in their everyday lives than more affluent families do, and this stress may affect children's development. Glen Elder Jr. first developed the family stress model to document how

economic loss affected people during the Great Depression.[4] According to this perspective, poor families face significant economic pressure as they struggle to pay bills and buy important goods and services, and are forced to cut back on daily expenditures. This economic pressure, coupled with other stressful events that are more prevalent in the lives of poor families, creates high levels of psychological distress in poor parents, including depressive and hostile feelings.[5]

Recent work in behavioral economics has broadened the family stress model by showing that poverty and scarcity not only create psychological distress but also deplete important cognitive resources.[6] Studies conducted mostly in developing countries have found that making economic decisions under conditions of scarcity reduces adults' ability to control their own behavior and renders them less able to pursue longer-term goals.

Psychological distress spills over into marriages and parenting. As couples struggle to make ends meet, their interactions tend to become more hostile and conflicted, and they withdraw from each other.[7] Parents' psychological distress and conflict, in turn, are linked with parenting practices that are, on average, more punitive, harsh, inconsistent, and detached, as well as less nurturing, stimulating, and responsive to children's needs. Such lower-quality parenting is likely to elevate children's physiological stress responses, and ultimately to harm children's development.[8]

To fully understand environmental stress as a pathway through which poverty may affect individuals, we need to go beyond the family to consider other sources of stress that poor children encounter every day. Compared with their more affluent peers, poor children are more likely to live in housing that is crowded, noisy, and characterized by defects such as leaky roofs, rodent infestations, or inadequate heating.[9] Poor families are more likely to live in neighborhoods characterized by high crime rates, boarded-up houses, abandoned lots, and inadequate municipal services.[10]

The schools that low-income children attend are more likely to be overcrowded and have structural problems (affecting, for example, noise, lighting, and ventilation).[11] Economically disadvantaged children also tend to be exposed to higher levels of air pollution from parents' smoking, traffic, and industrial emissions.[12] These environmental conditions create physiological and emotional stress in the lives of low-income children that may impair their socioemotional, physical, cognitive, and academic development. For example, poverty heightens a child's risk for lead poisoning, which has been linked to health, behavior, and neurological problems that may persist into adolescence and beyond.

Cognitive neuroscience has produced evidence that chronically elevated physiological stress may interfere with the development of poor children's stress response system and health, as well as the regions of their brains responsible for self-regulation (the ability to regulate attention and emotions). Researchers have documented that such stress harms brain development in animals. Exposure to stress, and increased levels of stress hormones such as cortisol, diminish animals' cognitive functioning, leading to impairments in brain structures such as the hippocampus, which plays an important role in memory.[13]

What empirical evidence supports family stress theory? Nonexperimental studies have found that low-income children have significantly higher levels of stress hormones than their wealthier counterparts and that early childhood poverty is associated with increased allostatic load, a measure of the physiological consequences of stress.[14] Higher levels of physiological stress have been linked not only to poorer cognitive functioning, but to poorer immunological functioning as well, putting children at risk for a host of inflammatory diseases later in life.[15] For example, recent work connects the body's stress system to brain regions that support cognitive skills, such as self-regulation and executive functioning (the ability to plan and carry out complicated tasks). Researchers have also found that heightened salivary cortisol, an indicator of an elevated stress response, partially accounts for the fact that poverty is associated with problems in both parenting and children's executive functioning.[16] Thus disparities in stress exposure and related stress hormones may explain to some extent why poor children have lower levels of cognitive ability and achievement as well as poorer health later in life.[17]

The biological links between low income and stress are compelling, but no methodologically strong studies have linked poverty to elevated and prolonged stress reactions in children. However, suggestive evidence has linked receiving food stamps in childhood to stress-related adult diseases.[18] Moreover, some rigorous studies have found poverty-stress connections in mothers. One of these tied expansions of the Earned Income Tax Credit (EITC) to data from the National Health Examination and Nutrition Survey.[19] Between 1993 and 1996, the generosity of the EITC increased sharply, particularly for mothers with two or more children. If higher income can reduce mothers' stress, the change in the EITC should have produced a bigger improvement for children and mothers in two-child low-income families than in single-child low-income families. And, indeed, the study found that when compared with mothers with just one child, low-income mothers with two or more children experienced larger reductions in biological indicators of health risks, and they reported better mental health. A study of increases in the Canadian Child Benefit also found that mothers' mental health improved. Evaluations of welfare and anti-poverty programs that increased both income and mothers' employment did not show similar improvements in mental health.[20]

Overall, the family stress perspective has advanced conceptually and empirically in recent years. On the conceptual side, a narrow focus on parents' mental health and parenting has been broadened by neurobiological evidence that too much stress can harm both parents and children, and by research in cognitive psychology that links stress, information processing, and decision making. Increasingly sophisticated studies suggest that income support can reduce mothers' stress. This research should continue to benefit from an explosion in neuroscience-based findings that shed light on the connections among poverty, stress, behavior, and development.

Resources and Investment

When economists think about how the family influences children's development, household production theory plays a central role. Gary Becker, in 1991's *A Treatise on the Family*, suggested that children's development is "produced" from a combination of endowments and parental investments. Endowments include genetic predispositions and the values and preferences that parents instill in their children. Parents' preferences, such as how much they value education and their orientation toward the future, combine with their resources to shape their investments.

Economists argue that time and money are the two basic resources that parents invest in their children. For example, investments in high-quality child care and education, housing in good neighborhoods, and rich learning experiences enhance children's development, as do investments of parents' time. Endowments and investments appear to affect development differently in different domains of children's development (for example, achievement, behavior, and health). Children's own characteristics also affect the level and type of investments that parents make in their offspring.[21] For example, if a young child is talkative and enthusiastic about learning, parents are more likely to purchase children's books or take the child to the library.[22]

Household production theory suggests that children from poor families lag behind their wealthier counterparts in part because their parents have fewer resources to invest in them.[23] Compared with more affluent parents, poor parents are less able to purchase inputs for their children, including books and educational materials for the home, high-quality child care and schools, and safe neighborhoods. Poor parents may also have less

Figure 2. Family Enrichment Expenditures on Children

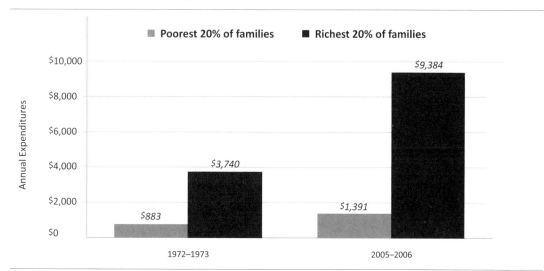

Source: Greg J. Duncan and Richard J. Murnane, "Introduction: The American Dream, Then and Now," in *Whither Opportunity? Rising Inequality, Schools, and Children's Life Chances*, ed. Greg J. Duncan and Richard J. Murnane (New York: Russell Sage, 2011), 3–23. Calculations are based on data from the U.S. Bureau of Labor Statistics' Consumer Expenditure Survey, http://www.bls.gov/cex.

Note: Amounts are in 2012 dollars.

time to invest in their children, because they are more likely to be single parents, to work nonstandard hours, and to have less flexible work schedules.[24] This too may have negative consequences for children. Evidence suggests that the amount of cognitive stimulation in the home environment varies with changes in family income.[25]

Compared with wealthier children, poor children have fewer child enrichment resources—for example, books, computers, high-quality child care, summer camps, and private schools—and the gap is growing wider. Forty years ago, low-income families spent about $880 (in 2012 dollars) per child annually on such resources, while higher-income families spent more than $3,700, already a substantial difference (figure 2).[26] By 2005–06, low-income families had increased their expenditures to about $1,400, but high-income families had increased theirs much more, to about $9,400 per child. The

difference in spending between the two groups had almost tripled in the intervening years. The largest spending differences were for activities such as music lessons, travel, and summer camps.[27]

Nonexperimental studies suggest that differences between poor children and wealthier children in the quality of their home environments account for a substantial portion of the association between poverty and children's educational achievement.[28] This is not surprising, because we know that environmental enrichment influences the structure and functioning of a wide range of brain areas in animals.[29] Disparities in the cognitive development of low- and middle-SES children are most pronounced in brain regions that are important for language, memory, and cognitive control.[30] These differences may stem in part from differences in exposure to enriching environments.[31]

All in all, the resource and investment perspective provides a conceptual framework for the interactions among family income, what parents spend to enrich their children's home learning environments, and the development of brain structures and functioning associated with learning. In light of sharp increases in both income inequality and the gap between what poor and higher-income parents spend on children's enrichment, the resource and investment perspective suggests that we should expect that, in the future, poor children will fall further behind higher-income children in terms of their school readiness.

Culture

In the 1960s, in his "culture of poverty" model, Oscar Lewis developed a sociological theory about how the norms and behavior of poor families and communities affect children.[32] Drawing from fieldwork with poor families in Latin America, he argued that the poor were economically marginalized and had no opportunity for upward mobility, and that people responded to their marginalized position with maladaptive behavior and values. The resulting culture of poverty was characterized by weak impulse control and an inability to delay gratification, as well as feelings of helplessness and inferiority. These adaptations manifested in high levels of female-headed households, sexual promiscuity, crime, and gangs. Although Lewis acknowledged that these behaviors emerged in response to structural factors, he thought that such values and behaviors were transmitted to future generations, and therefore became a cause of poverty: "By the time slum children are age six or seven they have usually absorbed the basic values and attitudes of their subculture and are not psychologically geared to take

full advantage of changing conditions or increased opportunities."[33]

Evidence suggests that poor people hold many middle-class values and beliefs, but that circumstances make it hard for them to behave accordingly.

Cultural explanations for the effects of poverty on children suggested that high levels of nonmarital childbearing, joblessness, female-headed households, criminal activity, and welfare dependency among the poor were likely to be transmitted from parents to children. In the mid-1980s and 1990s, scholars expanded the scope of this argument by paying closer attention to the origins of cultural and behavioral differences. For example, some emphasized the role of individual choice in the face of the liberal welfare state's perverse incentives, which rewarded single-mother households and joblessness among men.[34] Others stressed structural and economic factors: the concentration of neighborhood poverty, the social isolation of poor inner-city neighborhoods, and the deindustrialization of urban economies.[35] They contended that these structural factors undermine community norms and influence the behavior of inner-city adults and their children.

A common criticism of "culture of poverty" explanations is that they fail to differentiate people's behavior from their values and beliefs.[36] Evidence suggests that poor people hold many middle-class values and beliefs, but that circumstances make it hard for them to behave accordingly. For example, one study showed that poor women value marriage and recognize the benefits of raising children in a two-parent household.[37] However, their low wages, as well as black men's high rates of unemployment and incarceration, lead poor women to conclude that marriage is out of their reach. Notions of a unified culture of poverty do not account for this sort of disconnect between values and behaviors.

Annette Lareau's qualitative study of social class and family life identifies other differences in the cultural childrearing repertoires of high- and low-income families, including the degree to which middle-class parents "manage" their children's lives, while working-class and poor parents leave children alone to play and otherwise organize their activities on their own:

> "In the middle class, life was hectic. Parents were racing around from one activity to another … Because there were so many activities, and because they were accorded such importance, child's activities determined the schedule for the entire family … [In contrast, in working-class and poor families,] parents tend to direct their efforts toward keeping children safe, enforcing discipline, and, when they deem it necessary, regulating their behavior in certain areas. … Thus, whereas middle-class children are often treated as a project to be developed, working-class and poor children are given boundaries for their behavior and then allowed to grow.[38]"

Lareau called the middle-class pattern "concerted cultivation"—providing stimulating learning activities and social interactions that parents believe will promote their children's social and cognitive development. In contrast, the "natural growth" perspective of working-class and poor parents often stops at providing basic supports (for example, food, shelter, and comfort). Such differences in cultural repertoires give a distinct advantage to middle-class children and contribute to the intergenerational transmission of social class.

These cultural theories extend the resource and investment perspective. Class-related differences in the parenting practices of Lareau's families arise, in part, from income differences that let some parents support a much broader range of activities for their children. But some of the differences arise from fundamentally divergent beliefs about how children succeed and the best kinds of parenting practices. Such beliefs are unlikely to change in response to changes in family income that might be brought about by changes in policy.

Why Early Poverty May Matter the Most

The timing of poverty during childhood and adolescence may make a difference for how it shapes children's development. Emerging evidence from human and animal studies shows that during early childhood, the brain develops critically important neural functions and structures that will shape future cognitive, social, emotional, and health outcomes.[39] Two recent neuroscience studies show strong correlations between socioeconomic status and important aspects of young children's brain function.[40]

Flavio Cunha and James Heckman propose a model of the production of human capital that allows for distinct childhood stages during which investment may take place, as well as roles for the past effects and future development of both cognitive and socioemotional skills.[41] In this model, children are born with cognitive potential and temperament that reflect a combination of heredity and the prenatal environment. Cunha and Heckman emphasize that skill building interacts with investments from families, preschools and schools, and other agents. Their model suggests that we accumulate human capital in two ways. One is "self-productivity," in which skills developed in earlier stages bolster the development of skills in later stages. The other is "dynamic complementarity," in which skills acquired before a given investment increase that investment's productivity. These two principles combine to form the hypothesis that "skill begets skill." Cunha and Heckman's model predicts that economic deprivation in early childhood creates disparities in school readiness and early academic success that widen over the course of childhood.

Intensive programs that provide early care and educational experiences for high-risk infants and toddlers offer evidence to support the idea that the early years are a fruitful time to intervene. The best known are the Abecedarian program, a full-day, center-based educational program for children who were at high risk for school failure, starting in early infancy and continuing until school entry, and the Perry Preschool program, which provided one or two years of intensive, center-based education for preschoolers.[42] Both programs generated long-term improvements in subsequent education, criminal behavior, and employment, although other early-childhood education programs have shown more modest effects.

Income may matter the most for brain development in the early years, but increased income may also be beneficial for low-income

adolescents, particularly when they use it to help pay for postsecondary schooling. The sticker price of college has more than doubled in the past 20 years.[43] Although Pell Grants and other sources of financial aid drive down the net cost of college for low-income students, the cost of enrollment in public four-year colleges has risen faster than the amount available from grants. In contrast, the cost of attending a public community college has not increased over the past two decades for students from very low-income families because the amount of aid has expanded to cover the higher price. Of course, many low-income students and their parents either don't know how much aid is available or are discouraged by the extremely complex federal financial aid application form.[44]

Assessing Causal Effects of Poverty: Methods and Results

Studies that aim to estimate how income influences children's development differ in their methodological rigor. At one end are correlational studies that analyze associations between family income and children's outcomes, with few adjustments for confounding factors (that is, other important family conditions that might be correlated with income and child outcomes). These studies are common, particularly in neuroscience, but they are likely to be plagued by biases that lead researchers to overestimate income's causal effects. On the other end are experiments in which families are randomly assigned to receive additional income or not. If implemented correctly, experiments provide unbiased estimates of income's effects. But experimental studies are exceedingly rare, and sometimes they condition income support on behavior such as full-time work, which may exert its own influence on children's development. Almost as trustworthy as experiments are "quasi-experiments" in which income changes are beyond the control of the families involved. Examples are policy changes that increase the generosity of programs like the EITC.

Our review of the evidence on how increases in family income influence children and youth distinguishes among effects on achievement, attainment, behavior, and health. Readers should bear in mind that the policy implications of income support programs rest on collective impacts across all of these domains. Small impacts in several different domains of child functioning could add up to a total benefit that exceeds costs, even if no single component shows such a level of benefit.

School achievement, attainment, and behavior

The strongest evidence relates income increases to children's test scores (achievement) and the number of years of schooling they complete (attainment). The only large-scale randomized interventions to alter family income directly were the U.S. Negative Income Tax experiments, which were conducted between 1968 and 1982 with the primary goal of identifying how guaranteed income influenced parents' participation in the labor force. Three of the six experimental sites (Gary, Indiana, and rural areas in North Carolina and Iowa) measured achievement gains for children in elementary school, and two of the three found significant impacts.[45] In contrast, adolescents showed no differences in achievement. Impacts on school enrollment and attainment for youth were more uniformly positive. Both Gary and New Jersey—the only two sites that measured these outcomes—reported increases in school enrollment, high school graduation rates, or years of completed schooling.

Second- through eighth-grade teachers rated student "comportment" in the two rural sites; results showed income-induced improvements in one site but not the other.

Taken together, the Negative Income Tax studies appear to suggest that income is more important for the school achievement of pre-adolescents and for the school attainment of adolescents. None of the results offers evidence to support the "early is better" hypothesis, because no site tracked the achievement of children who had not yet entered school when the income "treatment" was being administered.

Welfare reform programs undertaken during the 1990s encouraged parents to work by providing income support to working-poor parents through wage supplements. Moreover, evaluations of some of these programs measured the test scores of at least some children who had not yet entered school when the programs began. One study analyzed data from seven random-assignment welfare and antipoverty policies, all of which increased parental employment, though only some increased family income.[46]

The combined impacts on children's school achievement of higher income and more work hours for mothers varied markedly by the children's age. Treatment-group children who were between the ages of four and seven when the programs took effect, many of whom made the transition to elementary school during the programs, scored significantly higher on achievement tests than their control-group counterparts. A sophisticated statistical analysis of the data on these younger children suggests that a $3,000 boost in annual income was associated with a gain in achievement scores of about one-fifth of a standard deviation—a modest but still statistically significant increase.[47] In contrast, a boost in income had no effect on children's rate of behavior problems, whether reported by parents or teachers.[48]

Elevated income did not appear to affect the achievement of children from eight to 11, and the achievement of children who were 12 and 13 seemed to be hurt by the programs' efforts to increase family income and parental employment. Another study using the same data examined very young children and found positive impacts for some ages but not others.[49]

Like the maternal stress study discussed above, another recent study took advantage of the increasing generosity of the EITC between 1993 and 1996 to compare children's test scores before and after it was expanded.[50] Most of the children in this study were between the ages of eight and 14, and none was younger than five. The researchers found improvements in low-income children's achievement in middle childhood that coincided with the EITC expansion.

A study conducted in Canada took advantage of variations in the generosity of the National Child Benefit program across Canadian provinces to estimate income's effects on children's achievement.[51] Among six- to 10-year-old children in low-income families, policy-related income increases had a positive and significant association with math scores and a negative association with the likelihood that a child would be diagnosed with a learning disability. Among four- to six-year-olds, the income increases were associated with higher scores on a test of receptive vocabulary for boys, but not for girls. Turning to behavior, higher income led to less aggression among four- to 10-year-olds, but it did not appear to affect other behaviors.

A third quasi-experimental study examined what happened after a tribal government in North Carolina opened a casino and began distributing about $6,000 annually to each adult member of the tribe.[52] A comparison of Native American youth with non-Native American youth, before and after the casino opened, found that receiving casino payments for about six years increased school attendance and high school graduation rates and decreased criminal behavior among poor Native American adolescents. The data did not include achievement test scores, nor any information on children under age nine.

These experimental and quasi-experiment studies offer three lessons. First, achievement gains depend at least in part on how old the children were when their families received additional income. Children making the transition to school and elementary school students generally enjoyed the most consistent achievement increases. For adolescents, the school achievement picture was muddier, with various studies finding positive, null, and even negative effects. Second, among adolescents, increased income appears to boost educational attainments such as high school graduation and completed years of schooling rather than test scores. Given the high cost of postsecondary education, it's not surprising that higher family income leads to more completed years of schooling. Third, we know far more about how boosting income affects achievement and schooling than we do about its effects on behavior problems, including childbearing and criminal activity.

Virtually none of the experimental literature on income effects has been able to estimate the impacts of changes in family income during the earliest years of life, when children are developing rapidly and may be especially sensitive to family and home conditions. Nor have these studies been able to examine how income changes during childhood affect outcomes measured in adulthood. This is particularly unfortunate, because policies directed at children often couch their goals in terms of lifetime effects, such as a middle-class standard of living or higher labor market earnings.

Achievement gains depend at least in part on how old the children were when their families received additional income.

Two recent nonexperimental studies, however, have linked early childhood income to adult outcomes.[53] Both use data from the Panel Study of Income Dynamics (PSID), focusing on children who were born in the early years of the study. Adult outcomes were collected when these children were in their 30s. The PSID measures income in every year of a child's life from before birth through age 15, making it possible to measure poverty and family income early in life (prenatal through the fifth year in one study, prenatal through the first year in the other) as well as later in childhood and in adolescence. Among families whose average income was below $25,000, one study found, an annual boost to family income early in the children's lives (birth to age 5) was associated with an increase in adult work hours, a rise in earnings, and a reduced likelihood of receiving food stamps (women, however, were no less likely to receive welfare). A boost in family income at other stages in children's lives, however, was not significantly related to the adults' earnings and work hours. For the most part, increased income at any stage of childhood did not affect whether the children would exhibit behavior problems (arrests and incarcerations for males; non-marital births for females).

Health

As Sherry Glied and Don Oellerich write in this issue of *Future of Children*, growing up in poverty is associated with poor health. In one study, only 70 percent of poor children were reported by their mothers to be in excellent or very good health, compared with 87 percent of wealthier children. Some evidence suggests that, in Western industrialized countries, economic disparities in health tend to increase from early childhood through adolescence.[54] It may be that income serves as a buffer, preventing early chronic health conditions from producing pervasive negative effects.[55] But not all researchers have found that the association between income and health becomes stronger as children grow older.[56]

In the United States, children from poor households have higher rates of chronic health conditions, such as asthma, diabetes, and problems with hearing, vision, and speech. According to reports from their parents, about 32 percent of poor children have at least one such condition, compared with 27 percent of wealthier children. Asthma is the most common chronic problem among poor children, followed by mental health and behavioral problems; attention deficit hyperactivity disorder is the most common mental health diagnosis. Finally, poor children are more likely than their more affluent peers to suffer from acute illness or to have health problems that require them to limit their activities.[57]

Table 2. Statistically Significant Associations between Income Increases during Childhood and Adult (Age 30–41) Outcomes, by Childhood Stage

Adult outcome (age 30–41)	Age when income is measured		
	Prenatal to age 2	*Age 3–5*	*Age 6–15*
Earnings	+Positive	Not significant	Not significant
Work hours	+Positive	Not significant	Not significant
Work limitations	−Negative	Not significant	Not significant
Arthritis	−Negative	Not significant	+Positive
Hypertension	−Negative	Not significant	Not significant
Depression	Not significant	Not significant	Not significant
General health	Not significant	Not significant	Not significant

Source: Kathleen M. Ziol-Guest et al., "Early Childhood Poverty, Immune-Mediated Disease Processes, and Adult Productivity," *Proceedings of the National Academy of Sciences* 109 (2012): 17289–93.

Correlations between childhood poverty and health are also found later in life. By age 50, compared with people whose incomes were twice the poverty line or greater, people who experienced poverty in childhood are 46 percent more likely to have asthma, 75 percent more likely to have high blood pressure, 83 percent more likely to have been diagnosed with diabetes, 125 percent more likely to have experienced a stroke or heart attack, and 40 percent more likely to have been diagnosed with heart disease. Economic disadvantage in adolescence has been linked to worse overall health and higher death rates in adulthood.[58] Adolescent poverty, measured from age 13 to 16, is associated with heightened risk for several chronic diseases in adulthood.[59]

Some studies have employed stronger statistical methods to reduce the influence of possible confounding factors and produce more trustworthy estimates of how income is associated with child health.[60] Specifically, two studies uncovered large and significant links between adolescent poverty and a variety of health problems in adulthood.[61] However, when the researchers compared the health of siblings who shared the same general family background but experienced different economic conditions during childhood, they found much smaller associations. However, none of these health studies measured income in early childhood, when, as we've seen, the link between income and health may be strongest.

Another group of researchers investigated the associations between mean family income in early, middle, and later childhood, on the one hand, and adult Body Mass Index (BMI), on the other. They found that, among poor people, higher income during their mother's pregnancy and their first year of life was associated with lower adult BMI, whereas higher income later in childhood was not.[62] A companion study considered whether chronic diseases in which the immune system plays a role, such as arthritis, affect the associations between poverty very early in life and adult economic outcomes.[63] Concentrating on families with incomes below $25,000, the researchers distinguished among three childhood stages—pregnancy through age two, ages three to five, and ages six to 15— and compared family income during each of these stages with the children's own earnings later in life. They found that increased family income from pregnancy to age two was significantly associated with higher earnings and longer work hours when the children reached ages 30 to 41, but family income at other stages of childhood was not (table 2). Similarly, when children's family income increased from pregnancy through age two (but not at the other stages of childhood), they were less likely as adults to experience high blood pressure, arthritis, or conditions that limited their daily living activities. Moreover, their reduced susceptibility to these three health problems partially explained their higher earnings and longer work hours as adults.

Despite the recent research that links income to both children's and adults' health, it is hard to show that these links are causal. Studies that link income with health have been far less rigorous than those that link income with achievement and behavior. Moreover, most studies that compare childhood family income with adult health have measured income during children's adolescent years. Although a few studies have suggested that early-life income can strongly affect adult health, the pattern of conflicting results produces more questions than answers.

Implications for Policy

Several recent rigorous studies suggest that childhood income does indeed improve at least some key child, adolescent, and adult outcomes. But we need a better understanding of how the timing of income boosts affects children's development, across a wide range of outcomes. If the effects differ, then policies that target specific stages of childhood or adolescence are likely to be more efficient than those that do not.

If the evidence ultimately shows that poverty early in childhood is most detrimental to development during childhood and adolescence, then it may make sense to consider income-transfer policies that provide more income to families with young children. In the case of work support programs like the EITC, this might mean extending more generous credits (or reallocating existing credits) to families with young children. In the case of refundable child tax credits, this could mean providing larger credits to families with young children.

Another step might be to ensure that sanctions and other regulations embedded in welfare policies do not deny benefits to families with very young children. Not only do young children appear to be most vulnerable to the consequences of poverty, but mothers with very young children are also least able to support themselves by working.

Assistance programs in several European countries offer time-limited income supports that depend on children's age. In Germany, a mother who works fewer than 20 hours per week can receive a modest parental allowance until her child is 18 months old. France guarantees a modest minimum income to most of its citizens, including families with children of all ages. Between 1976 and 2009, the Allocation de Parent Isolé (API) program supplemented this income for single parents with children under age three. In effect, the API acknowledges that families have a special need for income support during this period, especially if a parent wishes to forgo income from employment in order to care for very young children. Once children turn three, France's state-funded child care system alleviates some of the problems associated with a parent's transition to the labor force.

One way to deliver additional cash assistance is through payments that depend on the behaviors of parents and children. These strategies receive support because they encourage desirable behavior. The EITC is such a program, because it goes only to parents who work; unemployed parents do not receive a refundable tax credit. Conditional cash transfer (CCT) programs, used in a number of developing countries, constitute a more elaborate example. Mexico pioneered the CCT movement with a program originally called Progresa and now known as Oportunidades. This program gives parents direct cash payments that are linked to several positive behaviors, including whether their children attend school and preventive health care appointments, and whether they adopt specific child nutrition practices.[64] Although poor households in the program make more use of health and education services, evidence is mixed on whether the program improves children's health and education.[65] For example, school enrollment has improved, but achievement test scores have not. CCT programs have since been widely adopted in other developing countries. Evaluations show that some have improved children's health and nutrition, while others have not.

Oportunidades inspired New York City's Family Rewards program, which operated from 2007 to 2009 in the city's highest-poverty communities. Begun in the fall of 2007, the program tied cash rewards to children's education, families' preventive health care, and parents' employment.[66] As its creators hoped, the program reduced poverty and hardship and increased families' savings. However, children's results depended on their age. Elementary and middle school students whose families received the payments did not improve their school attendance or

overall achievement. But better-prepared high school students attended school more frequently, earned more course credits, were less likely to repeat a grade, and scored higher on standardized tests.

Increased income support can also take the form of in-kind benefits such as food stamps or housing vouchers. One study took advantage of geographic variation in the timing of the rollout of the Food Stamp Program (now called the Supplemental Nutrition Assistance Program) in the 1960s and 1970s. The researchers examined adult outcomes of people whose families received food stamps around the time they were born.[67] They found that access to food stamps in early childhood led to a significant reduction in the incidence of "metabolic syndrome" (obesity, high blood pressure, and diabetes) and, for women, an increase in economic self-sufficiency.

Though we emphasize that policies to boost income in early childhood may be important, we are not suggesting that this is the only policy path worth pursuing. Obviously, investments later in life and those that provide direct services to children and families may also be well advised. Regardless of the timing of the investment, economic logic requires that we compare the costs and benefits of the various programs that seek to promote the development of disadvantaged children throughout the life course. In this context, expenditures on income-transfer and service-delivery programs should be placed side by side and judged by their benefits, and by society's willingness to pay for the outcomes they produce, relative to their costs.

We conclude by noting again that the research we have reviewed focuses on the possible consequences for children and youth of income *changes*, and not just income increases. The wider discussion of policy has been cast in the optimistic light of benefits that might result from increasing the incomes of low-income families, particularly families with young children. It is important to remember, however, that reductions in the generosity of programs such the EITC can be expected to reduce children's success at school and increase their mothers' stress levels and mental health problems. With achievement and attainment gaps between low- and high-income children larger than any time in the past 40 years, we should think twice about policy changes that would further increase these gaps.

ENDNOTES

1. U.S. Census Bureau, "Income, Poverty, and Health Insurance in the United States: 2012," last modified September 28, 2013, http://www.census.gov/hhes/www/poverty/data/incpovhlth/2012/index.html.

2. Greg J. Duncan, Kathleen M. Ziol-Guest, and Ariel Kalil, "Early Childhood Poverty and Adult Attainment, Behavior, and Health," *Child Development* 81 (2010): 306–25, doi: 10.1111/j.1467-8624.2009.01396.x.

3. Katrine V. Loken, Magne Mogstad, and Matthew Wiswall, "What Linear Estimators Miss: The Effects of Family Income on Child Outcomes," *American Economic Journal: Applied Economics* 4, no. 2 (2012): 1–35, doi: 10.1257/app.4.2.1.

4. Glen H. Elder Jr., *Children of the Great Depression* (Chicago: University of Chicago Press, 1974); Glen H. Elder Jr., Tri van Nguyen, and Avshalom Caspi, "Linking Family Hardship to Children's Lives," *Child Development* 56 (1985): 361–75.

5. Ronald C. Kessler and Paul D. Cleary, "Social Class and Psychological Distress," *American Sociological Review* 45 (1980): 463–78; Jane D. McLeod and Ronald C. Kessler, "Socioeconomic Status Differences in Vulnerability to Undesirable Life Events," *Journal of Health and Social Behavior* 31 (1990): 162–72.

6. Dean E. Spears, "Economic Decision-Making in Poverty Depletes Behavioral Control," *B. E. Journal of Economic Analysis & Policy* 11, no. 1 (2011), article 72, doi: 10.2202/1935-1682.2973; Anandi Mani et al., "Poverty Impedes Cognitive Function," *Science* 341, no. 6149 (2013), 976–80.

7. Gene H. Brody et al., "Financial Resources, Parent Psychological Functioning, Parent Co-Caregiving, and Early Adolescent Competence in Rural Two-Parent African-American Families," *Child Development* 65 (1994): 590–605; Rand D. Conger and Glen H. Elder Jr., *Families in Troubled Times: Adapting to Change in Rural America* (New York: Aldine de Gruyter, 1994).

8. Rand D. Conger et al., "Economic Pressure in African American Families: A Replication and Extension of the Family Stress Model," *Developmental Psychology* 38 (2002): 179–93; Vonnie C. McLoyd, "The Impact of Economic Hardship on Black Families and Children: Psychological Distress, Parenting, and Socioemotional Development," *Child Development* 61 (1990): 311–46.

9. Gary W. Evans, Heidi Saltzman, and Jana L. Cooperman, "Housing Quality and Children's Socioemotional Health," *Environment and Behavior* 33 (2001): 389–99, doi: 10.1177/00139160121973043; Gary W. Evans, "The Environment of Childhood Poverty," *American Psychologist* 59 (2004): 77–92, doi: 10.1037/0003-066X.59.2.77.

10. Evans, "Environment of Childhood Poverty."

11. Ibid.

12. Ibid.

13. Bruce S. McEwen, "The Neurobiology of Stress: From Serendipity to Clinical Relevance," *Brain Research* 886 (2000): 172–89.

14. Sonia J. Lupien et al., "Can Poverty Get Under Your Skin? Basal Cortisol Levels and Cognitive Function in Children from Low and High Socioeconomic Status," *Development and Psychopathology* 13 (2001): 653–76; R. Jay Turner and William R. Avison, "Status Variations in Stress Exposure: Implications of Research on Race, Socioeconomic Status, and Gender," *Journal of Health and Social Behavior* 44 (2003): 488–505.

15. Gregory E. Miller, Edith Chen, and Karen J. Parker, "Psychological Stress in Childhood and Susceptibility to the Chronic Diseases of Aging: Moving toward a Model of Behavioral and Biological Mechanisms," *Psychological Bulletin* 137 (2011): 959–97, doi: 10.1037/a0024768.

16. Clancy Blair et al., "Salivary Cortisol Mediates Effects of Poverty and Parenting on Executive Functions in Early Childhood," *Child Development* 82 (2011): 1970–84, doi: 10.1111/j.1467-8624.2011.01643.x.

17. Martha J. Farah et al., "Childhood Poverty: Specific Associations with Neurocognitive Development," *Brain Research* 1110 (2006): 166–74.

18. Hilary Hoynes, Diane W. Schanzenbach, and Douglas Almond, "Long Run Impacts of Childhood Access to the Safety Net" (working paper, National Bureau of Economic Research, Cambridge, MA, 2012).

19. William Evans and Craig Garthwaite, "Giving Mom a Break: The Impact of Higher EITC Payments on Maternal Health" (working paper, National Bureau of Economic Research, Cambridge, MA, 2010).

20. Kevin Milligan and Mark Stabile, "Child Benefits, Maternal Employment, and Children's Health: Evidence from Canadian Child Benefit Expansions," *American Economic Review* 99, no. 2 (2009): 128–32; Greg J. Duncan, Lisa A. Gennetian, and Pamela Morris, "Parental Pathways to Self-Sufficiency and the Well-Being of Younger Children," in *Making the Work-Based Safety Net Work Better: Forward-Looking Policies to Help Low-Income Families,* ed. Carolyn Heinrich and John Karl Scholz, (New York: Russell Sage, 2009), 117–48.

21. Gary Becker, *A Treatise on the Family* (Cambridge, MA: Harvard University Press, 1991); Michael E. Foster, "How Economists Think about Family Resources and Child Development," *Child Development* 73 (2002): 1904–14.

22. Helen Raikes et al., "Mother-Child Book Reading in Low-Income Families: Correlates and Outcomes during the First Three Years of Life," *Child Development* 77 (2006): 924–53.

23. Becker, *Treatise on the Family*.

24. Eugene Smolensky and Jennifer A. Gootman, eds., *Working Families and Growing Kids: Caring for Children and Adolescents* (Washington, DC: National Academies Press, 2003).

25. Elizabeth Votruba-Drzal, "Economic Disparities in Middle Childhood: Does Income Matter?" *Developmental Psychology* 42 (2006): 1154–67.

26. Greg J. Duncan and Richard J. Murnane, "Introduction: The American Dream, Then and Now," in *Whither Opportunity? Rising Inequality, Schools, and Children's Life Chances,* ed. Greg J. Duncan and Richard J. Murnane, (New York: Russell Sage, 2011), 3–23.

27. Neeraj Kaushal, Katherine Magnuson, and Jane Waldfogel, "How Is Family Income Related to Investments in Children's Learning?" in *Whither Opportunity?*, Duncan and Murnane`, 187–206.

28. Greg J. Duncan and Jeanne Brooks-Gunn, "Family Poverty, Welfare Reform, and Child Development," *Child Development* 71 (2000): 188–96.

29. Henriette Van Praag, Gerd Kempermann, and Fred H. Gage, "Neural Consequences of Environmental Enrichment," *Nature Reviews: Neuroscience* 1 (2000): 191–98.

30. Farah et al., "Childhood Poverty," 166–74; Kimberly G. Noble, Bruce D. McCandliss, and Martha J. Farah, "Socioeconomic Gradients Predict Individual Differences in Neurocognitive Abilities," *Developmental Science* 10 (2007): 464–80.

31. Martha J. Farah, "Environmental Stimulation, Parental Nurturance and Cognitive Development in Humans," *Developmental Science* 11 (2008): 793–801.

32. Oscar Lewis, "The Culture of Poverty," in *On Understanding Poverty: Perspectives From the Social Sciences,* ed. Daniel P. Moynihan, (New York: Basic Books, 1969), 187–200.

33. Oscar Lewis, *La Vida: A Puerto Rican Family in the Culture of Poverty—San Juan and New York* (New York: Random House, 1966), xlv.

34. Lawrence M. Mead, *Beyond Entitlement: The Social Obligations of Citizenship* (New York: The Free Press, 1986).

35. Douglas S. Massey, "American Apartheid: Segregation and the Making of the Underclass," *American Journal of Sociology* 96 (1990): 329–57; William Julius Wilson, *The Truly Disadvantaged: The Inner City, the Underclass, and Public Policy* (Chicago: University of Chicago Press, 1987); William Julius Wilson, *When Work Disappears: The World of the New Urban Poor* (New York: Alfred A. Knopf, 1996).

36. Michele Lamont and Mario Luis Small, "How Culture Matters for the Understanding of Poverty: Enriching Our Understanding" in *The Colors of Poverty: Why Racial and Ethnic Disparities Persist*, ed. Ann Linn and David Harris, (New York: Russell Sage Foundation, 2008).

37. Kathryn Edin and Maria Kefalas, *Promises I Can Keep: Why Poor Women Put Motherhood before Marriage* (Berkeley: University of California Press, 2005).

38. Annette Lareau, *Unequal Childhoods: Class, Race, and Family Life* (Berkeley: University of California Press, 2003), 35, 66–7.

39. Robert M. Sapolsky, "Social Status and Health in Humans and Other Animals," *Annual Review of Anthropology* (2004): 393–418, doi: 10.1146/annurev.anthro.33.070203.144000; Eric I. Knudsen et al., "Economic, Neurobiological, and Behavioral Perspectives on Building America's Future Workforce," *Proceedings of the National Academy of Sciences* 103 (2006): 10155–62.

40. Farah et al., "Childhood Poverty"; Mark Kishiyama et al., "Socioeconomic Disparities Affect Prefrontal Function in Children," *Journal of Cognitive Neuroscience* 21 (2009), 1106–15. doi: 10.1162/jocn.2009.21101.

41. Flavio Cunha and James Heckman, "The Technology of Skill Formation" (working paper, National Bureau of Economic Research, Cambridge, MA, 2007).

42. Greg J. Duncan and Katherine Magnuson, "Investing in Preschool Programs," *Journal of Economic Perspectives* 27 (2013): 109–32, doi: 10.1257/jep.27.2.109.

43. College Board Advocacy and Policy Center, "Trends in College Pricing," accessed September 10, 2013, http://trends.collegeboard.org/college-pricing.

44. Eric P. Bettinger et al., "The Role of Application Assistance and Information in College Decisions: Results from the H&R Block FAFSA Experiment," *Quarterly Journal of Economics* 127 (2012), 1205–42, doi: 10.1093/qje/qjs017; Susan Dynarski and Judith Scott-Clayton, "Financial Aid Policy: Lessons from Research," *The Future of Children* 23, no. 1 (2013): 67–91.

45. Rebecca A. Maynard and Richard J. Murnane, "Effects of a Negative Income Tax on School Performance: Results of an Experiment," *Journal of Human Resources* 14 (1979): 463–76; Rebecca Maynard, "The Effects of the Rural Income Maintenance Experiment on the School Performance of Children," *American Economic Review* 67 (1977): 370–75; Charles Mallar, "The Educational and Labor Supply Responses of Young Adults on the Urban Graduated Work Incentive Experiment," in *The New Jersey Income Maintenance Experiment*, ed. Harold Watts and Albert Rees (New York: Academic Press, 1977).

46. Pamela Morris, Greg J. Duncan, and Elizabeth Clark-Kauffman, "Child Well-Being in an Era of Welfare Reform: The Sensitivity of Transitions in Development to Policy Change," *Developmental Psychology* 41 (2005): 919–32.

47. Greg J. Duncan, Pamela Morris, and Chris Rodrigues, "Does Money Really Matter? Estimating Impacts of Family Income on Young Children's Achievement with Data from Random-Assignment Experiments," *Developmental Psychology* 47 (2011): 1263–79, doi: 10.1037/a0023875.

48. Greg J. Duncan, Lisa A. Gennetian, and Pamela Morris, "Parental Pathways to Self-Sufficiency and the Well-Being of Younger Children," in *Work-Based Safety Net*, Heinrich and Scholz, 117–48.

49. Heather D. Hill and Pamela Morris, "Welfare Policies and Very Young Children: Experimental Data on Stage-Environment Fit," *Developmental Psychology* 44 (2008): 1557–71, doi: 10.1037/a0013913.

50. Gordon B. Dahl and Lance Lochner, "The Impact of Family Income on Child Achievement: Evidence from the Earned Income Tax Credit," *American Economic Review* 102 (2012): 1927–56, doi: 10.1257/aer.102.5.1927.

51. Kevin Milligan and Mark Stabile, "Do Child Tax Benefits Affect the Well-Being of Children? Evidence from Canadian Child Benefit Expansions," *American Economic Journal: Economic Policy* 3, no. 3 (2011): 175–205, doi: 10.1257/pol.3.3.175.

52. Randall Akee et al., "Parents' Incomes and Children's Outcomes: A Quasi-Experiment Using Transfer Payments from Casino Profits," *American Economic Journal: Applied Economics* 2, no. 1 (2010): 86–115, doi: 10.1257/app.2.1.86.

53. Greg J. Duncan et al., "Early-Childhood Poverty and Adult Attainment, Behavior, and Health," *Child Development* 81 (2010): 306–25; Kathleen M. Ziol-Guest et al., "Early Childhood Poverty, Immune-Mediated Disease Processes, and Adult Productivity," *Proceedings of the National Academy of Sciences* 109 (2012): 17289–93, doi: 10.1073/pnas.1203167109.

54. Anne Case, Darren Lubotsky, and Christina Paxson, "Economic Status and Health in Childhood: The Origins of the Gradient," *American Economic Review* 92 (2002): 1308–34; Janet Currie and Mark Stabile, "Socioeconomic Status and Child Health: Why Is the Relationship Stronger for Older Children?" *American Economic Review* 93 (2003): 1813–23; Jason E. Murasko, "An Evaluation of the Age-Profile in the Relationship between Household Income and the Health of Children in the United States," *Journal of Health Economics* 27 (2008): 1489–1502.

55. Case, Lubotsky, and Paxson, "Origins of the Gradient."

56. Edith Chen, Andrew D. Martin, and Karen A. Matthews, "Understanding Health Disparities: The Role of Race and Socioeconomic Status in Children's Health," *American Journal of Public Health* 96 (2006): 702–8, doi: 10.2105/AJPH.2004.048124; Janet Currie and Wanchuan Lin, "Chipping Away at Health: More on the Relationship between Income and Child Health," *Health Affairs* 26 (2007): 331–44; Rasheda Khanam, Hong Son Nghiem, and Luke B. Connelly, "Child Health and the Income Gradient: Evidence from Australia," *Journal of Health Economics* 28 (2009): 805–17; Carol Propper, John Rigg, and Simon Burgess, "Child Health: Evidence on the Roles of Family Income and Maternal Mental Health from a UK Birth Cohort," *Health Economics* 16 (2007): 1245–69; Steffen Reinhold and Hendrik Jürges, "Parental Income and Child Health in Germany," *Health Economics* 21 (2012): 562–79, doi: 10.1002/hec.1732.

57. Currie and Lin, "Chipping Away."

58. Anne Case, Angela Fertig, and Christina Paxson, "The Lasting Impact of Childhood Health and Circumstances," *Journal of Health Economics* 24 (2005): 365–89, doi:10.1016/j.jhealeco.2004.09.008.

59. Rucker C. Johnson and Robert F. Schoeni, "The Influence of Early-Life Events on Human Capital, Health Status, and Labor Market Outcomes over the Life Course" (working paper, National Poverty Center, University of Michigan, 2007).

60. Rucker C. Johnson and Robert F. Schoeni, "Early-Life Origins of Adult Disease: The Significance of Poor Infant Health and Childhood Poverty" (unpublished manuscript, Goldman School of Public Policy, University of California, Berkeley, 2007); Johnson and Schoeni, "Influence of Early-Life Events"; Dalton Conley and Neil G. Bennett, "Is Biology Destiny? Birth Weight and Life Chances," *American Sociological Review* 65 (2000): 458–67.

61. Johnson and Schoeni, "Early-Life Origins"; Johnson and Schoeni, "Influence of Early-Life Events."

62. Kathleen M. Ziol-Guest, Greg J. Duncan, and Ariel Kalil, "Early Childhood Poverty and Adult Body Mass Index," *American Journal of Public Health* 99 (2009): 527–32, doi: 10.2105/AJPH.2007.130575.

63. Ziol-Guest et al., "Early Childhood Poverty."

64. Santiago Levy, *Progress against Poverty: Sustaining Mexico's Progresa-Oportunidades Program* (Washington, DC: Brookings Institution Press, 2006).

65. Ariel Fiszbein, Norbert Schady, and Francisco Ferreira, *Conditional Cash Transfers: Reducing Present and Future Poverty* (Washington, DC: World Bank, 2009).

66. James Riccio et al., *Toward Reduced Poverty across Generations: Early Findings from New York City's Conditional Cash Transfer Program* (New York: MDRC, March 2010).

67. Hoynes, Schanzenbach, and Almond, "Long Run Impacts."

Parents' Employment and Children's Wellbeing

Carolyn J. Heinrich

Summary

Since modern welfare reform began in the 1980s, we have seen low-income parents leave the welfare rolls and join the workforce in large numbers. At the same time, the Earned Income Tax Credit has offered a monetary incentive for low-income parents to work. Thus, unlike some of the other two-generation mechanisms discussed in this issue of *Future of Children*, policies that encourage low-income parents to work are both widespread and well-entrenched in the United States.

But parents' (and especially mothers') work, writes Carolyn Heinrich, is not unambiguously beneficial for their children. On the one hand, working parents can be positive role models for their children, and, of course, the income they earn can improve their children's lives in many ways. On the other hand, work can impair the developing bond between parents and young children, especially when the parents work long hours or evening and night shifts. The stress that parents bring home from their jobs can detract from their parenting skills, undermine the atmosphere in the home, and thereby introduce stress into children's lives.

Unfortunately, it is low-income parents who are most likely to work in stressful, low-quality jobs that feature low pay, little autonomy, inflexible hours, and few or no benefits. And low-income children whose parents are working are more likely to be placed in inadequate child care or to go unsupervised. Two-generation approaches, Heinrich writes, could maximize the benefits and minimize the detriments of parents' work by expanding workplace flexibility, and especially by mandating enough paid leave so that mothers can breastfeed and form close bonds with their infants; by helping parents place their children in high-quality child care; and by helping low-income parents train for, find, and keep a well-paying job with benefits.

www.futureofchildren.org

Carolyn J. Heinrich is the Sid Richardson Professor of Public Affairs, an affiliated professor of economics and the director of the Center for Health and Social Policy at the Lyndon B. Johnson School of Public Affairs, University of Texas at Austin.

Carolyn J. Heinrich

Decades ago, highly regarded economists such as John Maynard Keynes predicted that technological advances would reduce the number of hours Americans worked by one-half to two-thirds.[1] It was also anticipated that we would enjoy three times the number of vacation days, allowing more time for leisure and to spend with our families. Alas, not only is the 40-hour workweek still standard, but parents are working more hours than ever. In 2011, among 34.3 million U.S. families with children, 87.2 percent had an employed parent, and in 58.5 percent of these families, both parents worked.[2] Some economists and historians argue that Americans are working more because they have chosen to consume more, but others suggest that we have to work more to support our families. In fact, women, whose participation in the workforce has been steadily rising, are now the main breadwinners in 40 percent of families, up from 11 percent in 1960.[3]

Social and policy changes that affect how much parents work have long been under way. In the 1960s, two-thirds of children had a parent who stayed at home; 40 years later, this was true for only one-third of children.[4] Public approval of mothers' working has grown steadily. A majority of U.S. adults (57 percent) now agree that both husbands and wives should contribute to family income, and 75 percent disagree with the idea that women should return to "traditional roles."[5]

Indeed, public policies have increased both expectations that parents will work and incentives for them to do so, particularly among low-income and single-parent families. Before 1979, women who received welfare were not expected to work if they had children under 16. Work requirements were then tightened, and by 1988, women with children older than two were expected to work if they received public assistance. Finally, Congress passed the Personal Responsibility and Work Opportunities Reconciliation Act of 1996 (PRWORA), which aimed to end dependence on government benefits by promoting job preparation, work, and marriage. Under PRWORA, states may exempt parents with children under age one from work requirements but are not obligated to exempt any parent who receives cash assistance.

The tightening of work mandates under welfare reform, along with greater incentives to work from successive expansions of the Earned Income Tax Credit (EITC), roused a public debate about whether parents' employment might enhance or harm their children's wellbeing. People on one side stressed the expected benefits of parents' work, including positive role models for children, higher self-esteem and a sense of control among working mothers, more productive family routines, and higher earnings. Others saw possible negative consequences, such as increased stress on parents, children placed in unsafe or unsuitable child care, and less monitoring of older children.[6] Many researchers have sought to use variations in the ways policies have been implemented over time and across states to shed light on the relationship between parents' work and children's wellbeing, particularly for lower-income families.

If more parents are working, what are the implications for their children's wellbeing? In this article, I investigate the pathways through which parents' employment affects their children, and I evaluate the evidence on the effects of parents' work. I then consider public policies intended to moderate the detrimental effects of parents' work and enhance the positive ones. Among the important findings:

- Although U.S. policies create strong incentives for parents to work and provide additional income support for low-earning parents that is beneficial to children, they are less effective in ensuring that children whose parents work have access to appropriate and stimulating early care environments.

- A preponderance of evidence shows that most children benefit if their mothers are their primary caregivers during their first year of life, and recent studies suggest that paid or partially paid leave of six weeks to six months would encourage more mothers to delay their return to work and breast-feed their children longer.

- Research finds that low-quality jobs (for example, those with low pay, irregular hours, or few or no benefits) are linked with higher work-related stress for parents, which in turn detracts from children's wellbeing. The effects of parents' work-related stress on children are particularly strong for single-mother families.

Presently, the parents whose work is most likely to have negative effects on their children are the same parents who are least able to take leave, cut their paid work hours, or otherwise secure the resources they need to provide for their children's wellbeing. As a nation, we could do more (possibly by simplifying federal tax provisions) to encourage employers to offer benefits such as paid sick leave, which enhance job quality and help parents balance work with the needs of their children.

How Parents' Employment Affects Children's Wellbeing

The broad societal support for women in the workforce does not necessarily hold true for mothers with young children. Only 12 percent of people surveyed in 2009 agreed that mothers with young children should work full-time, including only 13 percent of mothers with young children who were working full-time themselves. In fact, the first year of a child's life is when mothers are least likely to work full-time or to work at all.[7] The fact that people are more concerned about how mothers' work affects young children mirrors the findings of research in developmental psychology and neurobiology, which suggest that some periods of early childhood are particularly critical or sensitive for a child's brain development and long-term physical and mental health.[8]

How Parents' Work Can Decrease Children's Wellbeing

For some time, neurological research has told us that an infant's brain "blossoms" with new connections (that is, synapses) following birth, and that the rate at which these connections develop and are later pruned can be strongly influenced by the infant's early environment.[9] Research on the healthy development of children consistently shows that children need stable family relationships, with adults who are responsive, nurturing, and protective; physically safe environments that allow them to explore without risk or fear of harm; and adequate nutrition and health care.[10]

Focusing on mothers, one way that a mother's work might directly influence her child's development is through its effect on her ability to form a bond with her infant that promotes the child's security and attachment, as well as her ability to care for the child responsively and appropriately.[11] For example, if a mother's work requires frequent or long separations from her child, their bonding could be impeded—although many other factors could affect the outcome, such as the quality of the caregiver who substitutes for the mother or the mother's job-related stress. There are also varying perspectives regarding when maternal employment is more likely to affect the bonding process between mother and child. Some research suggests that a mother's return to work after their attachment is secure (rather than earlier in the bonding process) could be more disruptive to the child.[12]

When a mother returns to work may also affect how long she breastfeeds her infant or whether she starts breastfeeding at all. Research overwhelmingly documents that children benefit from breastfeeding exclusively in the first six months after birth and continuing some breastfeeding through their first year.[13] The benefits include better respiratory health; fewer ear and throat infections; lower incidence of allergies, diabetes, and other diseases; lower rates of childhood and adult obesity; and enhanced neurological development. One economic argument suggests that if a mother expects to go back to work relatively soon after a child's birth, the costs of learning and equipping for breastfeeding might exceed the perceived benefits and discourage the mother from starting. Upon returning to work, breastfeeding mothers need time, equipment, and accommodations for expressing milk; these may not be available, depending on the nature of their work and their employer. Mothers who reduce their work hours, request extended leaves, change employers, or quit working so that they can continue breastfeeding may lose current and future earnings. These factors likely contribute to the fact that low-income mothers have significantly lower rates of breastfeeding than do wealthier mothers.

Scientists widely agree that a child's first months are among the most sensitive for healthy development. But the trajectory of a child's development in the first three years of life is not fixed.[14] Jack Shonkoff, director of the Harvard Center on the Developing Child, and colleagues describe the process of development "as a function of 'nature dancing with nurture over time.'"[15] In other words, from conception onward, biology interacts with physical and social environments to shape a child's pathways and achievements. In this sense, the time that parents—both mothers and fathers—spend caring for children is likely to influence a child's development well beyond the initial bonding period, and in different ways depending on the children's age and circumstances. Parents' work can affect all of this.

For example, researchers have documented that children are more likely to spend time without parental supervision at younger ages if their parents are working, which may in turn harm the children's performance in school and increase their participation in risky behaviors.[16] Theories of how parents function and nurture their children suggest that ongoing stress at work may cause parents to withdraw from interacting with their children at home, or to be more vulnerable to stimuli that trigger conflict with their children. Researchers describe this as "role overload": working parents may be overwhelmed by the feeling that they can't accomplish everything they need to do, and, in this way, work stress becomes linked to stressful situations in the home.[17] Similarly, one parent's work stress might bubble over to the other, reducing the buffering influence that the other parent might have in the family.

More generally, family systems theory sees families as a "subsystem" (with marital, parental, and sibling ties) that is rooted in larger systems—for example, the community. Conditions or changes in these larger systems that affect one family member may also affect his or her relationships with other family members and, in turn, the way those family members function.[18] Research shows that parents feel pressured by external demands to work for pay, such as financial uncertainty, welfare requirements, or the rising cost of goods that are thought to benefit children (for example, child care, tutoring etc.).[19] These demands, in turn, may affect parents' job satisfaction, physical and mental health, coping resources and ability to provide socio-emotional support for their children. Long work hours, lack of autonomy, job insecurity, and a heavy workload are also associated with adult mental health problems (for example, anxiety and depression), and parents' mental health is believed to play a fundamental role in their children's mental and physical development.[20]

How Parents' Work Can Enhance Children's Wellbeing

At the same time, working parents earn money that they can use to improve how they care for their children and the quality of their children's environments. For example, they might spend money on nutrition, child care, health care, the safety of their physical surroundings, or opportunities for learning. Economists describe these expenditures as "inputs" for producing "child quality." Nobel Prize–winning economist Gary Becker's theory of "household production" laid the foundation for a large body of research that examines how parents allocate their time between work and children (or other activities, such as leisure), and how household budgets (which, of course, are affected by parents' employment) constrain or support the investments they want to make in their children. In this model, parents have to make trade-offs as they decide how much time

to spend at work versus at home with their children, and these decisions in turn depend on how much they earn (and the prices they have to pay for goods), their preferences for investing in their children's wellbeing (versus their own), and the "productivity" of their time with children versus the time they spend in other activities.[21]

Researchers who apply this economic model suggest, for example, that the amount of time parents spend with their children at home depends in part on how productive or efficient they are both at home and in the workplace. Parents for whom staying at home has higher opportunity costs (that is, those who are more productive in the workplace than at home) would be more likely to substitute hired child care for their own care of their children.[22] Family choices also depend on the overall family budget and wealth, and families with greater resources are expected to invest more in their children and potentially increase their children's chances of success. (However, parents have different preferences for investing resources in their children, so an increase in earnings or other sources of household income may not necessarily translate into a comparable rise in spending on the children.) With these ideas in mind, researchers have examined whether public policies that expand financial incentives to work or require parents to work (as in the case of the mid-1990s welfare reforms) have increased family income and, in turn, had positive effects on children.

In addition to how much time parents spend with their children (rather than at work) and when in their children's lives they trade off time at home with employment, what parents do in the time they spend with their children—or how they interact, and the quality of those interactions—is also very important to their children's wellbeing. Psychological and sociological theories suggest that the types of interactions parents have with their children can be influenced by a number of factors, both at work and elsewhere. For example, are there two parents in the household, and are both working? How involved is the mother vis-à-vis the father (or other caregiver) in hands-on care of the children? How do the quality of the parents' jobs, the stress they experience at work, their relationship as a couple and as a family, the children's gender, and other factors affect the parents' interactions with and availability to the children? In general, how central is child rearing in the lives of the parents and the family?[23]

For older children in particular, these theories also suggest that parents play an important part as role models through work and caregiving. Children and adolescents may change their own behavior and goals in response to the behavior modeled by their parents; for example, they might devote more time to their studies to increase their own future job prospects. In lower-income families where work replaces welfare, reliance on welfare may appear less attractive (or self-sufficiency more rewarding), and teenage childbearing and other risky activities may be reduced.[24] Once again, many factors may help determine how parents as role models influence their children's wellbeing.

How Parents' Job Loss Affects Children's Wellbeing

With lingering high unemployment and longer-term unemployment among working-age adults in the wake of the Great Recession, we need to know more about how parents' job loss affects children's wellbeing. In the context of family systems theory, parents' job loss presents a significant shock to the family subsystem. First, it reduces family income, sometimes substantially and permanently, constraining parents' ability to invest in their children.[25] The stress associated with job loss can also undermine parents' physical and mental health, which, in turn, can undermine children's health and family relationships. Job loss may also affect family structure—for example, parents may divorce[26]—compounding the blow to the family subsystem. At the same time, the strength and quality of marital and parent-child relationships, as well as the extent to which other social contacts and supports continue (that is, are not disrupted by the changes that follow job loss) may limit the negative effects that might otherwise spill over to the children.

In this section, I have described a number of ways that parents' employment may affect children's wellbeing, whether positively or negatively. An immense amount of research has examined these pathways and their implications for children's wellbeing. Next, I focus on the strongest evidence generated by these studies.

Evidence on How Parents' Work Affects Children's Wellbeing

It is especially challenging to causally link parents' employment to children's wellbeing, in part because of the many intricate and intimate family factors that come into play. Parents can't be randomly assigned to jobs, nor can children be randomly assigned to parents who work or don't work, so no controlled experiment can disentangle the influence of these factors. Some studies have relied on longitudinal data, such as the National Longitudinal Study of Youth (NLSY) and the Panel Study of Income Dynamics (PSID), that allow researchers to measure children's wellbeing over time and make adjustments for potential mediating variables. Even then, it is very difficult to determine the effects of parent's work on children's wellbeing with a fair level of confidence that the estimated effects are not biased by factors we are not observing or measuring.[27] In this review of the research, I take these limitations into account and indicate where there is consensus or greater confidence in the results, as well as where findings are still tentative or discrepant.

Effects of Mothers' Work on Children's Wellbeing

As we've seen, biological and developmental studies suggest that, in the first years of a child's life, we should be more concerned about mothers' work than fathers' work. This research has produced clear evidence that maternal stress affects infants' physiologic responses to stress, and that excessive or prolonged exposure to stress can harm a young child's socio-emotional and cognitive development. Work can be one source of sustained stress for mothers; through separation from their mothers during working hours, it can be a source of chronic stress for infants as well. However, if an available and caring adult helps children cope with stress (that is, protects children from its harmful effects), they can develop positive responses to stress that may help them deal with frustration and other adverse experiences later in life.[28]

An extensive review and summary of five decades of research on how maternal employment affects children's cognitive and behavioral development confirms the need to account for contextual factors—for example, the timing and nature of a mother's work, or the quality of care provided by others besides the mother—to discern plausible effects of mothers' work on their children.[29] Specifically,

there is a relatively strong consensus that higher-quality early child care (whether by parents or others) enhances children's cognitive and social development, as well as their later academic achievement and behavior.[30] That said, the strength and also the direction of these associations are moderated by other variables, including family structure, income, mother's education, and the child's age.

One fairly cohesive story that emerges from this interdisciplinary research is that, in single-parent or low-income families, the positive effects of additional income (and reduced financial stress) that are associated with maternal work are likely to outweigh the potential negative effects of less time caring for children, as long as the substitute care is not of poor quality—especially for children under five, who spend more time in child care. One study, using NLSY data, examined mothers who worked during their children's first three years. The researchers found that in low-income families, the children of these mothers had significantly fewer behavioral problems at ages 7–9 than did the children of other mothers, and that in single-parent families, such children had significantly higher reading scores at ages 3–4 and again at ages 7–12.[31] However, another study, which also used NLSY data, looked at single mothers who were affected by PRWORA's work mandates (which significantly increased their work hours and their use of child care) and found that mothers' work had a significant adverse effect on children's test scores at ages 3–6, reducing them by 2.6 percent on average.[32] This adverse effect appeared to be driven by the fact that three-fourths of the mothers were using informal child-care arrangements (that is, non–center-based care). Children who were placed in formal, center-based care showed no reduction in test scores. Other researchers, studying mothers who were leaving welfare, have not found a relationship between mothers going to work and preschool children's cognitive achievement or behavior. However, they did find that when mothers left welfare for work, adolescent children's reading skills and mental health improved, and their participation in risky behaviors (for example, using drugs and alcohol) decreased.[33]

Research suggests that the payoff for direct time investment in children (versus higher income from working) may be greater among more highly educated women, and not only for children in their early years. One study used PSID data to examine the relationship among the time mothers spent caring for their 7- to 13-year-old children, the time they spent working, and the children's educational attainment at ages 20–26. The researchers found that greater maternal child-care time produced benefits only for children whose mothers had 12 or more years of schooling.[34] Another study took advantage of a Swedish policy reform in 1988 that increased paid parental leave from 12 to 15 months to look at the relationship between the time mothers spent caring for their children and the children's educational achievements.[35] Assessing the impact of maternal care relative to the common alternative of subsidized child care, the researchers found a positive association between increased parental leave and children's scholastic performance at age 16 only for children whose mothers had a postsecondary education; subsidized child care did not have the same effect. The analysis showed that other possible moderating factors, such as mother's mental health or the children's health, did not play a role in the outcome.

Evidence on how maternal employment affects infants and very young children is likewise mixed, although a preponderance of findings suggests that children's cognitive development is enhanced if mothers are their primary caregivers in their first year and work less than full-time through age three.[36] One seminal study used data from the National Institute of Child Health and Human Development's Study of Early Child Care and Youth Development to see how the timing and intensity of mothers' employment affects children's cognitive development at age three years.[37] Children whose mothers worked at any time before they were nine months old scored lower on a school readiness measure, and the negative effect was largest for children whose mothers worked 30 or more hours per week. Consistent with the research discussed above, the study reported larger negative effects for married couples than for families headed by single parents, suggesting again that additional income from employment may have more beneficial effects for children in single-parent households. Another study similarly found that when mothers went to work in the first year of their children's lives, or worked longer hours in their second or third years, the children's reading and math scores suffered.[38]

Mothers who go to work sooner after a child's birth and work longer hours are less likely to breastfeed, which is particularly concerning given the substantial health benefits for children breastfed in the first six months to one year of their lives. Starting at about six weeks after the birth of a child, returning to work emerges as the top reason that mothers give for discontinuing breastfeeding.[39] Mothers say that the substantial time and commitment required to express their milk, and the lack of accommodations in many workplaces for pumping breast milk or breastfeeding, deter them from breastfeeding as long as they would like. Furthermore, recent research confirms that, compared with

Children's cognitive development is enhanced if mothers are their primary caregivers in their first year and work less than full-time through age three.

mothers who feed their children formula or breastfeed for less than six months, mothers who breastfeed for six months or longer experience a larger decline in their earnings in the year after giving birth and slower growth in earnings in the five years after childbirth.[40] This larger, longer-term reduction in earnings is explained by the fact that mothers who breastfeed for six months or longer tend to take more time off from work. But the research does not identify whether they take more time off because of their own changing views about work versus time with family or whether they feel pushed out because it's so hard to combine work with breastfeeding and infant care. Regardless, the economic penalty these mothers pay is cause for concern, considering that both the rate and duration of breastfeeding are significantly lower among poorer, less-educated working women than among wealthier, better-educated mothers (whether employed or unemployed).

Effects of Parents' Job Loss

Most researchers who study how parents' work affects children have focused primarily on how mothers allocate their time between work and child care, although they also emphasize that other family members, particularly fathers, play an important role in providing financial support, ensuring quality

substitute care, and buffering children from work-related stress. Studies of fathers suggest that, as with mothers, both the level of their involvement and their warmth and responsiveness determine the extent of their influence on children's behavior and academic achievement.[41]

Empirical evidence also shows that children are more likely to be affected by a father's job loss than by a mother's.[42] A parent's job loss can bring considerable financial and mental distress that reverberates through the family system. For example, in one study, Slovakian adolescents perceived lower support from fathers who experienced unemployment, likely because of the stress associated with the father's job loss.[43] But the amount of support they perceived from their mothers was not affected by either the father's or mother's job loss, and high support from the mother was particularly protective for the health of adolescents whose father lost his job. Similarly, other research has found that women experience less stress and fewer mental health problems in the face of their own unemployment than do men.[44]

To study the relationship between parents' job loss and children's development, researchers must disentangle the influence of parent characteristics, as well as parent-child interactions, that affect children's wellbeing even in the absence of job loss (for example, parents' mental health, marital or family relationship quality, etc.). When a company closes or downsizes, researchers can empirically examine the effects of job losses that are not associated with parents' individual characteristics. For example, one study from Norway examined the effects of this kind of abrupt parental job loss, occurring when children were in tenth grade, on the children's grade point averages

(GPAs) in their high school graduation year. Children whose fathers lost their jobs had a significantly lower graduation-year GPA, but a mother's job loss had no significant effects. Among children whose fathers had lower earnings before losing their jobs, and those who lived in communities with weaker job markets, the effect of fathers' job loss on GPA was nearly twice as large. Seeking the precise cause of the negative effect on GPA, the researchers were able to rule out explanations tied to loss of family income, changes in maternal employment or time inputs, and marital dissolution and relocation. Mental distress associated with job loss appeared to be the driving factor.

The Norwegian findings echo those of a U.S.-based study that used data on job loss and children's educational achievement from the 1996, 2001, and 2004 panels of the Survey of Income and Program Participation.[45] Focusing on short-term measures of children's educational progress, the researchers found that parents' job loss increased the likelihood that children would be retained in school by approximately 15 percent. Furthermore, this negative effect was more likely among children with less-educated parents (those with a high school degree or less). And a study of Canadian families, which included some fathers who lost their jobs when their company closed, found that parents' job loss diminished children's long-term labor market prospects. Sons who were 11 to 14 years old when their fathers lost a job saw their earnings as adults reduced by about 9 percent, on average; daughters also saw lower earnings later in life, though the reduction was imprecisely estimated. Like the Norwegian study, this study showed no link between this negative effect and divorce, residential relocation, or changes in mothers' earnings and employment; like the U.S.

study, it found that negative effects on children were more prevalent among families who had the lowest incomes before the parents' job loss. The study's authors could not say what best accounted for the detrimental long-term effect on children's economic prospects: the stress associated with parents' job loss, or the loss of family income itself.

Children in poorer or single-parent families face a greater likelihood that their parents' work will have harmful effects on their wellbeing.

Parents' Job Characteristics and Children's Wellbeing

Losing a job is a life-altering event for families, but research also suggests that other aspects of parents' work, such as job quality, can strongly affect how much time parents spend with children and the nature of their interactions. Theory and empirical research identify four key aspects of job quality as particularly germane to the effects of parents' work on children's wellbeing: the level of job security that parents perceive they have, which relates to feelings of financial stability; how much control parents have over what they do in their work; flexibility in work scheduling (for example, start and end times); and paid family leave (for example, maternity/paternity and other types of personal or family leave). Using an index of job quality based on these four dimensions and data from the Longitudinal Study of Australian Children, one team of researchers analyzed the relationship between job quality and a "child difficulties score," which measured children's distress, negative or oppositional behaviors, inattention or hyperactivity, and peer problems.[46] They found a strong relationship between job quality and children's difficulties that was mediated by parents' distress (both mothers' and fathers'); that is, when parents were more stressed, their children were more likely to experience difficulties. This relationship was particularly strong in single-mother families.

Among the four aspects of job quality, research shows, parents' work schedules and their degree of flexibility are particularly important for children. Studies of parents' shift work have found that preschool and elementary school children are significantly more likely to have behavioral problems when their parents work at night.[47] The researchers speculated that the mental stress of night work, as well as less effective parenting behaviors linked to such work schedules, might account for these detrimental effects. Several studies that used NLSY data to examine how parents' nonstandard work schedules affect children's wellbeing have found similar results.[48] Taking into account factors such as children's age, gender, and family income, nighttime work by both mothers and fathers has been found to be more harmful to children, and to parents' relationships with their children, than work on other shifts. Among adolescent children, there is a strong association between the number of years that their mothers and fathers work the night shift and risky behaviors. Night shift work reduces the amount of time mothers spend with their children, fathers' knowledge of children's whereabouts, fathers' closeness to their children, and the quality of the home environment. The relative importance of these factors varies with the age of the child, and the size of the effects also varies for some subgroups: boys, children in poorer or single-parent families, and whose

parents work in nonprofessional occupations experience the most negative effects.

In an Australian study that focused on children's health, researchers found that children whose parents, and particularly fathers, worked nonstandard schedules were significantly more likely to be obese or overweight, even after adjusting for household income and family and lifestyle factors.[49] The added pressure created by fathers' nonstandard work hours appeared to be borne largely by mothers, who in turn compromised in the family food environment (for example, by buying more fully prepared meals that tended to be higher in fat, sugar, and salt and larger in portion size). Another study, of adolescents, found a positive association between mothers' nonstandard work schedules and children's body mass index (BMI), suggesting that as children get older and have less adult supervision, mothers' work schedules grow increasingly important.[50] Other research suggests that parental supervision, which is affected by parental work hours and schedules, is particularly critical for children's wellbeing in low-income, single-parent families, or in families where parents' night and evening shift work is a condition of employment.[51] Parents who work nonstandard shifts may experience more physical and emotional stress, and parents' stress is in turn known to worsen parent-child interactions and children's behavior.[52]

The empirical evidence I've presented—from a range of studies in the United States and other countries that explore numerous ways parents' work might affect children—consistently suggests that children in poorer or single-parent families face a greater likelihood that their parents' work will have harmful effects on their wellbeing. Qualitative research further illuminates the many ways that the stress associated with economic struggles, poor job quality, lack of support at home, limited child care choices, and other factors can compound the difficulties that parents and children in these families face. For example, Ask the Children, a study involving more than 1,000 children in grades 3–12, supports the empirical finding that child-care arrangements may be especially critical to the development of children in lower-income families; children in lower-quality child care, which low-income families are more likely to use, are more affected by their mothers' behavior (particularly their warmth and responsiveness).[53] In addition, low-income parents are less likely to hold jobs with attractive attributes such as high job security and stability, autonomy in their work, meaningful work tasks, low frustration, and a supportive work-life culture, and they may be less likely to have positive feelings about their work roles. Ask the Children's data suggest that when parents value their work and think that they are doing the right thing for themselves and their families, whether by working or by staying home, their children are more likely to fare well, because this attitude will be reflected in their care and responsiveness. Furthermore, when parents have positive experiences at work, and in combining work and family responsibilities, the potential benefits for children of parents' serving as role models through their work—such as greater self-sufficiency and independence, social competence, and aspirations for their own schooling and career success—are more likely to be realized.

Policies That Address Parents' Work and Children's Wellbeing

The preceding sections have described ways that parents' work may affect children's wellbeing, as well as the evidence on both positive and negative effects of parents' work.

Few would dispute, for example, that parents' employment generates income that is key to promoting the health and wellbeing of children, the quality of their environments, and their prospects for future productivity and success in nurturing the next generation. At the same time, evidence of potential negative effects on children is also compelling, and the ways that parents' employment might bring about harm are complex and linked to family resources and functioning. Ideally, public policies would bolster the positive effects of parents' work on children's wellbeing and minimize the detrimental effects.

Data from the Organization for Economic Co-operation and Development (OECD) are frequently used to compare parental employment and work support policies across nations. OECD data for 18 developed countries show that employment rates among mothers in the United States are very comparable to those elsewhere. For example, in 2002, about 69 percent of U.S. mothers with children aged 6–14 were employed, equaling the OECD-18 average, while about 60 percent of U.S. mothers with children aged 3–5 and 56.6 percent with children under age three were employed, 3.5–4 percentage points below the OECD-18 averages.[54] As of 2009, approximately 70 percent of women aged 25–54 in the United States and in OECD countries were employed, suggesting that women with school-age children are participating in the labor force at about the same rate as working-age women across developed countries. Yet U.S. public policies that are intended to support working parents and their families look very different from those found elsewhere.

Income Support

The U.S. ranks third among 20 OECD countries in its support of families through cash transfers and tax benefits, which are closely linked to reductions in child poverty (as well as to parents' employment in the United States).[55] These income supports, which increased steadily from 1995 to 2005 through the expansion of the EITC earnings supplements, are particularly important for low-income parents. Parental employment is one of the most important factors in reducing the risk of child poverty, and numerous studies have found that the EITC promotes parental work, especially among single mothers, suggesting that these benefits may play a key role in improving children's wellbeing.[56] There is also growing evidence of strong positive linkages between earnings supplements for working parents and young children's educational performance, as well as their later educational attainment and labor market earnings.[57] Furthermore, we know that higher income is associated with better home environments. Still, researchers who explore the role of income in improving children's home environments and, in turn, children's behavior and academic readiness have found weaker evidence for a direct causal association between income and better child outcomes.[58] More generally, scholars who have synthesized the research and policy evidence appear to concur that policies that increase family income are less likely to improve children's wellbeing when support is weak for parental leave to care for children (for example, in the first year after birth or during illness) or for quality substitute care.[59]

Parental Leave

Worldwide, one of the most common policies to support working parents and their families is paid parental leave. In fact, the United States is among only four of 173 nations that do not guarantee paid parental leave, although the 1993 Family and Medical Leave Act (FMLA) gives some parents the right to take 12 weeks of unpaid leave after the birth (or adoption) of a child.[60] In a recent *Future of Children* article, Christopher Ruhm thoroughly reviewed state family leave policies, including those of six states that offer some form of paid leave (either short-term paid leave or temporary disability insurance).[61] His review makes clear the comparative generosity of European policies, which provide paid maternity leave for 14–20 weeks, at 70 to 100 percent of the mother's pre-childbirth wages.

Empirical studies of the relationship among family leave policies and children's material wellbeing, health and educational attainment find that paid parental leave, combined with generous public support for child care and early education, are significantly correlated with improved health and higher educational attainment among children.[62] One analysis, using 1969–94 data from 16 European countries, showed that associations between paid parental leave and children's health and wellbeing were strongest for infants aged 2–12 months, possibly because mothers who take paid leave are more likely to breastfeed.[63] One study examined a Canadian policy change that expanded paid parental leave, from 15 weeks of paid leave for mothers plus 10 weeks of paid leave that could be split between mothers and fathers to a total of 50 weeks of paid leave, of which 35 weeks could be shared between parents.[64] Looking specifically at how the change affected the amount of time mothers spent at home and how long they breastfed, the researchers found that after the change, mothers spent 2.3 more months at home (a 28 percent increase) and breastfed about one month longer. Mothers were also significantly more likely to say they stopped breastfeeding because they were introducing solid food, rather than because they were going back to work. And a recent analysis of California's paid parental leave policy, using 1999–2010 data from the Current Population Survey, found that even a far less generous policy (six weeks of partially paid leave) substantially increased maternity and family leave-taking (compared with unpaid leave under FMLA), especially among disadvantaged mothers, with no evidence of negative effects on mothers' future labor market earnings.[65]

Finally, a recent study examined a 1977 Norwegian policy reform that increased parental leave from 12 weeks of unpaid leave (the current U.S. policy) to four months of paid leave and 12 months of unpaid leave. Because several decades have passed since the reform took effect, the researchers were able to examine its longer-term effects. They found that children whose mothers spent more time with them during their first year of life, thanks to the expanded parental leave, were more likely to finish high school and had 5 percent higher earnings at age 30. These effects were larger for children whose mothers had less than 10 years of education; these children realized 8 percent higher earnings at age 30.

Child Care

The authors of the Norwegian study noted that, at the time of the 1977 parental leave reform, very little high-quality child care was available for children under two years (the primary alternative was grandparents or other informal care). Some of the research described earlier suggests that, depending on the quantity and quality, formal child care can have positive effects on children's cognitive development, and that it is potentially

most beneficial for disadvantaged children. Public spending on child care in the United States comes primarily through the Child Care and Development Fund (CCDF), a federal block grant that aims to help low-income families with work-related child care expenses. Parents can use these subsidies for formal child care, family day care or care provided in their own home or in the home of another family member; other than for the Head Start program, the rate of the subsidy is not tied to measures of program quality.[66] In fiscal year 2010, states spent $9.5 billion in combined federal and state funds on child care subsidies for low-income families, including CCDF funds as well as Temporary Assistance to Needy Families (TANF) transfers into CCDF.

The Child and Dependent Care Tax Credit is another form of subsidy that working parents can use for child care. The credit can refund 20 to 35 percent of day-care expenses and has no restrictions on the type of care parents can purchase. However, because this tax credit is nonrefundable (that is, it can't reduce the amount of tax owed to less than zero), low-income families who owe little or no income tax derive little benefit. Similarly, the cost of employer-provided dependent care is excluded from taxable income, another form of public support for child care that is not targeted to low-income families.

Overall, the United States spends less than other developed countries on its public child care programs (both in absolute terms and as a percentage of gross domestic product), and it has the lowest share of children enrolled in formal child care.[67] Research confirms that child care subsidies encourage mothers to work and increase parents' use of child care, although it also suggests that a preponderance of low-quality options, as well as lack of information about better-quality programs and their costs, may push low-income families toward informal or inferior child care. Still, evidence on the effects of child care subsidies on children's wellbeing is mixed. One recent study suggests that children with better-educated mothers who received subsidized care experienced substantial increases in behavioral problems, whereas children with less-educated mothers (a high school degree or less) were more likely to show improvements in positive social behaviors. The better-educated mothers not only worked more hours, but they were also less likely to enroll their children in center- and family-based care.[68]

Worker Supports and Workplace Flexibility

As we've seen, research has also revealed associations between parental job quality (that is, job security, flexibility, work schedules, etc.) and children's wellbeing, suggesting children's outcomes could be enhanced through policies that improve worker supports, reduce parents' job-related stress and increase parents' ability to respond to their children's needs. Employee benefits and supports such as paid sick leave, flexible work hours, time off for children's health and educational needs, breastfeeding breaks, premium pay for night shift work and paid vacation (in additional to paid parental leave and child care support) are mandatory in most advanced countries. But among these benefits and supports, only breastfeeding breaks are required in the United States (through legislation passed only in 2010). A group of scholars analyzed a global database of legislation that mandates these worker support policies for 175 countries and found no negative associations between more generous national policies and measures of

the nations' economic competitiveness.[69] In fact, their review of the research suggests that these policies have a number of potential benefits for employers, workers, and children, including increased employee retention and productivity, lower turnover and absenteeism, reduced business costs and increased profitability, lower parental stress, increased parental involvement with children, higher rates of child immunization, and improved child health, behavior, and cognitive achievement.

These findings raise the question of why the United States trails its developed-country peers (and some developing countries) in mandating worker benefits. One reason is that U.S. employers have strongly opposed legislation to increase benefits such as paid parental leave, sick leave, and other workplace flexibility provisions, on the grounds that the costs would be too high and would compromise their competitiveness.[70] But the Council of Economic Advisors (CEA) investigated workplace flexibility and found that few employers have accurate information about the costs and benefits of workplace flexibility policies.[71] In addition, because the costs and benefits of expanding workplace flexibility are likely to differ across industries and by employer size, it is difficult to assess how wider adoption of more generous worker supports might benefit or harm not only employers and workers, but also society and the U.S. economy overall. Furthermore, not only do we lack data on the prevalence of existing workplace flexibility practices, but employers and employees differ in their reports of whether such supports are available. The CEA used data from two surveys—one of employers and one of employees—to examine to what extent private sector employers are adapting their policies to changes in workforce participation (and the growing potential for work-family conflicts).

Carolyn J. Heinrich

More than half of employers indicated that they gave at least some workers the flexibility to change their work start and end times, but fewer than one-third of full-time workers and only 39 percent of part-time workers reported having this flexibility. Other research shows that just 30 percent of U.S. employees are offered paid sick leave that they can use for themselves or to care for family members.[72]

The CEA's finding that less-skilled workers are less likely than their more highly skilled counterparts to have workplace flexibility is especially worrisome. Parents in low-paid, low-skilled positions are also more likely to work a nonstandard shift as a requirement of their job (rather than for work–family balance).[73] And under FMLA, individual employees are eligible only if they worked at least 1,250 hours in the previous year, and employers with fewer than 50 workers do not have to provide unpaid leave. About half of workers do not qualify for unpaid family leave under FMLA, and these are more likely to be less-skilled, low-income workers.[74] In effect, the parents of families that are most at risk of seeing harmful spillover effects from work and disruptions to family routines are the same parents who are least able to take leave, cut their paid work hours, or reschedule them on occasion to accommodate their children's needs.[75]

Mitigating Negative Effects of Job Loss
For families, the most readily apparent impact of job loss and unemployment is a reduction in income. Workers who become unemployed through no fault of their own may receive unemployment insurance benefits, supported primarily through a tax on employers. This temporary financial assistance typically provides up to 50 percent

of prior weekly earnings, but the amount and duration are determined by state law. Following the 2007 recession, the length of time during which people could receive benefits was temporarily extended beyond the usual 26 weeks in most states. In addition, those without a job may receive employment and training services—including job-search and job-placement assistance, job counseling and assessment, vocational training, and support services—through federal funds from the Workforce Investment Act that are disbursed to states to help unemployed and dislocated workers find new jobs. Programs for dislocated workers, however, are among the least effective of public employment and training services. Research shows that they have modest effects on employment and are unlikely to help workers fully recover their lost earnings.[76]

In addition, our policy responses to job loss do not recognize or address the documented negative effects on other family members that are associated with the stress of job loss, and its implications for family functioning. Job counseling is available to the worker, but other support services are typically limited to individual, work-oriented supports such as transportation assistance. To better cope with stress and mitigate job loss's negative effects on children, family members may need psychological and family counseling, alcohol and drug abuse counseling, preventive health care (because they've lost health-care benefits), and food and nutritional assistance.[77]

Policy Recommendations
What new policies, or improvements to existing policies, would better support working parents, promote the positive effects of parents' work on children's wellbeing, and reduce the harmful consequences of parents'

work? The EITC, for example, is one of the most successful policies for supporting working families. The rate of participation is consistently high, and Congress recently expanded benefits for larger families and married couples. In addition, about half the U.S. states have enacted their own earned income credit policies that include expectations and incentives for parents to work. But although community outreach and tax programs for low-income workers have helped lower the costs of filing and receiving the benefit, an estimated 15 to 25 percent of eligible families are not claiming the EITC.[78] One way to get more families to claim the credit might be to simplify tax filing by consolidating the EITC with other tax provisions for families (for example, the Child and Dependent Care Credit) into a single credit, while also raising the income level at which benefits phase out to increase the level of support the credit provides for working parents.[79]

There are other opportunities to promote healthier working families and improve children's wellbeing. The United States stands apart from other developed countries in its near absence of policies that mandate employee work supports. Instead, U.S. employers determine on their own to what extent and to which employees they grant work flexibility or other family-oriented benefits. The result is that low-income or low-skilled workers and single parents, who may need additional support the most to improve nurturing and care arrangements for their children, are least likely to get such support.

Though research confirms that the first three to six months of an infant's life constitute a particularly sensitive time for the child's development and for bonding with caregivers, it is not definitively established that the caregiver should be the mother, full time, in every family. One policy option would be federally mandated paid leave for either mothers or fathers in the first weeks or months of a child's life. Since 2004, for example, California has mandated six weeks of partially paid leave (for a newborn, a foster or adopted child, or other family health needs), and this policy could be adopted nationwide. The latest research on California's leave policy shows substantial increases (three weeks on average) in use of maternity leave, with particularly large increases among less-educated, unmarried, and minority mothers. Studies in other countries such as Germany have not shown additional benefits for children (in terms of their educational success) or parents' income beyond six months of mandated parental leave, suggesting that a paid or partially paid leave of somewhere between six weeks and six months should be adequate to generate benefits for parents and children alike.[80]

Low-income or low-skilled workers and single parents, who may need additional support the most to improve nurturing and care arrangements for their children, are least likely to get such support.

An alternative to paid parental leave would be a fixed cash allowance provided by the federal government, or via federal cost-sharing with states, that would both augment and replace existing public investments in child care (that is, the Child and Dependent Care Credit, the

Exclusion for Employer-Provided Dependent Care Expenses, the Child Care and Development Fund, and the Title XX Social Services Block Grant) and let parents use the money either to purchase high-quality early child care or to offset the earnings they lose when they spend time out of the labor force after welcoming a new child into the family. This option would be more flexible for families. It could accommodate any adult family member's leave from employment to care for the child, and if the allowance were set at a fixed amount, it would cover a larger fraction of lost wages in families with lower income. In addition, families could make choices that would reflect their own circumstances, such as the availability of quality child-care providers, the implications of taking time off for their career progression, the age and health of other children in the family, and many others. Employers would be on equal footing nationally in terms of the costs of offering a basic family work support, and they could supplement the allowance with other benefits as their needs allowed. Like the EITC, the benefit could be phased out as family income increased.

How could a cash allowance be administered to ensure that children benefited from the funds? Parents could be required to document their leave from work (in conjunction with their employer), or if parents chose to use the allowance to purchase high-quality early child care, they could be required to document both their expenditures and the qualifications of the child-care provider. This type of work support should go hand in hand with more concerted policy efforts to inform parents about why choosing high-quality child care is important, to improve the information available to them so that they can make better choices, and to give them financial incentives to do so.

If implemented well, this type of flexible cash allowance should achieve the goal, articulated by David Blau, an economist and expert on child care policy, of subsidizing the costs of raising children "without favoring market child care costs over the forgone earnings cost of a parent who stays home to care for a child."[81]

Another area of family work support policy where the United States is clearly out of step with both developed and developing countries across the globe is the mandatory provision of paid sick leave. Data from the March 2012 National Compensation Survey (NCS), which measures employee benefits, show that paid sick leave was offered to 66 percent of civilian workers and 61 percent of those working in private industry, but to just 52 percent of workers in small private firms (those with fewer than 100 employees), 40 percent of workers in private-sector service occupations, and barely a quarter of part-time workers.[82] At the same time, research suggests not requiring some minimal paid sick leave benefit brings high costs for families and society alike. A recent *Future of Children* article indicated that parents with access to paid sick leave were more than five times as likely to be able to care for their sick children. This was especially important for families with a chronically ill child, for whom lack of access to paid sick leave posed a substantial risk that parents would lose their jobs.[83] Furthermore, research discussed earlier in this article provides convincing evidence of a strong connection between parents' and children's mental health, and a corresponding relationship between parents' involvement and responsiveness and children's cognitive achievement and behavior.

One option would be to elevate the provision of sick leave to be on par with the availability of health care insurance coverage. For example, the Affordable Care Act provides for a Health Coverage Tax Credit for employers who provide health insurance to employees; employers deduct the costs of these benefits and get the added bonus of a tax credit. Without mandating sick leave, a similar credit could give employers an incentive to offer it.

The United States currently uses its tax code to spur employers to provide a range of other benefits, including educational and tuition assistance, life insurance, commuting assistance, and more; these are nontaxable for employees and deductible by the firm. However, access and participation by employees follow consistent patterns—they are lowest for workers in small firms and service occupations and highest for workers in large firms and government agencies, presumably because administrative costs are influenced by organization size and employee tenure.[84] One possibility would be to explore reducing the administrative burden, for example, by giving employers a single deduction based on the generosity of the dollar-equivalent value of the menu of benefits they offer combined with their employee participation rate. The CEA study discussed earlier noted that one of the reasons for discrepancies between employers and employees in reporting the availability of workplace flexibility and other benefits is that employers do not necessarily make these benefits available to all employees; less-skilled, lower-income workers are more likely to be left out. Economic theory, however, suggests that caution may be warranted: workers could ultimately bear a larger fraction of these costs if there are trade-offs between wage offers from employers and these benefits. Although we still lack empirical work on this issue, a recent study that examined employer contributions to 401(k) plans found that associated reductions in wages were

much less (in percentage terms) for low-income than for higher-income workers.[85]

For parents who lose their jobs, unemployment insurance provides some temporary financial relief. Employment and training services are minimally effective in helping them find new jobs and do not help to fully replace lost earnings. A number of possible reforms to the unemployment insurance system have been proposed, including some that would shift more resources toward workers with larger, long-term wage losses. One such alternative would replace unemployment insurance with a combination of wage loss insurance—which would supplement the earnings of workers who can find only lower-wage employment after losing a job—and temporary earnings replacement accounts, to which workers would also make contributions. A larger share of the current unemployment insurance system's resources would, in effect, be redirected toward helping those experiencing significant long-term wage losses to maintain their living standards, with a smaller share going to short-term cash assistance for those enduring more limited bouts of unemployment or wage loss. Analyses suggest that this type of reform would reach more low-income families and would likely also strengthen parents' incentives to find new employment.[86] In addition, the need-based payments that may currently accompany an individual's job search in workforce development programs could be made more flexible, so that they could be used for any family member's needs during the period of unemployment (for example, for family, psychological, or substance abuse counseling).

Finally, the articles in this issue of the *Future of Children* share a focus on two generations—parents and their children— and this discussion of parents' employment and children's wellbeing has clearly shown how intimately and importantly parents' work participation is linked to their ability to effectively care for their children (and to their children's development). In this regard, policies that strengthen and support parents in their roles both as worker and parent could generate long-term benefits for the next generation, which in turn should advance the wellbeing of subsequent generations.[87]

One common model among programs that have an explicit two-generation focus includes three core components: high-quality early-childhood education; job training that gives parents opportunities to upgrade their workforce skills for high-demand occupations; and comprehensive family and peer support services.[88] The Tulsa County Career Advance program, in Oklahoma, initiated in 2009 by the Community Action Project (CAP), is an example of just such a two-generation intervention; it targets parents with children in Head Start and Early Head Start for workforce development services (see

the article in this issue by P. Lindsay Chase-Lansdale and Jeanne Brooks-Gunn). If these programs successfully help parents secure jobs with higher levels of job security, wages, and other attributes that improve how they feel about their work and the role models and encouragement they offer to their children, then the children may very well reap benefits beyond those associated with the education and stronger financial supports families realize through the programs. However, evaluations that are currently under way, such as the experimental evaluation of Enhanced Early Head Start, also point to difficulties in their implementation that may lessen these programs' effects.[89] As new, innovative strategies attempt to better engage parents, rigorous evaluations of these programs should continue, so that policy makers get the evidence they need to weigh these programs' costs and benefits, to assess whether they can be introduced more widely, and to determine their potential for net returns to society and to disadvantaged families.

ENDNOTES

1. Annalyn Kurtz, "The Four-Day Work Week," CNN Money, July 9, 2013, http://money.cnn.com/2013/07/09/news/economy/shorter-work-week/index.html.

2. U.S. Bureau of Labor Statistics, "Employment Characteristics of Families—2011," news release, April 26, 2012, http://www.bls.gov/news.release/archives/famee_04262012.pdf.

3. Wendy Wang, Kim Parker, and Paul Taylor, *Breadwinner Moms* (Washington, DC: Pew Research Center, 2013), http://www.pewsocialtrends.org/files/2013/05/Breadwinner_moms_final.pdf.

4. Jane Waldfogel, *What Children Need* (Cambridge, MA: Harvard University Press, 2006).

5. Pew Research Center, *The Harried Life of the Working Mother* (Washington, DC: Pew Research Center, 2009), http://www.pewsocialtrends.org/2009/10/01/the-harried-life-of-the-working-mother.

6. Greg J. Duncan and P. Lindsay Chase-Lansdale, eds., *For Better and for Worse: Welfare Reform and the Well-Being of Children and Families* (New York: Russell Sage Foundation, 2001).

7. Christopher J. Ruhm, "Parental Employment and Child Cognitive Development," *Journal of Human Resources* 39 (2004): 155–92.

8. Jack P. Shonkoff and Deborah A. Phillips, eds., *From Neurons to Neighborhoods: The Science of Early Childhood Development* (Washington, DC: National Academy Press, 2000); Rachel Lucas-Thompson, Wendy Goldberg, and JoAnn Prause, "Maternal Work Early in the Lives of Children and Its Distal Associations with Achievement and Behavior Problems: A Meta-Analysis," *Psychological Bulletin* 136 (2010): 915–42, doi: 10.1037/a0020875.

9. Mark H. Johnson, *Developmental Cognitive Neuroscience: An Introduction*, 2nd ed. (Oxford: Blackwell, 2005).

10. Jack P. Shonkoff et al., "Technical Report: The Lifelong Effects of Early Childhood Adversity and Toxic Stress," *Pediatrics* 129 (2012): e232–46, doi: 10.1542/peds.2011-2663.

11. Jay Belsky, "Emanuel Miller Lecture: Developmental Risks (Still) Associated with Early Childcare," *Journal of Child Psychology and Psychiatry* 42 (2001): 845–59.

12. P. Lindsay Chase-Lansdale and Margaret Tresch Owen, "Maternal Employment in a Family Context: Effects of Infant–Mother and Infant–Father Attachments," *Child Development* 58 (1987): 1505–12.

13. American Academy of Pediatrics, "Breastfeeding and the Use of Human Milk," *Pediatrics* 129 (2012): e827–41.

14. Paul A. Howard-Jones, Elizabeth V. Washbrook, and Sara Meadows, "The Timing of Educational Investment: A Neuroscientific Perspective," *Developmental Cognitive Neuroscience* 2 (2012): S18–29.

15. Shonkoff et al., "Lifelong Effects."

16. Waldfogel, *What Children Need*; Jeffrey Grogger and Lynn A. Karoly, *Welfare Reform: Effects of a Decade of Change* (Cambridge, MA: Harvard University Press, 2005).

17. Ann C. Crouter et al., "Linking Parents' Work Pressure and Adolescents' Well-Being: Insights into Dynamics in Dual-Earner Families," *Developmental Psychology* 35 (1999): 1453–61.

18. Martha J. Cox and Blair Paley, "Families as Systems," *Annual Review of Psychology* 48 (1997): 243–67, doi: 10.1146/annurev.psych.48.1.243.

19. Mark Evan Edwards, "Uncertainty and the Rise of the Work-Family Dilemma," *Journal of Marriage and Family* 63 (2001): 183–96.

20. Geraldine Downey and James C. Coyne, "Children of Depressed Parents: An Integrative Review," *Psychological Bulletin* 108 (1990): 50–76.

21. Gary S. Becker, *A Treatise on the Family* (Cambridge, MA: Harvard University Press, 1981).

22. Robert T. Michael, "Education and the Derived Demand for Children," *Journal of Political Economy* 81 (1973): S128–64.

23. Steven Nock and Paul W. Kingston, "Time with Children: The Impact of Couples' Work-Time Commitments," *Social Forces* 67 (1988): 59–85.

24. Grogger and Karoly, *Welfare Reform*.

25. Christopher J. Ruhm, "Are Workers Permanently Scarred by Job Displacements?" *American Economic Review* 81 (1991): 319–24.

26. Kerwin K. Charles and Melvin Stephens Jr., "Job Displacement, Disability, and Divorce," *Journal of Labor Economics* 22 (2004): 489–522.

27. Ruhm, "Parental Employment."

28. Shonkoff et al., "Lifelong Effects."

29. Lucas-Thompson, Goldberg, and Prause, "Maternal Work."

30. Ellen S. Peisner-Feinberg et al., "The Relation of Preschool Child-Care Quality to Children's Cognitive and Social Developmental Trajectories through Second Grade," *Child Development* 72 (2001): 1534–53; Deborah L. Vandell et al., "Do Effects of Early Child Care Extend to Age 15 Years? Results from the NICHD Study of Early Child Care and Youth Development," *Child Development* 81 (2010): 737–56, doi: 10.1111/j.1467-8624.2010.01431.x. NICHD Early Child Care Research Network and Greg Duncan, "Modeling the Impacts of Child Care Quality on Children's Preschool Cognitive Development," *Child Development* 74 (2003): 1454–75.

31. Elizabeth Harvey, "Short-Term and Long-Term Effects of Early Parental Employment on Children of the National Longitudinal Survey of Youth," *Developmental Psychology* 35 (1999): 445–59.

32. Raquel Bernal and Michael P. Keane, "Child Care Choices and Children's Cognitive Achievement: The Case of Single Mothers," *Journal of Labor Economics* 29 (2011): 459–512.

33. P. Lindsay Chase-Lansdale et al., "Mothers' Transitions from Welfare to Work and the Well-Being of Preschoolers and Adolescents," *Science* 299 (2003): 1548–52, doi: 10.1126/science.1076921.

34. Linda Datcher-Loury, "Effects of Mother's Home Time on Children's Schooling," *Review of Economics and Statistics* 70 (1988): 367–73.

35. Qian Liu and Oskar Nordström Skans, "The Duration of Paid Parental Leave and Children's Scholastic Performance," *B. E. Journal of Economic Analysis and Policy* 10, no. 1 (2010): Article 3.

36. Wendy A. Goldberg et al., "Maternal Employment and Children's Achievement in Context: A Meta-Analysis of Four Decades of Research," *Psychological Bulletin* 134 (2008): 77–108, doi: 10.1037/0033-2909.134.1.77; Vandell et al., "Effects of Early Child Care."

37. Jeanne Brooks-Gunn, Wen-Jui Han, and Jane Waldfogel, "Maternal Employment and Child Cognitive Outcomes in the First Three Years of Life: The NICHD Study of Early Child Care," *Child Development* 73 (2002): 1052–72.

38. Ruhm, "Parental Employment."

39. Michael Baker and Kevin Milligan, "Maternal Employment, Breastfeeding and Health: Evidence from Maternity Leave Mandates," *Journal of Health Economics* 27 (2008): 871–87.

40. Phyllis L. F. Rippeyoung and Mary C. Noonan, "Is Breastfeeding Truly Cost Free? Income Consequences of Breastfeeding for Women," *American Sociological Review* 77 (2012): 244–67, doi: 10.1177/0003122411435477.

41. James A. Levine and Todd L. Pittinsky, *Working Fathers: New Strategies for Balancing Work and Family* (New York: Harcourt Brace & Co., 1997).

42. Crouter et al., "Linking Parents' Work Pressure"; Mari Rege, Kjetil Telle, and Mark Votruba, "Parental Job Loss and Children's School Performance," *Review of Economic Studies* 78 (2011): 1462–89, doi: 10.1093/restud/rdr002; Phillip Oreopoulos, Marianne Page, and Ann Huff Stevens, "The Intergenerational Effects of Worker Displacement," *Journal of Labor Economics* 26 (2008): 455–83.

43. Maria Bacikova-Sleskova et al., "Parental Support and Adolescents' Health in the Context of Parental Employment Status," *Journal of Adolescence* 34 (2011): 141–9, doi: 10.1016/j.adolescence.2010.01.003.

44. Lucia Artazcoz et al., "Unemployment and Mental Health: Understanding the Interactions Among Gender, Family Roles and Social Class," *American Journal of Public Health* 94 (2004): 82–8; Rand D. Conger et al., "Husband and Wife Differences in Response to Undesirable Life Events," *Journal of Health and Social Behavior* 34 (1993): 71–88.

45. Ann Huff Stevens and Jessamyn Schaller, "Short-Run Effects of Parental Job Loss on Children's Academic Achievement," Economics of Education Review 30 (2011): 289–99, 10.1016/j.econedurev.2010.10.002.

46. Lyndall Strazdins et al., "Job Quality and Inequality: Parents' Jobs and Children's Emotional and Behavioural Difficulties," *Social Science & Medicine* 70 (2010): 2052–60, doi: 10.1016/j.socscimed.2010.02.041.

47. Lyndall Strazdins et al., "Unsociable Work? Non-Standard Work Schedules, Family Relationships, and Children's Well-Being," *Journal of Marriage and Family* 68 (2006): 394–410, doi: 10.1111/j.1741-3737.2006.00260.x.

48. Wen-Jui Han, "Shift Work and Child Behavioral Outcomes," *Work, Employment, and Society* 22 (2008): 67–87, doi: 10.1177/0950017007087417; Wen-Jui Han, Daniel P. Miller, and Jane Waldfogel, "Parental Work Schedules and Adolescent Risky Behavior," *Developmental Psychology* 46, No. 5 (2010): 1245–67, doi: 10.1037/a0020178.

49. Stephanie L. Champion et al., "Parental Work Schedules and Child Overweight and Obesity," International *Journal of Obesity* 36 (2012): 573–80, doi: 10.1038/ijo.2011.252.

50. Daniel P. Miller and Wen-Jui Han, "Maternal Nonstandard Work Schedules and Adolescent Overweight," *American Journal of Public Health* 98 (2008): 1495–1502, doi: 10.2105/AJPH.2007.123885.

51. Sara S. McLanahan, "Parent Absence or Poverty: Which Matters More?" in Greg J. Duncan and Jeanne Brooks-Gunn, eds., *Consequences of Growing up Poor* (New York: Russell Sage Foundation, 1997): 35–48.

52. Anne Roeters, Tanja Van Der Lippe, and Esther S. Kluwer, "Work Characteristics and Parent-Child Relationship Quality: The Mediating Role of Temporal Involvement," *Journal of Marriage and Family* 72 (2010): 1317–28, doi: 10.1111/j.1741-3737.2010.00767.x.

53. Ellen Galinsky and Judy David, *Ask the Children: What America's Children Really Think About Working Parents* (New York: William Morrow, 1999).

54. Organisation for Economic Co-operation and Development (OECD), "Mothers in Paid Employment," in *Society at a Glance 2006: OECD Social Indicators* (Paris: OECD Publishing, 2007): 173–211, doi: 10.1787/soc_glance-2006-10-en.

55. Daniel Engster and Helena Olofsdotter Stensöta, "Do Family Policy Regimes Matter for Children's Well-Being?" *Social Politics* 18 (2011): 82–124, doi: 10.1093/sp/jxr006; Lee Rainwater and Timothy Smeeding, *Poor Kids in a Rich Country: America's Children in Comparative Perspective* (New York: Russell Sage Foundation, 2003).

56. Nada Eissa and Hilary W. Hoynes, "Behavioral Responses to Taxes: Lessons from the EITC and Labor Supply," *Tax Policy and the Economy* 20 (2006): 73–110.

57. Greg J. Duncan, Pamela A. Morris, and Chris Rodrigues, "Does Money Really Matter? Estimating Impacts of Family Income on Young Children's Achievement with Data from Random-Assignment Experiments," *Developmental Psychology* 47 (2011): 1263–79, doi: 10.1037/a0023875; Raj Chetty, John N. Friedman, and Jonah Rockoff, *New Evidence on the Long-Term Impacts of Tax Credits* (Washington, DC: Internal Revenue Service, Statistics of Income Paper Series, 2011), www.irs.gov/pub/irs-soi/11rpchettyfriedmanrockoff.pdf.

58. Lawrence M. Berger, Christina Paxson, and Jane Waldfogel, "Income and Child Development," *Children and Youth Services Review* 31 (2009): 978–89, doi: 10.1016/j.childyouth.2009.04.013.

59. OECD, "Promoting Child Development"; Engster and Stensöta, "Family Policy Regimes."

60. Jody Heymann, *Forgotten Families: Ending the Growing Crisis Confronting Children and Working Parents in the Global Economy* (Oxford: Oxford University Press, 2006).

61. Christopher J. Ruhm, "Policies to Assist Parents with Young Children," *The Future of Children* 21, no. 2 (2011): 37–68.

62. Engster and Stensöta, "Family Policy Regimes"; Sakiko Tanaka, "Parental Leave and Child Health across OECD Countries," *Economic Journal* 115 (2005): F7–28, doi: 10.1111/j.0013-0133.2005.00970.x.

63. Christopher J. Ruhm, "Parental Leave and Child Health," *Journal of Health Economics* 19 (2000): 931–60.

64. Baker and Milligan, "Maternal Employment, Breastfeeding, and Health."

65. Maya Rossin-Slater, Christopher J. Ruhm, and Jane Waldfogel, "The Effects of California's Paid Family Leave Program on Mothers' Leave-Taking and Subsequent Labor Market Outcomes," *Journal of Policy Analysis and Management* 32 (2013): 224–45, doi: 10.1002/pam.21676.

66. Jean Kimmel and Emily P. Hoffman, eds., *The Economics of Work and Family* (Kalamazoo, MI: W. E. Upjohn Institute for Employment Research, 2002).

67. Ruhm, "Policies to Assist Parents."

68. Chris M. Herbst and Erdal Tekin, *The Impact of Child Care Subsidies on Child Well-Being: Evidence from Geographic Variation in the Distance to Social Service Agencies* (working paper, National Bureau of Economic Research, Cambridge, MA, August 2010), http://www.nber.org/papers/w16250.pdf.

69. Alison Earle, Zitha Mokomane, and Jody Heymann, "International Perspectives on Work-Family Policies: Lessons from the World's Most Competitive Economies," *The Future of Children* 21, no. 2 (2011): 191–210.

70. Ibid.

71. Council of Economic Advisers, *Work-Life Balance and the Economics of Workplace Flexibility* (Washington, DC: Executive Office of the President, 2010), www.whitehouse.gov/files/documents/100331-cea-economics-workplace-flexibility.pdf.

72. Vicky Lovell, *No Time to Be Sick: Why Everyone Suffers When Workers Don't Have Paid Sick Leave* (Washington, DC: Institute for Women's Policy Research, 2004), http://www.iwpr.org/publications/pubs/no-time-to-be-sick-why-everyone-suffers-when-workers-don2019t-have-paid-sick-leave.

73. Han, Miller, and Waldfogel, "Parental Work Schedules and Adolescent Risky Behavior."

74. Ruhm, "Policies to Assist Parents."

75. Rosalind C. Barnett, "Home-to-Work Spillover Revisited: A Study of Full-Time Employed Women in Dual-Earner Couples," *Journal of Marriage and Family*, 56 (1994): 647–56; Pedro Carneiro, Katrine V. Løken, and Kjell G. Salvanes, *A Flying Start? Maternity Leave Benefits and Long Run Outcomes of Children* (discussion paper, Institute for the Study of Labor [IZA], Bonn, Germany, 2011), http://ftp.iza.org/dp5793.pdf.

76. Carolyn J. Heinrich et al., "A Nonexperimental Evaluation of WIA Programs," in Douglas J. Besharov and Phoebe H. Cottingham, eds., *The Workforce Investment Act: Implementation Experiences and Evaluation Findings* (Kalamazoo, MI: W. E. Upjohn Institute, 2011): 371–406.

77. Ariel Kalil and Patrick Wightman, "Parental Job Loss and Children's Educational Attainment in Black and White Middle-Class Families," *Social Science Quarterly* 92, (2011): 57–78; Ramsay Liem and Paula Rayman, "Health and Social Costs of Unemployment: Research and Policy Considerations," *American Psychologist* 37 (1982): 1116–23.

78. Steve Holt, *Ten Years of the EITC Movement: Making Work Pay Then and Now* (Washington, DC: Metropolitan Policy Program at Brookings, 2011), http://www.brookings.edu/~/media/research/files/papers/2011/4/18%20eitc%20holt/0418_eitc_holt.pdf.

79. Urban Institute and Brookings Institution Tax Policy Center, "Taxation and the Family: What is the Earned Income Tax Credit?" in *The Tax Policy Briefing Book: A Citizens' Guide for the 2012 Election and Beyond* (2012), http://www.taxpolicycenter.org/briefing-book/key-elements/family/eitc.cfm.

80. Christian Dustmann and Uta Schonberg, "Expansions in Maternity Leave Coverage and Children's Long-Term Outcomes," *American Economic Journal: Applied Economics* 4, no. 3 (2011): 190–224, doi: 10.1257/app.4.3.190.

81. David Blau, "Federal Child Care Policy: An Evaluation and Proposal for Reform," in Jean Kimmel and Emily P. Hoffman, eds., *The Economics of Work and Family* (Kalamazoo, MI: W. E. Upjohn Institute for Employment Research, 2002): 7–42.

82. U.S. Bureau of Labor Statistics, "Employee Benefits in the United States—March 2012," news release, July 11, 2012, http://www.bls.gov/news.release/ebs2.nr0.htm.

83. Earle, Mokomane, and Heymann, "International Perspectives"; S. Jody Heymann, Sara Toomey, and Frank Furstenberg, "Working Parents: What Factors Are Involved in Their Ability to Take Time Off from Work When Their Children Are Sick?" *Archives of Pediatrics and Adolescent Medicine* 153 (1999): 870–74.

84. U.S. Bureau of Labor Statistics, "Employee Benefits."

85. Robert Turner, "Fringe Benefits," in Joseph J. Cordes, Robert D. Ebel, and Jane G. Gravelle, eds., *The Encyclopedia of Taxation and Tax Policy* (Washington, DC: Urban Institute Press, 1999); Eric J. Toder and Karen E. Smith, "Do Low-Income Workers Benefit from 401(k) Plans?" (working paper, Center for Retirement Research at Boston College, October 3, 2011), doi: 10.2139/ssrn.1937795.

86. Jeffrey Kling, *Fundamental Restructuring of Unemployment Insurance: Wage-Loss Insurance and Temporary Earnings Replacement Accounts* (policy brief, Brookings Institution Hamilton Project, September 2006), http://www.brookings.edu/~/media/research/files/papers/2006/9/unemployment%20 kling/200609kling_pb.pdf.

87. P. Lindsay Chase-Lansdale and Jeanne Brooks-Gunn, "Two-Generation Programs in the Twenty-First Century," *Future of Children* 24, no. 1 (2014): 13–40; Robert G. St. Pierre, Jean I. Layzer, and Helen V. Barnes, "Two-Generation Programs: Design, Cost, and Short-Term Effectiveness," *Future of Children* 5, no. 3 (1995): 76–93.

88. Ray Marshall Center for the Study of Human Resources, *Dual Generation Strategy Initiative* (research brief, University of Texas, Lyndon B. Johnson School of Public Affairs, February 2012), http://www.utexas. edu/research/cshr/pubs/pdf/Dual-Gen_Research_Brief.FINAL.3-19-12.pdf.

89. JoAnn Hsueh and Mary E. Farrell, *Enhanced Early Head Start with Employment Services: 42-Month Impacts from the Kansas and Missouri Sites of the Enhanced Services for the Hard-to-Employ Demonstration and Evaluation Project* (Washington, DC: U.S. Department of Health and Human Services, Administration for Children and Families, Office of Planning, Research and Evaluation, 2012).

Family Assets and Child Outcomes: Evidence and Directions

Michal Grinstein-Weiss, Trina R. Williams Shanks, and Sondra G. Beverly

For poor families, the possession of assets—savings accounts, homes, and the like—has the potential not only to relieve some of the stress of living in poverty but also to make a better future seem like a real possibility. If children in families that own certain assets fare better than children in families without them, then helping poor families build those assets would be an effective strategy for two-generation programs.

Indeed, write Michal Grinstein-Weiss, Trina Williams Shanks, and Sondra Beverly, plenty of evidence shows that assets are connected to positive outcomes for poor children. For example, young people who have any college savings at all, even a very small amount, are more likely to go to college; children in households with assets score higher on standardized achievement tests; and children of homeowners experience fewer behavioral problems. But this evidence comes from longitudinal data sets and is therefore correlational.

Looking for causal relationships, the authors examine the results of experimental programs that opened various types of savings accounts for poor people and matched their contributions. Several of these trials included a control group that did not receive a savings account, making it possible to attribute any positive outcomes directly to the savings accounts rather than to their owners' personal characteristics. These programs dispelled the myth that poor people can't save; participants were generally able to accumulate savings. It's too early to tell, however, whether assets and asset-building programs have long-term effects on children's wellbeing, though one experiment found positive impacts on disadvantaged children's social-emotional development at age four. The most promising programs share several features: they are opened early in life; they are opened automatically, with no action required from the recipients; and they come with an initial deposit.

www.futureofchildren.org

Michal Grinstein-Weiss is an associate professor of social work and associate director of the Center for Social Development at Washington University in St. Louis. Trina R. Williams Shanks is an associate professor of social work and a faculty associate of the Institute for Social Research's Survey Research Center at the University of Michigan. Sondra Beverly is a senior scholar at the Center for Social Development at Washington University in St. Louis. The authors wish to thank Margaret Clancy, Krista Holub, Clint Key, and Michael Sherraden for helpful comments; Jenna Tucker for help summarizing the evidence on college savings; Liz S. Lee for invaluable help throughout the process; and Chris Leiker and Diane Wyant for excellent editing.

Michal Grinstein-Weiss, Trina R. Williams Shanks, and Sondra G. Beverly

O ver the past 20 years, scholars have noted that assets have benefits beyond those associated with income and that U.S. asset policies disproportionately benefit economically secure families. Several initiatives have emerged to enable low-income families to accumulate assets. In this article, we consider two questions: whether family assets improve children's wellbeing, and, if they do, whether asset-building programs increase saving and assets, leading to improvements in the wellbeing of children from low-income families.

Evidence strongly suggests that children who grow up in families with assets are better off than children who grow up in families without them. But we need more research to determine how much of this pattern is due to asset holding and how much is due to family and other characteristics that typically accompany asset holding. Evidence also indicates that asset-building programs can increase family assets and psycho-social outcomes, though we need to learn more about the extent and nature of these impacts and the pathways through which they work. The evidence discussed below shows that the greatest potential benefits to low-income children come from programs with automatic, universal features—for example, programs that automatically open an account for a child when he or she is born and provide automatic deposits.

Assets as Financial Resources

A central premise of asset-building research has been that poverty and wellbeing are not determined solely by income.[1] Many families spend much of their income on short-term consumption, but assets are different. They function as both a stock of resources for the future and a safety net. Assets can finance investments that are difficult to make with income alone—for example, in education, a home, or a small business.

Measuring Assets

Assets come in different forms and can be measured in many ways. Researchers sometimes examine asset ownership alone (that is, whether a family holds a particular asset). But if the data allow, they consider the value of assets. To measure the value of total assets, researchers combine the value of financial assets (for example, stocks, pensions, and funds in bank accounts) with the value of tangible, nonfinancial assets (for example, homes, businesses, and vehicles). Net worth, an assessment of both assets and liabilities, is typically measured as the value of assets minus debts. To capture immediately available resources, some examine narrower measures of *liquid* assets—that is, measures of assets that can be quickly converted to cash. In this article, we consider a variety of assets but focus on special savings accounts and the funds they hold.

Children in families with assets are much more likely to be protected from the most severe consequences of financial crisis.

Distribution of Assets

In the United States, the distribution of assets is highly skewed by income and race. In 2010, the median net worth was more than $286,000 for households in the highest fifth of the income distribution and less than $6,200 for households in the lowest fifth.[2] In

2009, the typical African Amerian household had just $5,677 in net worth and the typical Hispanic household had $6,325 while the typical white household had $113,149.[3]

Recognizing the value of assets for families and society, state and federal governments have created policies that promote asset building. The federal government spends more than $500 billion per year on such policies, but they are extremely regressive (for example, the home-mortgage interest deduction and 401(k) retirement plans primarily help people who have enough assets and income to benefit from reducing their tax liability).[4] In 2009, the bottom 60 percent of taxpayers received only 4 percent of the federal budget for asset-building programs.[5] Some programs have emerged in response to growing wealth inequality and policies that disproportionately benefit the economically secure. These programs seek to help low- and moderate-income (LMI) families build assets. These programs are intended to complement, not replace, programs that boost income. They are grounded in theories about the effects of assets, and also in a political economic view of fairness in public policy—if we use public resources to support asset building, these expenditures should include the whole population.

Pathways: How Assets May Help Parents Help Children

As other articles in this issue demonstrate, human development is a complex process influenced by many factors. The cumulative effect of these factors is more influential than the effect of any single one, even persistent income poverty or asset poverty.[6] However, the effects of assets and asset poverty may be understudied and underestimated. We suggest four pathways by which assets may affect children's wellbeing.

Pathway 1: Assets May Provide a Cushion

Assets, especially liquid assets, commonly lessen the impact of hardship or distress. Without a cushion to protect a family, a financial crisis may trigger a series of negative events. For example, if a vehicle breaks down and the family can't afford to fix it, lack of transportation may lead to job loss. Families may create a vicious cycle of debt by using expensive financial services (for example, payday loans and subprime credit cards) to solve short-run crises.[7] Financial crises can also make it difficult for families to pay rent, forcing them to move and to experience real stress in the process. Moving children to new neighborhoods and schools is disruptive and potentially harmful. Moreover, even a minor crisis can trigger substantial reductions in a family's standard of living. These experiences may undermine children's wellbeing, either directly or by reducing the quality of parent-child interaction. Children in families with assets are much more likely to be protected from the most severe consequences of financial crisis.[8]

Pathway 2: Assets May Reduce Parental Stress

Even families that have not encountered a financial crisis may experience economic pressure.[9] Parents may worry, for example, about not having enough to pay bills and meet their children's basic needs. Parents try but sometimes fail to minimize the effects of stress; children may bear the brunt. Stress can increase marital conflict, decrease marital warmth, and reduce parental nurturing. For children, these conditions can lead to poor cognitive development, poor social interactions, poor health, and poor academic performance.[10] As Ross Thompson writes in this issue of *Future of Children*, high levels of daily stress can disrupt a child's brain architecture and hamper development. We theorize that assets offer a sense of security and limit the effects of parental stress, thereby increasing the likelihood that household interactions will be positive.

Housing is also relevant. Some families can afford to purchase homes in safe neighborhoods with good schools and municipal services. Owning or renting in neighborhoods with high crime rates, inadequate schools, and poor services likely exposes families to stress.[11]

Pathway 3: Assets May Help Parents Invest in Children

The first two pathways highlight the value of contingency savings and the economic security that assets can provide, but assets also let families invest in children; parents' wealth influences children's educational and occupational opportunities.[12] For example, low-income families with a small stock of assets may be able to pay for a summer camp that is out of other families' reach. Families with greater wealth can make greater investments in their children. Those able to purchase homes in "good" neighborhoods can give children access to good schools and other desirable resources that often have large, lasting effects on mobility and life chances.[13]

Pathway 4: Assets May Change Attitudes and Expectations

Michael Sherraden has hypothesized that assets change attitudes, creating an orientation toward the future and increasing personal efficacy (attitudes can also influence the accumulation of assets).[14] As Marcia Shobe and Deborah Page-Adams write, assets may "provide people with otherwise unattainable opportunities to hope, plan, and

dream about the future for themselves and their children."[15] The opportunity to envision the future may be especially powerful for low-income families forced by resource constraints to focus on day-to-day living. Envisioning, working toward, and achieving a goal may increase hope and future orientation, producing other changes in attitudes and behaviors.[16] Also, the basic financial knowledge and skills associated with owning simple accounts and assets may affect financial attitudes (for example, about banks and budgeting) as well as expectations about the financial future.

Empirical work supports Sherraden's hypothesis that assets increase personal efficacy and future orientation (and vice versa).[17] Research has shown that parents with assets have higher expectations for their children's education than do parents without assets.[18] We theorize that parents who are hopeful and thoughtful about the future interact with children and others differently than do parents with other outlooks. For example, parents who have higher expectations for their children's education are probably more likely to support children's academic development, talk more about higher education, and engage more with teachers and schools.

Evidence from National Data Sets

National data sets began to collect reliable data on assets in the early 1980s, but these data provide only correlational evidence; relationships should not be interpreted as causal.[19] Elsewhere in this article, we summarize evidence from experiments that test causality.

Wealth and Children's Outcomes

Early studies found that income from investments and assets better predicts children's test scores and years of education than does income from other sources.[20] Dalton Conley tested the hypothesis that most racial disparities in children's outcomes are actually class differences, defined primarily by wealth. Using data from the Panel Study of Income Dynamics (PSID), he found that parents' net worth predicts a young adult's net worth and that parents' education is the strongest predictor of how far their children will go in school. The value of equity in the parents' primary residence, the net value of their businesses, and the value of their liquid assets are also strong predictors of whether their children will go to college.[21]

Later studies confirm that household assets are associated with children's academic performance and educational outcomes. Data from the PSID show that parents' net worth is positively associated with applied problem (math) scores for children aged 3–12.[22] Data from the National Longitudinal Survey of Youth show a similar relationship between household assets and math achievement scores.[23] Verbal achievement scores are better among children in households with assets than among those in households with no assets.[24] Building on his earlier work, Conley found that family net worth is significantly associated with the total number of years children spend in school; a doubling of assets is associated with an 8.3 percentage-point increase in a child's chances of going to college. If the child enrolls in college, a doubling of family assets increases the chance that he or she will graduate by 5.6 percentage points.[25] Other studies have shown similar results.

A few studies suggest that household wealth plays a role in health and socioemotional outcomes. One of the authors of this article, Trina Williams Shanks, used the PSID Child Development Supplement to examine how assets affect behaviors measured with the Behavior Problem Index.[26] She found that the number of behavior problems declines as family net worth grows but that it increases with increases in families' credit-card and other unsecured debt. Other researchers have found that parental saving for a child's college expenses before the child's first birthday is positively associated with his or her self-esteem at age 23.[27]

Homeownership and Children's Outcomes

Some researchers have specifically considered how family homeownership affects children. Family homeownership is positively associated with children's academic performance and chances of graduating from high school, and it is negatively associated with the chances of teenage and out-of-wedlock childbearing.[28] Children of homeowners are less likely than children of renters to experience emotional and behavioral problems, including depression.[29] But some have noted that the duration of homeowning (or residential stability), not whether parents own or rent, is likely the more relevant predictor of behavioral problems.[30]

Some have questioned the benefits of homeownership, noting that few studies recognized potential risks such as neighborhood selection, difficulty in meeting mortgage payments, and mortgage default.[31] Others have argued that homeownership studies may be biased by unobserved differences between homeowners and renters, such as personality traits that help people successfully navigate the mortgage process.[32]

The effects of homeownership seem to differ by race and ethnicity. One study found that homeownership is positively associated with academic outcomes for low-income white children and reading comprehension scores for low-income Hispanic children but that neither association holds for African American children.[33] These findings suggest that researchers should routinely consider who benefits most from homeownership and under what circumstances.

Regardless of homeownership's effects on children's outcomes, helping adult children buy their first home is a common way for parents to transfer wealth to the next generation. This intergenerational transmission significantly influences whether families transition to homeownership.[34] Four percent of first-time home buyers finance all of their down payment with funds from relatives, and 20 percent receive some such help. Among buyers who receive family help, such gifts account for 50 percent of the average down payment.[35]

College Savings and Children's Outcomes

Some data sets allow researchers to distinguish overall household wealth from money set aside in a child's name for future schooling. Money set aside in this way raises children's and parents' college expectations and helps affirm a college-bound identity (meaning that children see college as a possibility). Such savings link current activities to a future goal, making college seem relevant and important, and perhaps improving persistence in school.[36]

Analyzing PSID data, researchers found that 81 percent of adolescents with college savings expect to graduate from college but that only 39 percent of those without college savings expect this.[37] Parents' and young people's college savings during the children's teenage years predict whether, as young adults, the

children will attend and finish college; this relationship seems to work via educational expectations.[38] College savings and educational expectations appear to work in tandem. By itself, neither appears to have any effect on whether a child will attend college. Yet adolescents who have both college savings and high expectations are significantly more likely than others to attend college.[39] Furthermore, college savings and expectations may work in a virtuous circle: the presence of one may increase the other over time.[40]

The size of young people's college savings does not necessarily make a difference. One researcher controlled for the amount of savings in an account, finding that adolescents with any college savings at all are more likely to go to college than are those without such savings. Adolescents with between $1 and $499 in such savings were significantly more likely to graduate. Because college savings under $500 cannot substantially defray the cost of a degree, the researcher concluded that the effects of college savings are likely psychological.[41]

Evidence from Short-Term Asset-Building Programs

The findings from national data sets suggest a plausible link between assets—wealth, homeownership, and college savings—and children's outcomes, but these studies cannot prove causality. Studies summarized below provide stronger evidence by comparing participants in an asset-building program with nonparticipants. Because some of these groups were formed by randomly assigning people to one group or the other, the groups are similar, and comparisons let researchers estimate what would have happened without a program.

Individual Development Accounts

Individual Development Accounts (IDAs) were the central feature of the first asset-building program offered to low-income individuals in the United States. Developed in response to asset-building policies that favor high-income households, the original proposal saw IDAs as universal, progressive, lifelong savings plans that would begin as early as birth. However, they have been implemented in the United Sates as short-term savings programs for low-income adults and youth.[42] These programs aim to help participants accumulate assets as a way to increase long-term wellbeing and financial self-sufficiency.[43] Participants are encouraged to save money in IDAs, and they receive matching funds when they withdraw savings to purchase a home, pay for college or job training, or invest in a microenterprise. The programs usually require participants to attend financial-education classes. Also, IDA case managers steer participants to other support programs that can help them clear debts, build or repair credit, and claim tax credits (for example, the Earned Income Tax Credit). Matching rates vary, but they are typically one to one or two to one (that is, $1 or $2 of matching funds for every $1 saved); the funds come from federal or foundation grants.

Over the past two decades, the popularity of IDAs has grown rapidly here and abroad. In 1998, Congress established the Assets for Independence Program (AFI). From 1999 through 2010, the Department of Health and Human Services awarded approximately $190 million in grants to fund more than 68,000 IDAs.[44]

American Dream Demonstration. The American Dream Demonstration (ADD) was the first large-scale test of IDAs in the United States. Between 1998 and 2002, more than 2,000 LMI individuals participated in 14 privately funded local IDA programs. The demonstration used a variety of research methods, including a random-assignment experiment with more than 1,100 people at the IDA program in Tulsa, Oklahoma.

Adolescents with any college savings at all are more likely to go to college than are those without such savings.

Members of the experiment's control group were not eligible to participate in the IDA program at the Tulsa ADD site during the four years of the study but could receive homeownership counseling and referrals to other agencies. The treatment group could receive an IDA, financial education, and case management. Treatment participants who opened IDAs earned matches for their deposits: two to one for home purchases and one to one for home repairs, small business investment, postsecondary education, or retirement savings. Account holders could make unmatched withdrawals at any time. Over the program's three years, participants who saved enough to earn the maximum match could accumulate $6,750 (plus interest) for a home purchase or $4,500 (plus interest) for the other qualified uses.

Do IDA Programs Increase Saving and Wealth? Because IDA programs support short-term saving for particular purchases, most studies of the ADD examine assets purchased by participants. But data on saving in IDAs can also be revealing. Many assume that the poor cannot save, but ADD data show that they can and do save in IDAs. The average ADD participant deposited $16.60 (after withdrawals) per month, saved about 42 cents for every dollar eligible for a match, and deposited money in the IDA about every other month. From the start of the demonstration until its end (December 31, 2001), participants saved an average of $32.44 each month and, with an average match rate of about two to one, accumulated an average of $1,609 in IDAs.[45]

Many assume that the poor cannot save, but ... they can and do save in IDAs.

Patterns of saving in IDAs can be explained mostly by program characteristics, such as the monthly cap on the amount eligible for matching funds, the availability of direct deposit, and financial education, and not by the individual's characteristics.[46] It is important to note that all IDA holders in the ADD chose to sign up for the program and so probably saved more than typical low-income people would have.

Three studies examined the Tulsa IDA program's effect on wealth, which they measured as net worth (assets minus debts), not just savings in IDAs. Findings were mixed: One study found that IDAs do not increase wealth.[47] The other two adjusted for outliers (cases with unusual asset and liability values) and found the opposite.[48] Research on net worth is commonly subject to errors in participants' reports on assets and liabilities. These errors make it difficult to detect changes in net worth.[49]

Two more studies examined how IDAs affect various aspects of household wealth. One evaluated the Canadian *Learn$ave* demonstration, the largest IDA experiment to date, which randomly assigned nearly 5,000 people to treatment or control groups. Though it had no significant effect on net worth and total savings, *Learn$ave* affected the overall composition of participants' financial assets. Treatment participants had higher average bank account balances and lower retirement savings than did control-group members. It seems that treatment participants saved more at the beginning and then later drew on those savings to invest in education or a small business, and that may have led to the lower retirement savings among treatment participants. In addition, treatment participants were more likely to set financial goals and make household budgets.[50] Another study analyzed data to compare Assets for Independence IDA participants with a control group drawn from the 2001 Survey of Income and Program Participation, comprising people who shared similar demographic characteristics. It found that the AFI IDA program did not affect savings, home equity, or consumer debt.[51]

In sum, the evidence suggests that short-term IDA programs do not increase overall savings or wealth, with the caveat that survey data from these studies may be flawed. However, because IDA programs aim to support short-term saving for specific purchases, we would not expect IDAs to produce large increases in savings or wealth. It is worth noting that, despite their low incomes, ADD IDA participants saved about $200 per year in IDAs. It's also noteworthy that an IDA program increases financial goal-setting, ongoing saving, and budgeting.

Do IDA Programs Increase Asset Purchases? Evidence suggests that they do. Data show that *Learn*$ave increased enrollment in training and education programs.[52] The AFI study indicates that rates of homeownership, business ownership, and enrollment in postsecondary education are higher for treatment participants than for a comparison group.[53] Also, evidence identifies differences between IDA home buyers and other low-income home buyers: the former receive loans with more favorable terms and more often make loan payments on time.[54]

Evaluations of ADD indicate that, by the Tulsa IDA program's end, homeownership increased among people who rented when the program began.[55] The increase was 7–11 percentage points larger among those in the treatment group than among counterparts in the control group.

Ten years after random assignment, and six years after the ADD IDA program ended, study participants at the Tulsa site completed follow-up surveys. Over the decade, homeownership increased for both the treatment and control groups. Growth continued into the housing crisis that began with the Great Recession in 2007, but the control group caught up, and the difference in homeownership rates was no longer statistically significant. In addition, researchers observed effects for certain subgroups. The program increased both rates and duration of homeownership among participants whose annual income at the start of the program exceeded the median for the sample ($15,384). However, other subgroup analyses identified no differences, so this could be a random result. Some participants were homeowners when the program began, and the value of treatment members' homes rose more than that of control members' homes. Treatment participants were less likely to forgo needed repairs and provided significantly lower estimates of the cost of unmade repairs, indicating that some of their IDA savings went into home repair, which was an allowed use.[56]

ADD also had a noteworthy effect on the education of adults in the treatment group. In the 10 years from the program's inception to the follow-up survey, rates of enrollment in any educational program were higher for adults in the treatment group than for counterparts in the control group, even though only 7.6 percent of treatment participants reported using an IDA for education.[57] Treatment participation did not affect level of education or degree completion. But among those who reported a high-school education or less when they entered the program, ADD increased the likelihood of gaining some college. In addition, the positive impact on several education outcomes (likelihood of enrollment, acquisition of a degree or certificate, increase in educational level) was larger for males than for females. Given the declining educational attainment of low-income males and the growing attainment gap between low-income males and low-income females, this is an important finding.

Do IDA Programs Affect Parents and Children? In in-depth interviews, ADD participants reported generally positive effects.[58] They said that having an IDA increased their feelings of short- and long-term security, self-confidence, and hope for the future, as well as their ability to set and achieve goals and their sense of responsibility. They also reported heightened civic attitudes (for example, acting altruistically, engaging in the community, and helping others) and reduced levels of stress. Over 40 percent of IDA participants with children reported feeling reassured that their savings would help to pay for their children's education, improve their children's living environment, or generally provide for their children's future. Others said that participation helped them to teach their children good money-management habits and how to save. Some couples reported that they argued less because both agreed on savings goals. The choice between providing for children's current needs and saving for their future weighed heavily on parents, especially those in very poor families. Evidence suggests that families put children's basic needs first and focus on saving only after children's needs are met.[59]

Overall, participants have positive feelings about their IDAs. Setting and achieving financial goals can be powerful experiences. Building assets can help people see themselves differently and may lead others to view them with respect. Short-term evidence shows that participants indeed save money and purchase assets, particularly homes. But long-term follow-up evidence, collected several years after the IDA program ended, is not as favorable regarding homeownership. IDAs were proposed not as short-term savings projects, but rather as lifelong accounts. If LMI families had lifelong accounts instead of short-term ones, the effects on education, homeownership, child wellbeing, and other outcomes might be different.

Evidence on LMI Homeownership: Community Advantage Program

Begun in 1998, the Community Advantage Program (CAP) was a policy demonstration project designed to make homeownership possible for LMI households. It has provided evidence of LMI homeownership's effects on a host of outcomes. The project has helped more than 46,000 LMI households buy homes by underwriting 30-year fixed-rate mortgages for borrowers who otherwise would have received a subprime mortgage or been unable to purchase a home. Borrowers put little or nothing down and received near-prime interest rates. To qualify for a CAP loan, applicants met stringent eligibility criteria.[60] Most homeownership research focuses on middle- and higher-income households; CAP provides one of the first opportunities to study how homeownership affects LMI households.[61]

The Center for Community Capital evaluated CAP, interviewing 3,700 CAP homeowners in 1998, shortly after they purchased homes. The center began follow-up interviews in 2003 and has conducted them annually since. To identify the effects of homeownership and to examine the transition from renting to ownership, the center has also interviewed a comparison group of nearly 1,500 renters who met CAP income guidelines and lived in the same neighborhoods as CAP homeowners. However, the center did not randomly assign participants to a treatment or comparison group, and important differences probably remain between the groups. The CAP evaluation offers the best available data on the impact of LMI homeownership programs.

Did CAP Increase Assets? Evidence showed that CAP homeowners made substantial financial gains and generally fared well even during the housing crisis. By the fourth quarter of 2012, the median annual increase in the price of CAP homes was 1 percent and the median annual return on equity was 22 percent. Since receiving loans, CAP homeowners have seen a median increase in equity of about $18,000.[62] Also, most kept up with their mortgage payments: rates of delinquency and default were 10–20 percentage points lower than the rates for subprime loans in the same period.[63] One of the authors of this article, Michal Grinstein-Weiss, working with a group of colleagues, compared CAP homeowners and renters; she found that, between 2005 and 2008, CAP homeowners saw greater increases in net worth and assets.[64] Other researchers extended the analysis to compare the 2010 net worth of owners and renters who were in the same income categories in 2005.[65] In each income group, homeowners had a significantly higher net worth after five years. The results were the same when the two groups were divided into categories by their 2005 wealth rather than by their 2005 income, suggesting that the housing investment protected the wealth of CAP homeowners through the financial crisis better than renting protected the wealth of renters.

The choice between providing for children's current needs and saving for their future weighed heavily on parents, especially those in very poor families. Evidence suggests that families put children's basic needs first and focus on saving only after children's needs are met.

Did CAP Affect Parents and Children?
Three studies examined differences between CAP homeowners and renters in parents' behaviors and children's outcomes. The results are mixed. One found that LMI homeownership is not associated with parental attitudes and behaviors, but another identified several beneficial effects, including a greater likelihood that parents would read to their children and that children would participate in organized activities.[66] The third study indicated that homeownership's effects on child behavior increase with urban density.[67] Together, these findings suggest that homeownership has limited effects on parents' behaviors but some effect on children's behaviors, particularly when the home is in an urban area.

Additional evidence from CAP suggests that LMI homeownership is associated with individual- and community-level benefits. Therefore, homeownership may indirectly affect children. For example, CAP homeowners had greater access to social capital than did renters; the homeowners belonged to more neighborhood groups and were connected to more people who could help in a time of need.[68] Also, CAP homeowners were less likely to experience mental-health problems and to live in neighborhoods where crime was seen as a problem.[69]

In summary, early findings from CAP do not provide strong evidence that the parenting behaviors of CAP homeowners are better than those of counterparts who rent. Nor is there strong evidence that CAP participation leads to better outcomes for children.

Evidence from Child Development Account Programs
Child Development Account (CDA) programs are designed to support long-term—even lifelong—asset building. Like IDAs, CDAs are special savings or investment accounts for developmental purposes, such as the

purchase of supplemental childhood education, postsecondary education, a home, or a business. However, CDAs differ from IDAs in important ways.

Proposals for CDAs envision special accounts that are opened early, automatically, and with a sizable initial deposit. For example, CDAs could be opened automatically at birth for every child born in the United States and could receive an initial deposit of $500–$1,000. Also, a CDA is meant to be a lifelong development tool that is held and used for multiple purposes. Like IDAs, CDAs are designed to be progressive: the greatest incentives go to the most disadvantaged. Some CDA programs offer low-income people initial seed deposits, matches on deposits, and deposits at certain milestones, such as when the child enters kindergarten or graduates from high school.[70]

Most CDA programs so far focus on saving for postsecondary education, and many make use of existing state 529 college-savings plans (that is, special tax-favored investment accounts for higher education). CDAs may influence education-related attitudes and behaviors of both parents and children. These attitudes and behaviors may in turn influence educational outcomes, including postsecondary education and training.

With William Elliott and Michael Sherraden, one of the authors of this article, Sondra Beverly, has suggested several pathways through which CDAs might shape education-related attitudes, behaviors, and achievements. First, a CDA might make parents and children feel that college is important and expected. Second, it might make them feel that planning and saving for college are important. Third, a CDA might give parents and children a place to deposit money when they are motivated and able to save for college. Fourth, CDAs might increase the financial capability of parents and children. If some or all of these pathways exist, CDAs might encourage parents and children to view the children as college bound.[71]

This issue of *Future of Children* emphasizes two-generation programs, and all of the pathways we propose for CDAs influence youth directly and indirectly through their parents. Moreover, the pathways do not operate solely through accumulation of assets. Owning a college-savings account sets the stage for future asset accumulation. And, as we have seen, some research suggests that simply having an account may affect educational outcomes, regardless of how much money is in it. Nor do the pathways operate solely through individual behavior: positive impacts may occur even if accounts are opened and assets are deposited automatically, as long as parents and children know that the accounts and assets exist.[72] As children age, parents might use a CDA to model goal-setting, budgeting, and saving for their children, in preparation for the time when the children take ownership of the account.[73] Two large-scale CDA demonstrations in the United States have provided important evidence: the Saving for Education, Entrepreneurship, and Downpayment (SEED) national initiative and SEED for Oklahoma Kids (SEED OK).

The SEED National Initiative
The SEED national initiative was a multi-method test of asset-building accounts implemented for youth through 12 community-based organizations. The initiative gave SEED sites flexibility in designing programs and targeted groups of youth who were diverse in terms of age, race, ethnicity, and region.[74]

One SEED site in the Detroit area was selected for a large study called Michigan SEED (MI SEED). The site included 14 Head Start centers. Researchers identified the demographic characteristics of families in each center and matched centers with similar characteristics to create seven matched pairs. They randomly assigned one center in each pair to the treatment group and the other to the comparison group. Parents of children enrolled in the treatment centers were encouraged to open a CDA—specifically, a Michigan 529 college-savings account (SEED account). Because SEED provided an $800 initial deposit, the child's account was eligible for a $200 match from the state. In addition, the SEED program provided a one-to-one match, up to $1,200, for personal deposits into the account. If the family saved up to the $1,200 match cap, the account would hold $3,400 at the end of the four-year program. Treatment-group parents were also offered financial education sessions and case management. Families in the comparison group received no information on 529 accounts, were not eligible for the initial deposit or the savings match, and were offered no financial education or case management. Data on MI SEED come from quarterly account information, a 2004 baseline survey with parents, and a 2008 follow-up with them. Because they were enrolled in Head Start programs, we know that most MI SEED families had low incomes.[75]

SEED OK

SEED OK differs from the SEED national initiative in important ways. In SEED OK, CDAs were opened for newborns and were opened automatically unless parents opted out. In addition, households invited to participate in the study were selected from the population of households with newborns in Oklahoma, and individuals, not Head Start centers, were randomly assigned to the treatment or the control group.[76]

In collaboration with SEED OK, the state treasurer's office opened an Oklahoma 529 College Savings Plan account for every child in the treatment group. SEED OK deposited $1,000 into each account. These special Oklahoma 529 accounts—the SEED OK accounts—hold all deposits from SEED OK and are owned by the state of Oklahoma; withdrawals may be used only for the named beneficiary's postsecondary education. Promotional materials and a time-limited $100 incentive encouraged treatment-group parents to open and save in a separate Oklahoma 529 account for their infant's college expenses. In addition, SEED OK offered LMI families a one-to-one or one-half–to–one savings match on personal deposits into the account (up to a maximum match of $250 per year). Parents in the control group received no information from SEED OK about Oklahoma 529 accounts, were not eligible for the special SEED OK account or initial deposit, and were offered no SEED OK financial incentive. However, they could open their own Oklahoma 529 account, as can any U.S. citizen. Data on SEED OK come from account records, birth certificates, two survey waves, and in-depth interviews with a subsample of participants. More than two-thirds of SEED OK participants had household income below twice the federal poverty level.[77]

Do CDA Programs Increase Account Holding?

It is relevant to ask whether CDA programs affect account holding because, as we have seen, owning a college-savings account may shape the education-related attitudes and behaviors of parents and children—perhaps even if accounts are opened automatically. In both MI SEED and SEED OK, treatment-group families were more likely than comparison families to have 529 accounts. By about 15 months after SEED OK began, 99.9 percent of the treatment-group children had a state-owned SEED OK account in their name (one mother opted out, citing religious reasons), compared to none of the control-group children. In addition, 16 percent of treatment participants and 1 percent of control participants had opened their own Oklahoma 529 accounts for their child.[78]

Economically secure parents are more likely than disadvantaged ones to open their own 529 accounts. By about 30 months after SEED OK began, high-income treatment parents (incomes at or above 400 percent of the federal poverty guideline) were 4.5 times as likely as their low-income counterparts (incomes below 200 percent of poverty) to have opened an Oklahoma 529 account for their child. The difference was even greater among control-group parents, who were not eligible for SEED OK incentives.[79] In MI SEED, all families had low incomes, and case managers had to meet one-on-one with parents to encourage them to open accounts. Acceptance was slow, despite the fact that opening an account triggered a $1,000 deposit.[80]

As we note above, opening accounts automatically increases account holding. Automatic opening also eliminates variation in access to accounts by socioeconomic status. Although these observations may seem obvious, they have important ramifications: a CDA program with automatic account opening brings the potential benefits of CDAs to all families,

and it does so without the expense of outreach and account-opening incentives.

Do CDA Programs Increase Savings and Asset Accumulation?

What do we know about how CDA programs affect accumulation of assets? Largely because of the sizable initial deposits, CDAs have a large impact on the early accumulation of assets for college. For example, about four years after MI SEED began, the average total in SEED accounts was $1,483 and the median was $1,131.[81] (Because we lack data on the comparison group's Michigan 529 accounts, we cannot assess how MI SEED affected college assets.) In SEED OK, about 30 months after the program began, 99.9 percent of treatment children had some Oklahoma 529 assets, compared to only 2.1 percent of control children. Treatment children had much more: $1,130 versus $76, on average. For children in the treatment group, the automatic initial deposit eliminated much of the variation by socioeconomic status in the assets accumulated.[82]

The fact that these patterns were planned does not make them less meaningful. Account ownership and asset accumulation are primary goals of CDA programs. CDAs are envisioned as universal and progressive tools with automatic features and incentives. Thus, early results from MI SEED and SEED OK include outcomes directly related to automatic account opening, initial deposits, and savings matches. People do not have to take action themselves for an outcome to be meaningful.[83]

Do CDAs increase personal saving (that is, saving by individuals, excluding deposits from MI SEED or SEED OK)? The evidence is incomplete. First, data on parents' saving often includes information only on saving in Michigan or Oklahoma 529 accounts; findings on personal saving and CDA programs' role may be skewed if parents saved elsewhere. We believe that parents who saved were quite likely to do so in 529 accounts because of the incentives (for example, tax breaks in both states and savings matches for LMI treatment-group families), but we have no data to support this. Second, information is only sometimes available on saving by people other than parents (for example, 529 contributions by grandparents and other relatives). Third, we have information only about very early saving for college, because children in the programs were younger than 10. Personal saving behavior—and the impact of CDA programs—may change as children age and college grows closer.

Still, evidence from MI SEED and SEED OK suggests that personal saving for young children's future college expenses was modest. Over the four years when parents could receive the MI SEED savings match, 31 percent of SEED accounts received personal deposits. Across all 495 MI SEED accounts, the average net contribution per quarter ranged from -$67 to $1,500 (a negative value indicates that participants withdrew some of the initial deposit). The mean quarterly contribution was $16.[84] This information on savings comes from the Michigan 529 plan and is likely accurate but is available only for SEED treatment-group accounts.

A second source of information—parents' survey responses—is probably much less accurate, but the information is available for both the treatment and comparison groups. Responses indicated the amount of savings set aside by parents and others: over four years, the MI SEED program increased by

$484 (on average) the savings that parents set aside for their child's education but decreased by $188 the savings that others set aside for the child's education. The average amount set aside for children in the treatment group by all sources was not significantly different than that for children in the comparison group.[85] Thus it is not clear that MI SEED increased the amount of personal savings for children's future college expenses.

In SEED OK, about 30 months after the program began (SEED OK children were younger than four), treatment participants were four times as likely as control-group members (8.5 percent versus 2.1 percent) to have personal savings in their own OK 529 account—a pattern that held across socio-economic subgroups. However, treatment participants' average personal 529 savings ($109) were modest and just slightly larger than control members' average ($76).[86]

In our view, modest savings levels are to be expected, even in the treatment groups. Many parents had low incomes, and children's college education probably seemed a distant goal. We note that only 18 MI SEED account holders (3.6 percent of the total) withdrew any of the $800 initial deposit, despite the economic downturn, and that 48 MI SEED account holders (9.7 percent) saved $1,200—enough to earn the maximum match.[87] Also, as we note above, the most important early impacts to examine in SEED OK are that 529 accounts exist and assets are held for treatment children several years later. As Sherraden wrote, "From the outset, the guiding vision and purpose of SEED OK has been to test the impacts of a universal and progressive CDA policy structure. Individual saving behavior alone can never result in universal and progressive asset accumulation—no one would believe this is remotely possible. Therefore, SEED OK, as a policy demonstration, does not focus on individual savings behavior alone, or even primarily."[88]

Well-designed asset-building programs and policies can encourage a wide variety of families to save, with some positive effects.

Do CDA Programs Affect Parents and Children?

We will not be able to assess how CDAs affect postsecondary education and training for many years. However, researchers continue to analyze the effects of CDAs on parents' and children's attitudes and behaviors related to education.

Early evidence from MI SEED is mixed. Four years after MI SEED began (when children were six to eight years old), parents who had opened CDAs were more likely than parents in the comparison group to view college as important. But the groups reported similar levels of parental stress, neither felt more capable of managing their parenting responsibilities, and neither was more likely to provide children with stimulating activities and materials.[89]

Early evidence from SEED OK suggests that the CDA with automatic account opening and initial deposit improved children's social-emotional development. When children were about four years old, those in the treatment group had better scores

than those in the control group, and the CDAs' impact was greater for disadvantaged children.[90] The effect of the CDA is similar in size to at least one estimate of the effect of the Head Start program on early social-emotional development.[91] Additional analyses of SEED OK's impacts are under way at this writing.

Other evidence concerning SEED OK comes from in-depth interviews with mothers in the treatment group (when children were two to three years old) and does not result from comparing mothers in the treatment group with counterparts in the control group. These interviews suggest that the SEED OK account and initial deposit made some treatment-group mothers more hopeful about their children's future and perhaps more motivated to support their children's education.[92] Yet mothers could identify many barriers that might prevent children from completing college (for example, having babies, falling in love, and being adversely influenced by peers). Also, although many expressed confidence that they would "find a way" to put their children through school, the mothers did not seem well informed about how to finance college.[93]

Clearly, it is too soon to draw firm conclusions about the effects of CDAs on parents and children. Early evidence gives some indication that CDAs affect parents' attitudes and behaviors in ways that could improve their children's social-emotional development and perhaps later educational outcomes, especially when CDAs are opened automatically and have automatic initial deposits. As time passes, CDA programs may affect attitudes and behaviors differently. Fortunately, SEED OK is a well-designed and well-implemented experiment, with the potential to track children's development and academic progress into their early school years and beyond.

Summary of Evidence

At the beginning of this article, we posed two key questions: Do family assets improve child wellbeing? And can asset-building programs increase saving and assets, leading to improvements in the wellbeing of children from low-income families?

In this review, we present evidence that children in families with assets have better outcomes than those in families without assets. In particular, family assets are associated with positive educational outcomes, including academic achievement, postsecondary enrollment, and college graduation. As some studies suggest, assets may also be positively associated with children's behavior and health. Research continues to explore these relationships. Although most of the studies use longitudinal data (that is, they measure assets at one point in time and outcomes at a later date) and so are more rigorous than cross-sectional studies (which measure assets and outcomes at a single point), this evidence is correlational and cannot demonstrate causality. People who have savings and assets probably differ from people who lack them, and it can be difficult to distinguish the effects of assets from the effects of other unobserved variables that are associated with assets. In other words, it is plausible that family assets improve wellbeing, but evidence from national data sets does not settle the matter conclusively.

Evidence from policy demonstrations— especially experiments in which people are randomly assigned to treatment and control groups—can provide clearer evidence about the effects of assets and asset-building programs. The American Dream Demonstration IDA program appears to have increased homeownership among initial renters by the time the three-year program ended. Within six years of its end, the program had positive effects on outcomes tied to two of IDAs' five allowable uses: baseline homeowners saw improvements in the value of their homes, and educational attainment improved among males. In addition, among households whose income was above the median but still low, the program may have increased the rate and long-term duration of homeownership.

Overall, short-term IDA programs appear to have had some lasting effects on asset investments by some subgroups, yet some of the positive results, such as homeownership rate and duration, ceased to be statistically significant several years after the programs ended. We do not know what would have happened if an IDA program lasted longer. However, research on IDA programs shows that low-income people can save in IDAs if a support structure and subsidies are in place. Research also suggests that program features like ease of use (for example, automatic features) and expectations (for example, savings targets, such as match caps) have combined effects that together are more strongly associated with savings performance than are individual participants' characteristics. In general, there is reason to believe that well-designed asset-building programs and policies can encourage a wide variety of families to save, with at least some positive effects.[94]

Our conclusions about LMI homeownership programs must be tentative, because the only large demonstration, CAP, did not randomly assign participants to treatment and control groups. Instead, the CAP treatment group consists of people who purchased homes with the program's support, and researchers created a comparison group from renters with similar characteristics (for example, they had similar incomes and lived in the same neighborhoods). Early findings offer no strong evidence that CAP participation or purchasing a home led to improvements in parenting behavior or children's outcomes. But they do suggest that CAP homeowners have greater access to social capital than do CAP renters and tend to have better mental health. In addition, CAP homeowners saw greater increases in their net worth between 2005 and 2008.

Research on CDAs is in its infancy, and these are intrinsically long-term accounts. We will not be able to assess how CDAs affect postsecondary education and training for many years. In the meantime, research can examine how CDAs affect parents' and children's attitudes and behaviors. One study shows that a universal and automatic CDA with an initial deposit improved children's early social-emotional development. And, in in-depth interviews, some parents reported that CDAs make them more hopeful about their children's future and more motivated to support their education.

Evidence from CDAs also shows that better-off families fare better than disadvantaged ones if savings outcomes depend on individual behavior. That is, families with social and economic advantages, including high levels of income, education, and financial sophistication, are more likely than less-privileged counterparts to participate in asset-building programs and take advantage

of saving incentives. However, the evidence also suggests that policies and institutional supports—features like those in universal and progressive CDAs—can offset socioeconomic advantage.

Thus, if we want to increase the number of low-income families that have accounts and accumulate assets, we cannot simply encourage them to open accounts and save—we need automatic account opening and automatic subsidies. Evidence from SEED OK demonstrates that a universal CDA program with such features is feasible, at low administrative costs, by building on an existing college savings plan, and that it can include the entire population.

Conclusions

Overall, there is reason to believe that children who grow up in families with assets are better off than those who grow up in otherwise similar families without them. There is also reason to expect that asset-building programs increase family assets and improve children's outcomes. Long-term asset-building programs—especially early, universal, and progressive programs—seem most likely to improve the wellbeing of low-income children. It is also possible that subsidized asset holding has positive impacts in itself, regardless of personal saving. Survey and qualitative evidence supports the link between asset holding and children's wellbeing, and recent experimental evidence affirms positive effects on social-emotional development for the most disadvantaged children. In the coming years, we can expect the SEED OK experiment to provide additional evidence.

ENDNOTES

1. Michael Sherraden, *Assets and the Poor: A New American Welfare Policy* (New York: M. E. Sharpe, 1991).

2. Jesse Bricker et al., "Changes in U.S. Family Finances from 2007 to 2010: Evidence from the Survey of Consumer Finances," *Federal Reserve Bulletin* 98, no. 2 (2012), http://www.federalreserve.gov/pubs/bulletin/2012/pdf/scf12.pdf.

3. Rakesh Kochhar, Richard Fry, and Paul Taylor, *Wealth Gaps Rise to Record Highs between Whites, Blacks, and Hispanics* (Washington, DC: Pew Research Center, 2011).

4. Reid Cramer, Rachel Black, and Justin King, *The Assets Report 2012: An Assessment of the Federal "Asset-Building" Budget* (Washington, DC: New America Foundation, 2012), http://assets.newamerica.net/sites/newamerica.net/files/policydocs/AssetsReport2012.pdf.

5. Beadsie Woo, Ira Rademacher, and Jillien Meirer, *Upside Down: The $400 Billion Federal Asset-Building Budget* (Baltimore: Annie E. Casey Foundation, 2010), http://www.aecf.org/~/media/Pubs/Initiatives/Family%20Economic%20Success/U/UpsideDownThe400BillionFederalAssetBuildingBudget/033%2010_UpsideDown_final.pdf.

6. Leslie Morrison Gutman, Arnold J. Sameroff, and Robert Cole, "Academic Growth Curve Trajectories from 1st Grade to 12th Grade: Effects of Multiple Social Risk Factors and Preschool Child Factors," *Developmental Psychology* 39 (2003): 777–90, doi: 10.1037/0012-1649.39.4.777.

7. Michael S. Barr, *No Slack: The Financial Lives of Low-Income Americans* (Washington, DC: Brookings Institution Press, 2012).

8. Signe-Mary McKernan, Caroline Ratcliffe, and Katie Vinopal, *Do Assets Help Families Cope with Adverse Events?* (Washington, DC: Urban Institute, 2009), http://www.urban.org/UploadedPDF/411994_help_family_cope.pdf.

9. Trina R. Williams Shanks and Christine Robinson, "Assets, Economic Opportunity and Toxic Stress: A Framework for Understanding Child and Educational Outcomes," *Economics of Education Review* 33 (2013): 154–70, doi: 10.1016/j.econedurev.2012.11.002.

10. Rand D. Conger and M. Brent Donnellan, "An Interactionist Perspective on the Socioeconomic Context of Human Development," *Annual Review of Psychology* 58 (2007): 175–99, doi: 10.1146/annurev.psych.58.110405.085551.

11. Gary W. Evans, "The Environment of Childhood Poverty," *American Psychologist* 59 (2004): 77–92, doi: 10.1037/0003-066X.59.2.77.

12. Fabian T. Pfeffer and Martin Hällsten, *Mobility Regimes and Parental Wealth: The United States, Germany, and Sweden in Comparison* (Ann Arbor: University of Michigan, Institute for Social Research, 2012), http://www.psc.isr.umich.edu/pubs/pdf/rr12-766.pdf.

13. Thomas M. Shapiro, *The Hidden Cost of Being African American: How Wealth Perpetuates Inequality* (New York: Oxford University Press, 2004), 11.

14. Sherraden, *Assets and the Poor*.

15. Marcia Shobe and Deborah Page-Adams, "Assets, Future Orientation, and Well-Being: Exploring and Extending Sherraden's Framework," *Journal of Sociology and Social Welfare* 28 (2001): 119.

16. Ibid.

17. Guatam N. Yadama and Michael Sherraden, "Effects of Assets on Attitudes and Behaviors: Advance Test of a Social Policy Proposal," *Social Work Research* 20 (1996): 3–11, doi:10.1093/swr/20.1.3.

18. Trina R. Williams Shanks and Mesmin Destin, "Parental Expectations and Educational Outcomes for Young African American Adults: Do Household Assets Matter?" *Race and Social Problems* 1 (2009): 27, doi: 10.1007/s12552-009-9001-7; Min Zhan and Michael Sherraden, "Assets and Liabilities, Educational Expectations, and Children's College Degree Attainment," *Children & Youth Services Review* 33 (2011): 846–54, doi: 10.1016/j.childyouth.2010.12.006.

19. See Caroline Ratcliffe et al., "Assessing Asset Data," in *Asset Building and Low-Income Families*, ed. Signe-Mary McKernan and Michael Sherraden (Washington, DC: Urban Institute Press, 2008), 239–70.

20. Martha S. Hill and Greg J. Duncan, "Parental Family Income and the Socioeconomic Attainment of Children," *Social Science Research* 16 (1987): 39–73, doi: 10.1016/0049-089X(87)90018-4; Susan E. Mayer, *What Money Can't Buy: Family Income and Children's Life Chances* (Cambridge, MA: Harvard University Press, 1997).

21. Dalton Conley, *Being Black, Living in the Red: Race, Wealth, and Social Policy in America* (Berkeley: University of California Press, 1999).

22. Trina R. Williams Shanks, "The Impacts of Household Wealth on Child Development," *Journal of Poverty* 11 (2007): 93–116, doi: 10.1300/J134v11n02_05.

23. Amy J. Orr, "Black-White Differences in Achievement: The Importance of Wealth," *Sociology of Education* 76 (2003): 281–304, doi: 10.2307/1519867.

24. Trina R. Williams Shanks, *Diverging Pathways: How Wealth Shapes Opportunity for Children* (Oakland: Insight Center for Community Economic Development, 2011), http://www.insightcced.org/uploads/CRWG/DivergingPathwaysReport-InsightCenter.pdf.

25. Dalton Conley, "Capital for College: Parental Assets and Postsecondary Schooling," *Sociology of Education* 74 (2001): 59–72, doi: 10.2307/2673145.

26. Williams Shanks, "Impacts of Household Wealth."

27. William Axinn, Greg J. Duncan, and Arland Thornton, "The Effects of Parents' Income, Wealth, and Attitudes on Children's Completed Schooling and Self-Esteem," in *Consequences of Growing up Poor*, ed. Greg J. Duncan and Jeanne Brooks-Gunn (New York: Russell Sage, 1997), 518–40.

28. Daniel Aaronson, "A Note on the Benefits of Homeownership," *Journal of Urban Economics* 47 (2000): 356–69, doi: 10.1006/juec.1999.2144; Min Zhan and Michael Sherraden, "Assets, Expectations, and Children's Educational Achievement in Female-Headed Households," *Social Service Review* 77 (2003): 191–211, doi: 10.1086/373905; Richard K. Green and Michelle J. White, "Measuring the Benefits of Homeowning: Effects on Children," *Journal of Urban Economics* 41 (1997): 441–61, doi: 10.1006/juec.1996.2010; Conley, *Being Black*.

29. Michael H. Boyle, "Home Ownership and the Emotional and Behavioral Problems of Children and Youth," *Child Development* 73 (2002): 883–92, doi: 10.1111/1467-8624.00445; John Cairney, "Housing Tenure and Psychological Well-Being during Adolescence," *Environment and Behavior* 37 (2005): 552–64, doi: 10.1177/0013916504270697.

30. Donald R. Haurin, Toby L. Parcel, and R. Jean Haurin, "Does Homeownership Affect Child Outcomes?" *Real Estate Economics* 30 (2002): 635–66, doi: 10.1111/1540-6229.t01-2-00053.

31. William Rohe, Shannon van Zandt, and George McCarthy, "Home Ownership and Access to Opportunity," *Housing Studies* 17 (2002): 51–61, doi: 10.1080/02673030120105884.

32. David Barker and Eric A. Miller, "Homeownership and Child Welfare," *Real Estate Economics* 37 (2009): 279–303, doi: 10.1111/j.1540-6229.2009.00243.x; Scott Holupka and Sandra J. Newman, "The Effects of Homeownership on Children's Outcomes: Real Effects or Self-Selection?" *Real Estate Economics* 40 (2012): 566–602, doi: 10.1111/j.1540-6229.2012.00330.x.

33. Holupka and Newman, "Effects of Homeownership."

34. Robert D. Dietz and Donald R. Haurin, "The Social and Private Micro-Level Consequences of Homeownership," *Journal of Urban Economics* 54 (2003): 401–50, doi: 10.1016/S0094-1190(03)00080-9; Amanda Helderman and Clara H. Mulder, "Intergenerational Transmission of Homeownership: The Roles of Gifts and Continuities in Housing Market Characteristics," *Urban Studies* 44 (2007): 231–47, doi: 10.1080/00420980601075018.

35. Gary V. Engelhardt, "House Prices and Home Owner Saving Behavior," *Regional Science and Urban Economics* 26 (1996): 313–36, doi: 10.1016/0166-0462(95)02118-3.

36. Daphna Oyserman, "Not Just Any Path: Implications of Identity-Based Motivation for Disparities in School Outcomes," *Economics of Education Review* 33 (2013): 188, doi: 10.1016/j.econedurev.2012.09.002

37. William Elliott III, "Children's College Aspirations and Expectations: The Potential Role of Children's Development Accounts (CDAs)," *Children & Youth Services Review* 31 (2009): 274–83, doi: 10.1016/j.childyouth.2008.07.020.

38. William Elliott III and Sondra G. Beverly, "The Role of Savings and Wealth in Reducing 'Wilt' between Expectations and College Attendance," *Journal of Children and Poverty* 17 (2011): 165–85, doi: 10.1080/10796126.2011.538375.

39. William Elliott III, Gina Chowa, and Vernon Loke, "Toward a Children's Savings and College-Bound Identity Intervention for Raising College Attendance Rates: A Multilevel Propensity Score Analysis," *Sociology Mind* 1 (2011), 192–205, doi: 10.4236/sm.2011.14025.

40. William Elliott III et al., "The Age Old Question, Which Comes First? A Simultaneous Test of Children's Savings and Children's College-Bound Identity." *Children & Youth Services Review* 33 (2011): 1101–11. doi: 10.1016/j.childyouth.2011.02.001.

41. William Elliott III, "Small-Dollar Children's Savings Accounts and Children's College Outcomes," *Children & Youth Services Review* 35 (2013): 572–85, doi: 10.1016/j.childyouth.2012.12.015.

42. Michael Sherraden, "Rethinking Social Welfare: Toward Assets," *Social Policy* 18 (1988): 37–43; Sherraden, *Assets and the Poor*; Sherraden, "Asset Building Research and Policy: Pathways, Progress, and Potential of a Social Innovation," in *The Assets Perspective*, ed. Reid Cramer and Trina R. Williams Shanks (New York: Palgrave Macmillan, forthcoming).

43. Sherraden, "Rethinking Social Welfare"; Sherraden, *Assets and the Poor*.

44. Office of Community Services, *Report to Congress: Assets for Independence Program; Status at the Conclusion of the Eleventh Year Results through September 30, 2010* (Washington, DC: U.S. Department of Health and Human Services, Administration for Children and Families, 2009), http://www.acf.hhs.gov/sites/default/files/ocs/11th_afi_report_to_congress.pdf.

45. Mark Schreiner and Michael Sherraden, *Can the Poor Save? Saving and Asset Building in Individual Development Accounts* (New Brunswick, NJ: Transaction, 2007).

46. Ibid.

47. Gregory Mills et al., "Effects of Individual Development Accounts on Asset Purchases and Saving Behavior: Evidence from a Controlled Experiment," *Journal of Public Economics* 92 (2008): 1509–30, doi: 10.1016/j.jpubeco.2007.09.014.

48. Mark Schreiner and Michael Sherraden, "Detecting Effects on Net Worth Is Nettlesome Work: Fragility in a Randomized Experiment with Individual Development Accounts," *Journal of Income Distribution* 21(2012): 116–35; Chang-Keun Han, Michal Grinstein-Weiss, and Michael Sherraden, "Assets beyond Savings in Individual Development Accounts," *Social Service Review* 83 (2009): 221–44, doi:10.1086/600861.

49. Schreiner and Sherraden, "Detecting Effects."

50. Norm Leckie et al., *Learning to Save, Saving to Learn: Learn$ave Individual Development Accounts Project Final Report* (Ottawa: Social Research and Demonstration Corporation, 2010), http://www.srdc.org/uploads/learnSave_final_EN.pdf.

51. Gregory Mills et al., Assets for Independence Act Evaluation: Impact Study Update (Cambridge, MA: Abt Associates, 2003), http://www.abtassociates.com/reports/2003159999428_47206.pdf.

52. Leckie et al., *Learning to Save*.

53. Mills et al., Assets for Independence.

54. Ida Rademacher et al., *Weathering the Storm: Have IDAs Helped Low-Income Homebuyers Avoid Foreclosure?* (Washington, DC: CFED and Urban Institute, 2010), http://www.urban.org/UploadedPDF/412064_weathering_the_storm.pdf.

55. Michal Grinstein-Weiss, Jung-Sook Lee, Johanna K. P. Greeson, Chang-Keun Han, Yeong H. Yeo, and Kate Irish, "Fostering Low-Income Homeownership through Individual Development Accounts: A Longitudinal, Randomized Experiment," *Housing Policy Debate* 19 (2008), 711–39, doi: 10.1080/10511482.2008.9521653; Chang-Keun Han et al., "Assets beyond Savings;" Mills et al., "Effects."

56. Michal Grinstein-Weiss et al., "Long-Term Impacts of Individual Development Accounts on Homeownership among Baseline Renters: Follow-Up Evidence from a Randomized Experiment," *American Economic Journal: Economic Policy* 5 (2013): 122–45, doi: 10.1257/pol.5.1.122.

57. Michal Grinstein-Weiss et al., "Long-Term Effects of Individual Development Accounts on Postsecondary Education: Follow-Up Evidence from a Randomized Experiment," *Economics of Education Review* 33 (2013): 58–68, doi: 10.1016/j.econedurev.2012.12.007.

58. Margaret S. Sherraden and Amanda Moore McBride, *Striving to Save: Creating Policies for Financial Security of Low-Income Families* (Ann Arbor: University of Michigan Press, 2010).

59. Margaret S. Sherraden et al., *Saving in Low-Income Households: Evidence from Interviews with Participants in the American Dream Demonstration* (St. Louis, MO: Center for Social Development, Washington University, 2005), http://csd.wustl.edu/Publications/Documents/IDIPResearchReport2005.pdf.

60. Roberto G. Quercia, Allison Freeman, and Janneke Ratcliffe, *Regaining the Dream: How to Renew the Promise of Homeownership for America's Working Families* (Washington, DC: Brookings Institution Press, 2011).

61. Amy B. Shlay, "Low-Income Homeownership: American Dream or Delusion?" *Urban Studies* 43 (2006): 511–31, doi: 10.1080/00420980500452433.

62. Quercia et al., *Regaining the Dream*.

63. Ibid.

64. Michal Grinstein-Weiss et al., "Homeownership and Wealth among Low- and Moderate-Income Households," *Housing Policy Debate* 23 (2013): 259–79, doi: 10.1080/10511482.2013.771786.

65. Allison Freeman and Janneke Ratcliffe, "Setting the Record Straight on Affordable Homeownership," working paper, Center for Community Capital, University of North Carolina at Chapel Hill, May 2012, http://ccc.sites.unc.edu/files/2013/02/SettingRecordStraightAffordableHO.pdf.

66. Michal Grinstein-Weiss et al., "The Impact of Low- and Moderate-Wealth Homeownership on Parental Attitudes and Behavior: Evidence from the Community Advantage Panel," *Children & Youth Services Review* 31 (2009): 23–31, doi: 10.1016/j.childyouth.2008.05.005; Michal Grinstein-Weiss et al., "Homeownership and Parenting Practices: Evidence from the Community Advantage Panel," *Children & Youth Services Review* 32 (2010): 774–82, doi: 10.1016/j.childyouth.2010.01.016.

67. Michal Grinstein-Weiss et al., "Homeownership, Neighbourhood Characteristics, and Children's Positive Behaviours among Low- and Moderate-Income Households," *Urban Studies* 49 (2012): 3545–63, doi: 10.1177/0042098012443861.

68. Kim Manturuk, Mark Lindblad, and Roberto G. Quercia, "Friends and Neighbors: Homeownership and Social Capital among Low- to Moderate-Income Families," *Journal of Urban Affairs* 32 (2010): 471–88, doi: 10.1111/j.1467-9906.2010.00494.x; Michal Grinstein-Weiss et al., "Social Capital and Homeownership in Low- to Moderate-Income Neighborhoods," *Social Work Research* 37 (2013): 37–53.

69. Kim Manturuk, "Urban Homeownership and Mental Health: Mediating Effect of Perceived Sense of Control," *City & Community* 11 (2012): 409–30, doi: 10.1111/j.1540-6040.2012.01415.x; Mark R. Lindblad, Kim R. Manturuk, and Roberto G. Quercia, "Sense of Community and Informal Social Control among Lower Income Households: The Role of Homeownership and Collective Efficacy in Reducing Subjective Neighborhood Crime and Disorder," *American Journal of Community Psychology* 51 (2013): 123–39, doi: 10.1007/s10464-012-9507-9.

70. Reid Cramer and David Newville, *Children's Savings Accounts: The Case for Creating a Lifelong Savings Platform at Birth as a Foundation for a "Save-and-Invest" Economy* (Washington, DC: New America Foundation, 2009), http://www.newamerica.net/sites/newamerica.net/files/policydocs/CSAPolicyRationale_0.pdf; Michael Sherraden, "Asset Building Research."

71. Sondra G. Beverly, William Elliott III, and Michael Sherraden, *Child Development Accounts and College Success* (St. Louis, MO: Washington University, Center for Social Development, 2013), http://csd.wustl.edu/Publications/Documents/P13-27.pdf.

72. Ibid.

73. Trina R. Williams Shanks et al., "Assets and Child Well-Being in Developed Countries," *Children & Youth Services Review* 32 (2010): 1488–96, doi: 10.1016/j.childyouth.2010.03.011.

74. Michael Sherraden and Julia Stevens, eds., *Lessons from SEED: A National Demonstration of Child Development Accounts* (St. Louis, MO: Center for Social Development, Washington University, 2010), http://csd.wustl.edu/Publications/Documents/SEEDSynthesis_Final.pdf.

75. Trina R. Williams Shanks, Lewis Mandell, and Deborah Adams, "Financial Education and Financial Access: Lessons Learned from Child Development Account Research," *Innovations* 8 (2013): 167–83, doi: 10.1162/INOV_a_00171.

76. Yunju Nam et al., "Do Child Development Accounts Promote Account Holding, Saving, and Asset Accumulation for Children's Future? Evidence from a Statewide Randomized Experiment," *Journal of Policy Analysis and Management* 32 (2012): 6–33, doi: 10.1002/pam.21652.

77. Ibid.

78. Ibid.

79. Sondra G. Beverly et al., "Are Child Development Accounts Inclusive? Early Evidence from a Statewide Experiment," working paper, Center for Social Development, Washington University, 2012, http://csd.wustl.edu/publications/documents/wp12-30.pdf.

80. Vernon Loke, Margaret Clancy, and Robert Zager, *Account Monitoring Research at Michigan SEED* (St. Louis, MO: Center for Social Development, Washington University, 2009), http://csd.wustl.edu/Publications/Documents/RP09-62.pdf.

81. Ibid.

82. Beverly et al., "Are Child Development Accounts Inclusive?"

83. Sherraden, "Asset Building Research."

84. Loke, Clancy, and Zager, *Account Monitoring Research.*

85. Ellen L. Marks et al., *Building Assets: An Impact Evaluation of the MI SEED Children's Savings Program* (Research Triangle Park, NC: RTI International, 2009), http://www.rti.org/pubs/mi_seed_report.pdf.

86. Beverly et al., "Are Child Development Accounts Inclusive?"

87. Marks et al., *Building Assets.*

88. Sherraden, "Asset Building Research."

89. Marks et al., *Building Assets.*

90. Jin Huang, Michael Sherraden, Youngmi Kim, and Margaret Clancy, "Effects of Child Development Accounts on Early Social-Emotional Development: An Experimental Test," *JAMA Pediatrics* 168. Published electronically January 27, 2014. doi: 10.1001/jamapediatrics.2013.4643.

91. Michael Puma et al., *Head Start Impact Study: Final Report* (Washington: U.S. Department of Health and Human Services, Administration for Children and Families, 2010), http://www.acf.hhs.gov/sites/default/files/opre/hs_impact_study_final.pdf.

92. Karen Gray et al., *Interviews with Mothers of Young Children in the SEED for Oklahoma Kids College Savings Experiment* (St. Louis, MO: Center for Social Development, Washington University, 2012), 57, http://csd.wustl.edu/Publications/Documents/RP12-53.pdf.

93. Ibid, 48.

94. Sherraden, "Asset Building Research."

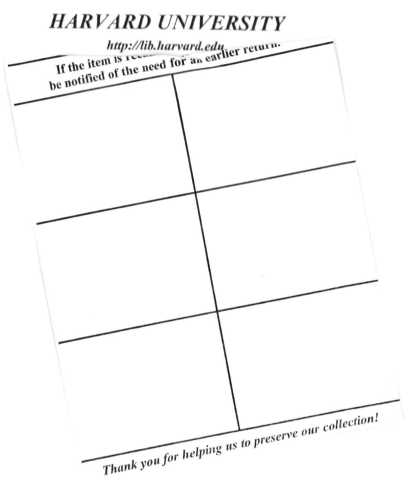

HARVARD UNIVERSITY

http://lib.harvard.edu

If the item is rec... ...earlier return.
be notified of the need for an earlier return.

Thank you for helping us to preserve our collection!